D1689662

NomosTextbook

The textbook series presents selected topics from the social sciences and humanities program. Published are outstanding topics relevant to English-language teaching from all program areas, such as political science, sociology, social work, or media and communication studies. The selection of books is based on the curricula of the respective disciplines. Renowned experts provide a compact introduction to the topics of the respective subject.

Claudia Lohrenscheit | Andrea Schmelz
Caroline Schmitt | Ute Straub [Eds.]

International Social Work and Social Movements

Nomos

This English edition is based on the book "Internationale Soziale Arbeit und soziale Bewegungen", Nomos 2023, ISBN 978-3-8487-6407-5. Parts of the translation into English were created with support of machine translation and/or artificial intelligence. This textbook was written for the German-speaking world in 2022/23. In the translation presented here, German-language citations have been translated, original sources left, and supplemented where possible with relevant English-language sources. The textbook was proof-read by a native speaker.

All contributions to this volume have undergone an independent peer review process.

The Deutsche Nationalbibliothek lists this publication in the Deutsche Nationalbibliografie; detailed bibliographic data are available on the Internet at http://dnb.d-nb.de

ISBN   978-3-7560-1389-0 (Print)
          978-3-7489-1931-5 (ePDF)

British Library Cataloguing-in-Publication Data
A catalogue record for this book is available from the British Library.

ISBN   978-3-7560-1389-0 (Print)
          978-3-7489-1931-5 (ePDF)

Library of Congress Cataloging-in-Publication Data
Lohrenscheit, Claudia | Schmelz, Andrea
Schmitt, Caroline | Straub, Ute
International Social Work and Social Movements
Claudia Lohrenscheit | Andrea Schmelz
Caroline Schmitt | Ute Straub (Eds.)
212 pp.
Includes bibliographic references and index.

ISBN   978-3-7560-1389-0 (Print)
          978-3-7489-1931-5 (ePDF)

Online Version
Nomos eLibrary

1st Edition 2024

© Nomos Verlagsgesellschaft, Baden-Baden, Germany 2024. Overall responsibility for manufacturing (printing and production) lies with Nomos Verlagsgesellschaft mbH & Co. KG.

This work is subject to copyright. All rights reserved. No part of this publication may be reproduced or transmitted in any form or by any means, electronic or mechanical, including photocopying, recording, or any information storage or retrieval system, without prior permission in writing from the publishers. Under § 54 of the German Copyright Law where copies are made for other than private use a fee is payable to "Verwertungsgesellschaft Wort", Munich.

No responsibility for loss caused to any individual or organization acting on or refraining from action as a result of the material in this publication can be accepted by Nomos or the editors.

Table of Contents

I. INTRODUCTION

I.1 Utopias of a Good Life for All People: International Social Work and Social Movements — 7
Claudia Lohrenscheit, Andrea Schmelz, Caroline Schmitt & Ute Straub

I.2 (Re-)Visions and Challenges: International Social Work and Social Movements — 19
Ute Straub

II. INTERNATIONAL SOCIAL WORK IN SOCIAL MOVEMENTS

II.1 "Your Body Is a Battleground" Women's Movements, Queer Feminism and Gender Justice — 41
Claudia Lohrenscheit

II.2 Racism and Postcolonial Resistance — 61
Susan Arndt & Mario Faust-Scalisi

II.3 The Global Movements for Children's Rights - with an Interview with Manfred Liebel — 75
Claudia Lohrenscheit

II.4 Global Migration, Refugees and Protest Movements: International Social Work Approaches — 91
Andrea Schmelz

II.5 Solidarity Cities. Urban Citizenship and Artivism as a Practice of Inclusive Solidarity — 111
Caroline Schmitt

II.6 Environment, Ecology, Climate and Sustainability: Global Movements towards Ecosocial Transformation — 131
Andrea Schmelz

II.7 Indigenous Movements in International Social Work — 151
Monika Pfaller-Rott & Ute Straub

II.8 Nothing About Us Without Us: Social Movements of People with Disabilities — 169
Ernst Kočnik, Rahel More & Marion Sigot

II.9 Divided Humanity, Divided World – Questions and Perspectives for a Peace-oriented Diversity Education as Global Citizenship ... 187
Hans Karl Peterlini

III. OPPORTUNITIES, LIMITS, PERSPECTIVES

Outlook: Making Conditions Dance. International Social Work and Social Movements as Alliance Partners ... 205
Claudia Lohrenscheit, Andrea Schmelz, Caroline Schmitt & Ute Straub

Index ... 211

I. Introduction

I.1 Utopias of a Good Life for All People: International Social Work and Social Movements

Claudia Lohrenscheit, Andrea Schmelz, Caroline Schmitt & Ute Straub

1. Introduction

This textbook aims to familiarise students with the basic concepts of international social work and to provide an insight into the interconnections between international social work and social movements. The background to this are the worsening global inequalities and the question which tasks a social work that thinks beyond national borders[1] has with a view to war, violence and flight, the climate crisis, sexism, racism and populism, discrimination and marginalisation of people with disabilities, LGTBIQ+ (Lesbian, Gay, Trans, Bi, Intersex, Queer+) or BIPoC (Black, Indigenous, and People of Colour) and how it can work with social movements.

The continuing reports of war and violence in the world, natural disasters or the Covid 19 pandemic and the destruction of planet Earth illustrate the complex challenges of our time. They leave many people with little hope for the future and sometimes lead to helplessness or the feeling that they can achieve little. Social movements refuse to give in to resignation. They stand for the politics of hope and have always fought for a transformation of inequality. In doing so, they are oriented towards real utopias and create these.

Social work is about acting in the interest of the addressees, supporting them in the face of problems and the loss of security in a world that has become confusing. This is linked to the task of building and helping to shape communities that strengthen the ability to act, creating sustainable support networks, and advocating for social change, human rights, inclusion, participation, equality, justice, equity and solidarity. The mission of social work in a global world is not limited to nation states. It neither stops at different origins or other diversity dimensions such as our sexual identity, our world view, or different physical, psychological or neuro-diverse conditions. Social work is there for all people, especially for those who are pushed to the margins of society. In our interconnected world, it must necessarily be internationally oriented. This textbook wants to broaden the scope even more and thinks beyond the human being to include the planet earth in social work – a perspective that is becoming increasingly important in the face of the climate crisis and makes clear that human beings should not dominate above nature and are not rulers over it but part of it.

---

1 The term "social work" in this volume includes both social work and social pedagogy degree programmes. The term "social workers" also refers to social work and social pedagogy professionals.

When we think about who draws attention to the massive challenges in our world, such as the extinction of species, the violation of human rights in the accommodation of refugees, or femicides, i.e. the murder of girls and women because of their gender – to name just a few examples –, it is not always social work that first comes to mind. It is often social movements that denounce social ills and speak up when human rights are violated and the planet is destroyed. Social work can therefore learn from the "fire" of social movements (Harms 2015) to intersectionally stand up for human rights and socio-ecological justice as tangible utopias with creative and rebellious forms of protest. For social work, alliances with international protest movements such as Black Lives Matter, Solidarity Cities, Friday for Future or with indigenous activists can become places of solidarity and resistance.

2 Social movements as a yardstick

Social movements are fluid associations of people that arise when a need for social action becomes apparent in the eyes of those involved. Sociologist Friedhelm Neidhardt (1985) writes that social movements function in their respective social contexts as "disruptive events" that question what is supposedly taken for granted. They intervene in social routines with the aim of changing them. For this, they need to be perceived publicly. They need an approval among the population that goes beyond the movement, a certain form of acceptance, so that they can actually achieve their goals. If social movements reach their goal or if the intervention is difficult and even violently crushed, they can sometimes disappear, but they can also be revived.

The educationalist Susanne Maurer (2019: 367) highlights the difficulty of clearly defining and typifying social movements – characteristics that apply to one movement may be irrelevant to other social movements. Accordingly, it can be stated that one feature of social movements is precisely their heterogeneity. Nevertheless, loose cornerstones can be formulated: for example, the founding dates and memberships of social movements are less clear than those of highly formalised associations. Procedures and processes are characterised by a higher degree of fluidity. Above all, social movements are about reacting to a certain matter, a certain social condition, setting themselves apart from it and developing alternative ways of seeing and dealing with it. Roth and Rucht (2002: 297) point out as a special feature of social movements the distinction from short-term initiatives, on the one hand, but also the difference from more formalised contexts, on the other hand. One feature of social movements is a certain duration and permanence, which potentially enables a collective identity. In the authors' eyes, a social movement is only a social movement as long as it is not transformed into formalised structures such as a party, a club, or an association.

Alliance partnerships between social work and social movements are not yet a matter of course, even at the international level, although both share fundamental commonalities. As intersections of social work and social movements, Sabine Stövesand identifies in particular common core principles such as empowerment, participation, anti-discrimination, democratisation, participation, and self-determination (Stövesand 2014: 35). However, the International Federation of Social Workers had to accept justified criticism that its global action plan, the Global Agenda, lacked interaction with social movements. Instead, the focus is on international organisations such as the United Nations (UN), the African Union (AU), or the European Union (EU) instead of targeted alliances with globalisation-critical social movements and civil society actions (such as the Occupy Movement, Earth Day, World Day for Social Justice), which deal with the actual causes of global inequality in a neoliberal world order (Gray/Webb 2014). Social work can learn from social movements to direct its perspective towards socio-ecological and intersectional real utopias of social change and to strengthen the imagination that another world is possible.

3. Spaces of possibility, gap-fillers and "shrinking spaces". Social movements as part of civil society

Social movements are considered part of civil society. The term civil society has a long tradition (Zimmer 2021). In ancient Greece, it was used to describe the free coexistence of citizens in the political community – but it should be noted that enslaved people and women were excluded from this. In the further course of history, the understanding differentiated. According to Geissel and Freise (2015), general welfare and action-related definitions can be distinguished from interest- and area-related definitions. Definitions related to the general good and action understand civil society as a bundle of civil modes of action that are, for example, oriented towards the common good and are non-violent. Interest- and sector-related definitions mean by civil society the area between the state, the market, and the private sphere. This area is sometimes also described as the third sector and used synonymously with the term "non-profit sector".

The textbook focuses on the potentials that social movements within civil society open up. It is an impressive testimony to how many people around the world are involved in social movements and civil society organisations. Civil society is more alive than ever – this is our thesis and observation! Particularly the recent developments of the climate protests of Fridays for Future, the mass movements against racism and sexism, and the uprising against the Russian war of aggression against Ukraine are proof of the multiple solidarity-based engagement of groups and individuals, as can be seen, for example, in the reception, support, and accompaniment of refugees from Ukraine. However, this positive results cannot and should not hide the sometimes contradictory developments. For example, struggles for emancipation have always met with strong resistance and hostility (Schutzbach 2021: 112) and have to develop enormous forces to achieve their goals, if this is possible at all. On the one hand, civil society groups and social movements take on tasks that should actually be handled by state organisations. These forms of "substitute action" are described in the most recent academic debate as collaborations (Terkessides 2015); this means that civil society cooperation and solidarity-based engagement step in wherever the state withdraws or provides services too late, in insufficient quantities or not at all. On the other hand, international scientific and human rights organisations have been analysing *shrinking (action) spaces* of civil society for years. All over the world, social movements and civil society actors have less and less space for manoeuvre. The current "Atlas of Civil Society" published in German by Brot für die Welt e.V. (2022)[2] shows that today only three percent of the world's population live in countries with open civil societies, while two thirds live in authoritarian countries.

The 194 states examined are divided into five categories (open, impaired, restricted, repressed, closed). Oppression and violence can be found on all continents and in many countries and cities: in Brussels as well as in Budapest, in repressive states as well as in (still) democratic states. In concrete terms, this means that social spaces beyond the state, the private sphere, and the economy are being touched – spaces in which associations, social movements, non-governmental organisations (NGOs), but also churches, religious communities, and foundations etc. operate. Democratic states based on the rule of law guarantee freedom of assembly and association as the basis of a free civil society; authoritarian states restrict them or ban them altogether. But "if the space for action, also known as civic space, is eroded by repression or violence, the central social corrections are lost. Progressive social change is replaced by creeping disenfranchisement. Social movements can exert less and less political pressure, powerful people cannot be held accountable" (Jakob 2022: 12, translation by the authors). As a result, critical reporting is hardly possible any more, governments are no longer democratically controlled and, at worst, become corrupt and authoritarian. Inequality, poverty, and violence increase. "When protests are no longer possible, mismanagement and corruption flourish. (...) The repression here is as varied as it is rampant. It can be deadly, even when people are only demanding things that are taken for granted" (ibid.: 12–13, translation by the authors). In 2022, the NGO Front Line Defenders documented almost 800 human rights defenders in acute danger, including arbitrary arrests, killings and attempted killings, enforced disappearances, torture practices, and sexual violence.[3]

Germany is currently still one of the three percent of states that are characterised as "open". But here, too, sea rescuers are not only criminalised by populist parties and climate protectors are sometimes stigmatised as terrorists. As one of the strongest leading countries in the European Union, the failure to take effective political steps against the dismantling of democratic rights at the EU's external borders and in the countries bordering the Mediterranean must also be criticised. Italy and Austria were downgraded from "open" to "impaired". The reasons for this include election victories of the right-wing parties Lega and FPÖ as well as political measures that restrict the degree of freedom of civil society in both countries.

---

[2] The original "State of Civil Society Report" has been developed and published once a year for more than ten years by the South African NGO Civicus. Civicus, based in Johannesburg, is a global alliance of civil society organisations with over 10,000 members worldwide (see: https://civicus.org/ (retrieved at 28.02.2024).

[3] See: https://www.frontlinedefenders.org/en/violations (retrieved at 28.02.2024); similar data and figures can also be found at Amnesty International or Reporters Without Borders with regard to specific professional groups such as journalists.

4. Making the conditions dance

In this textbook, together with all the authors, we take up the ambivalence of social movements with their practices and effectiveness and their simultaneous limitation, criminalisation, and destruction. Social movements want to move society and change current social conditions. Symbolically for the inspiration that emanates from social movements, we, the editors, refer to the image of dance at various points in this textbook.

We understand dance both literally and as a metaphor for movement, because, after all, social movements are at the centre of this volume. Moreover, dance, just like the music associated with dance, is a universal language that can be understood everywhere and intuitively, that connects people, even across borders and continents, and that can create new imaginaries and utopias. According to Lutz (2018: 41, translation by the authors), "dancing thoughts and people who give the round dance its own melody" are needed to make social conditions dance.

There are many dancing thoughts and melodies in this volume. The very concrete examples range from queer feminism to gender justice (cf. Lohrenscheit's chapters in this volume). Among others, the feminist collective Las Tesis from Chile is presented, which inspired feminist social movements internationally with its performance "Un violador en tu camino" (a rapist on your way). This choreography criticises patriarchal violence as a combination of domestic and state, individual and structural violence. The text states, among other things: "It was not my fault where I was or what I wore; the rapist is you." The dance/performance was performed in public places in numerous cities in the Americas, Europe, Asia, and on the African continent, and Las Tesis organised accompanying workshops to learn the choreography, but also to advance the discussion of sexism and violence against women, for example in 2020 and 2022 in Berlin under the title "Together we burn the fear".[4] The creative and resistant potential of dance, performance, and movement is not a new development. Not without reason do we know numerous historical examples of dance bans. For example, the tango was banned in Argentina at the time of the dictatorship, or swing in fascist Nazi Germany. Such anti-dance demonstrations of power can be traced back to the Middle Ages, where dancing women were persecuted as witches for allegedly performing satanic dances. "Strike. Dance. Rise!" is still an appeal that moves women* and FLINTA[5] in particular today. Social movement researcher Kristina Stein-Hinrichsen shows this in her current publication "Tanzen als Widerstand" (Dancing as Resistance) (2022), using the example of "One Billion Rising", among others. This choreographic intervention in public space is a worldwide campaign against violence towards girls and women, originally initiated by the New York artist Eve

---

[4] The events were organised in cooperation between the Rosa Luxemburg Foundation and the HAU – Hebbel am Ufer theatre; see: https://www.hebbel-am-ufer.de/archiv/zusammen-verbrennen-wir-die-angst (retrieved at 28.02.2024).
[5] FLINTA stands for: Women, Lesbians, Inter, Non-binary, Trans and Agender people (cf. Schutzbach 2021: 16).

Ensler. "Dance, dance, otherwise we are lost"[6] – this is how we editors would like to put it, following Wim Wenders' film for Pina Bausch, and we hope that our textbook can contribute to making conditions dance more again in (international) social work as well.

5. Creative forms of protest

A fascinating component of this textbook is the variety of different forms of protest used by social movements, as reported by the various authors in this volume. These range from classical peaceful protests such as public demonstrations or blockades and human chains to creative forms of resistance through theatre, dance, or performance art (cf. Schmitt's contribution in this volume) to provocative, sometimes violent actions such as those currently occurring in the context of climate protests, for example, when activists stick their hands to the asphalt during street blockades, risking injury themselves in the process. From a historical perspective, it also becomes apparent that the creativity of social movements is limitless. Some forms of protest arise more by chance or in the process, others are prepared for a long time and are strategically planned. One of the world's first social movements was the anti-slavery movement at the turn of the 18th century (cf. Tilly/Tarrow 2015: 4). Already at this time, the abolitionists tried to stir up public opinion against the slave trade with the help of demonstrations, petitions, with lectures and even a boycott of sugar as one of the most important products obtained through the exploitation of slave labour. With success, so "that politicians finally bowed: In February 1807, the British Parliament became the first colonial power to criminalise the trade in slaves" (Köpke 2008, translation by the authors).

Another early example of resistance that arose in the process is the so-called "hat pin danger" reported by Katharina Schulzbach (2021: 25f.). When the young tourist Leoti Baker visited New York in 1903 and was propositioned and also touched by a man on the way in a stagecoach, she stabbed him with her hatpin. "In the period that followed, newspapers reported similar incidents around the country of women defending themselves against public harassment with hatpins, and soon there was heated debate" (ibid.: 26, translation by the authors). However, rather than focusing on protecting women from sexual harassment, the debate took on the "hatpin menace", and indeed bans were imposed in many cities, and women were imprisoned and had to pay fines for wearing hatpins, even if they only wore them as a fashion accessory.

As these two quite different historical examples show, social movements often need a long breath. Some issues seem inexhaustible, some goals seem almost unattainable, and yet social movements do not stop fighting for their rights, their dreams, for a better life, a better world. Sometimes this also leads to activist burn-out. This is what the climate activists at Fridays for Future are currently

---

[6] The Filmmuseum Potsdam writes: "'Dance, dance, otherwise we are lost', Pina Bausch had told her dancers time and again. After her unexpected death, Wim Wenders stuck to a jointly planned film project and worked closely with Pina Bausch's ensemble. The result is a moving homage to the 'inventor of a new art' (W. Wenders)."

reporting – no wonder, because in relation to their lifespan they have already spent a large part of their lives in the social movement. Other movements that span long periods of time, such as the anti-racist and civil rights movements, have developed their own term for this: racial battle fatigue, i.e. fatigue in the face of ongoing struggles against racism and discrimination. At the same time, social movements with their various forms of protest are always a demonstration and public representation of power, strength, and self-confidence. Even if they cannot always achieve their political goals and even if these are often far away, they still carry the potential for empowerment, for community and strength that comes from acting together.

6. Insights into the diversity of social movements

The following chapters provide insight into this power of collective action, which arises in different contexts and unfolds in diverse fields and forms of action. They do not aim to work through individual movements peu à peu but to highlight the interconnections and references between social movements and international social work based on a variety of topics. The diversity of social movements is great, which means that the selection made must necessarily remain inadequate. Please feel inspired to research other social movements not covered in this volume.

This introduction is followed by a detailed approach to the subject of this volume. In the chapter "International Social Work and Social Movements", *Ute Straub* sets out the conceptual, historical and theoretical foundations of this volume, which make it possible to link the subject of 'social movements' with international social work and to place social movements and international social work in a relationship. Definitions are followed by a historical review of how social movements have contributed to the professionalisation of social work, where there have been overlaps, but also demarcations. The article then looks at current developments and the significance of social movements within the debates on international social work. The central starting point is an understanding of social work as a human rights profession that takes up the issues of social movements and positions itself, among other things, at the annual International Day of Social Work and Social Development in statements and in committee work at the UN. In this context, it is important not to take for granted the gaps that are dealt with through the solidarity-based engagement of movements, and also not to release the state from its social responsibility. As the agendas of social movements shine where support is lacking or remains insufficient, this is always connected with the question of whether these voids can be transferred into an institutionalised framework of support, for example into services to be provided by the welfare state. The article reveals this area of tension and asks: Can international social work contribute to building and maintaining social structures – in cooperation with social movements and NGOs? This leads to the concluding question: Is social work itself a movement?

This basic introduction is followed by nine chapters devoted to individual social movements and their references to social work.

Claudia Lohrenscheit looks in her contribution "Your Body Is a Battleground. Women's Movements, Queer Feminism and Gender Justice" at interventions by social movements against sexism and violence against women and LGBTIQ+. An examination of violence against marginalised persons (groups) is one of the core issues of social work at home as well as in numerous countries around the globe. However, Lohrenscheit points out in her chapter that these topics are not naturally anchored in curricula and practice at universities. She therefore provides a basic introduction to questions of gender justice and takes a look at three current examples of how social movements advocating for gender justice and queer feminist goals; these are firstly the social struggles against femicide (murders of women), secondly the resistance against the criminalisation of abortion and for reproductive rights, and thirdly the struggles for the human rights of intersex people.

The contribution "Anti-Racism and Postcolonial Theory" by *Susan Arndt* and *Mario Faust-Scalisi*, like Claudia Lohrenscheit, takes up a topic that needs to be further anchored in social work curricula. In their contribution, Arndt and Faust-Scalisi deal with decolonisation movements and the anti-apartheid movement and reflect on the significance of postcolonial theory at universities and for concrete practical action in world society. The contribution gives an insight into definitions and understandings of racism, postcolonialism, Black Studies, and Critical Whiteness Studies. In doing so, it takes protest and achievements of social movements – especially with a view to historical and current developments in Germany – as a starting point.

The global movement for children's rights and the human right to education are the focus of the chapter "The Global Movements for Children's Rights". *Claudia Lohrenscheit* chooses to start with a discussion of the United Nations Convention on the Rights of the Child, which is one of the most well-known and globally recognised human rights conventions. This also applies to social work, but in the curricula at German-speaking universities the focus is mostly on national child and youth welfare law, albeit with reference to children's rights. Here, a look at the global movement for children's rights and the right to education can be helpful in discovering new perspectives and critically questioning dominant attitudes. This becomes particularly clear in the interview with *Manfred Liebel*, who has been working academically, politically, and as an activist for children's rights and children's movements for decades. He shows that children and young people themselves stand up for the respect of their rights, even if they do not always do so in language of, or with reference to, children's rights. Furthermore, some important personalities in this framework are introduced, such as Janusz Korczak from a historical perspective and Malala Yousafzai as a current example. The author continues to focus on the human right to education, which is central for children and young people but, beyond that, as a right to human rights education and lifelong learning, affects everyone at any time and in any place.

Andrea Schmelz also deals with the unlimited validity of human rights for all people, regardless of their origin or their own experiences of migration and flight, in her chapter "Global Migration, Refugees and Protest Movements: International

1.1 Utopias of a Good Life for All People: International Social Work and Social Movements

Social Work Approaches". Schmelz introduces the field of flight and migration, which is fundamental to international social work. Particularly in Europe but also elsewhere, this field is shaped by policies of migration control and racism. The chapter looks at emerging fields of tension and potential alliances between social work and activist movements. With brave protests, refugees and migrants demand their rights, defend themselves against racist exclusion, criminalisation, and violence, and are supported by solidarity movements. The approaches of Social Workers without borders, political social work, and human rights-based social work critical of racism show perspectives on how social work can ally with refugees and migrants, critically reflecting and transforming power and inequality relations. Social work can learn from the political self-help work of refugee women in Women in Exile (WiE), which exemplifies the resistance, self-empowerment, and political creativity of the many initiatives around the world, where men, women, and children in contexts of global refugee migration fight on a daily basis against repression and inequality.

Following Schmelz, the chapter "Solidarity Cities. Urban Citizenship and Artivism as a Practice of Inclusive Solidarity" by *Caroline Schmitt* deals with visionary approaches that counter the drawing of boundaries in the city and in the countryside and show concrete practices for an inclusive coexistence. Her article focuses on solidarity-based urban movements that advocate for a city for all people, regardless of diversity dimensions such as residence status, nationality, and origin. Urban solidarity movements have been called sanctuary cities since the 1980s in the USA and have also spread to Canada. At the latest since the 'Long Summer of Migration' they have also become known in Europe under the term solidarity cities. After an introduction to the history and concerns of sanctuary and solidarity cities, the chapter is dedicated to the concept and practice of municipal city cards as an expression of urban solidarity. Using the Züri City Card as a case study, the possibilities and challenges of urban citizenship are discussed, before an artistic approach takes centre stage. The example of the "Weekends for Moria Carinthia/Koroška" will show how solidarity alliances generate attention for social grievances with artistic actions and create a public sphere in the city (artivism). Finally, the importance of solidarity-based urban movements for international social work will be discussed and linked to the approaches of popular social work and municipal pedagogy.

The idea of cities based on solidarity is in principle open to thinking beyond people. The question of how cities, municipalities, regions, and countries can be made "green" and sustainable is also necessary. The discussion in this volume, which has so far focused primarily on people, is expanded accordingly. The world is moving from a climate crisis to a climate disaster; locally and globally the ecosocial transformation can no longer be postponed. This is what climate activism is campaigning for with increasingly radical protests. Everywhere on the planet, the impact of the climate crisis for the well-being and health of people, animals, plants, and the whole environment is tangible and visible. What still seems to need explanation in Germany has a firm place in social work discourses at the international level. Thus, the chapter "Environment, Ecology, Climate and Sustainability: Global Movements towards Ecosocial Transformation" by *Andrea Schmelz* highlights the connections between environmental and climate movements and a "green", ecosocial transformation in international social work. The author elaborates on how environmental and climate justice movements have historically emerged as a frame of reference in social work. She introduces the discourses and approaches of Green Social Work, Ecosocial Work, and Ecological/Environmental Social Work. As a global pioneer of the environmental movement, she portrays Wangari Matthai (1940–2011), a climate, women's, human rights and peace activist from Kenya who became a global icon of the environmental and climate movement. The Green Belt Movement (GBM), which she initiated, focuses on the interaction of sustainable, ecosocial community development and women's empowerment in Kenya and has inspired many projects worldwide.

Among others, it is indigenous communities that are associated with practices of sustainable living on this planet and are discussed in social work as pathfinders. At the same time, they are also the ones who have to vehemently defend their rights to land and rights to their way of life. This paradox is the subject of the article "Indigenous Movements in International Social Work" by *Monika Pfaller-Rott* and *Ute Straub*. Indigenous approaches are an element of "social work of the South". Local and indigenous systems of help and traditions of support have long been disregarded or suppressed in the course of colonisation and professional imperialism. Social work has contributed significantly to the loss of cultural roots and thus to the loss of an identity-forming framework that is indispensable for personal development. In recent years, the "forgotten knowledge" (Smith 2005) has experienced a renaissance due to the louder and more self-confident voices from the Global South in the form of liberation movements and movements for the rights of indigenous peoples, which also includes the demand to include indigenous approaches as equals in the canon of social work approaches. These approaches have given and continue to give impulses for the further development of social work and are discussed in this article in connection with *Ecosocial Work* and *Green Social Work*. As an example, insight is given into the actions and life's work of Rigoberta Menchú Tum, a Quiché Maya from Guatemala, as one of the most important representatives and initiators of indigenous movements.

The subsequent contribution by *Ernst Kočnik, Rahel More* and *Marion Sigot* entitled "Nothing about Us without Us: Social Movements of People with Disabilities" deals with social movements of people with disabilities and their significance for social work. The political slogan "Nothing about us without us" is indicative of the demand for self-determination. The links between human rights and social work with movements critical of psychiatry, the self-determined life movement, and the people-first movement are outlined with international references. This is followed by short portraits of three activists who are part of social movements and the presentation of the Austrian association "Counselling, Mobility and Competence Centre (Beratungs-, Mobilitäts- und Kompetenzzentrums – BMKz)" in Klagenfurt and the inclusive working group "Mensch Zuerst Kärnten". The

BMKz is part of the Self-Determined Living Initiative and the Personal Assistance project, which will also be presented.

Hans Karl Peterlini concludes the insight into different social movements with his contribution "Divided Humanity, Divided World – Basic Questions and Perspectives for a Peace-Oriented Diversity Education as Global Citizenship Education". The debate on questions of war and peace (Peters 2019), which has so far been insufficiently conducted in social work, is appreciated against the background of the many wars and conflicts in the world. The war in Ukraine has once again led to a broader search on how peace policy and peace education perspectives can be taken into account in social work and strengthened and shaped against the background of the social work mandate. This chapter aims to offer suggestions in this regard. It opens up offers for reflection from the perspective of educational science oriented towards diversity education and invites us to relate these to international social work. The article discusses fundamental questions of an international peace movement such as: How do violence and war arise in thinking and in structures? What do positive and negative peace mean and what does peace mean as a process? In this context, the power of divisions between an 'us' and the 'others', between the sexes and between humans, animals, and nature is discussed. The consequence of this is a loss of compassion for the respective split-off other, against which war is then waged and violence perpetrated. As a counter-model, the article discusses a sense of planetary responsibility in the sense of global citizenship. Portraits of Edgar Morin, a pioneer of a Citizenship of the Earth, and Sima Samar, a peace and human rights activist, reveal living examples of such a consciousness.

7. Continuing and shaping debates and practices

If you, dear reader, have joined the authors of the individual chapters on a journey into the multifaceted engagement of social movements, and if references to international social work have been negotiated in the process, the dance that opened with this volume has come to an end for the time being. In the final chapter "Making Conditions Dance: International Social Work and Social Movements as Allies", we reflected on how to continue with the discussion, which further dances international social work can bring to the dance floor together with social movements and other partners, and which challenges arise – especially from anti-democratic and human rights violating movements. It seems important to us to always think of international social work as a visionary project with a view to the future that combines a critique of social conditions with a willingness to change and an open-minded thinking beyond the here and now.

Changes are always embedded in intergenerational dialogues, dialogues with as many different actors as possible and, ideally, in networks that develop an effect together. We hope that this volume can contribute to such a perspective and look forward to exchanging ideas with you.

Literatur

Brot für die Welt (Hrsg.) (2022): Atlas der Zivilgesellschaft. Freiheitsrechte unter Druck. Schwerpunkt Digitalisierung. Berlin.

Gray, Mel/Webb, Stefen A. (2014): No issue, no politics: towards a New Left in Social Work Education. In: Noble, Carol/Strauss, Helle/Littlechield, Brian: Global Social Work Education. Crossing Borders, Blurring Boundaries. Sydney: Sydney University Press, 327–340.

Harms, Linda (2015): What should Social Work learn from „The fire of social movements that burns at the heart of society". In: Critical and Radical Social Work Journal 3, H. 1, 19–34.

Jakob, Christian (2022): Zivilgesellschaft unter Druck. In: Südlink. Das Nord-Süd-Magazin H. 4, 12–15.

Köpke, Monika (2008): Das Ende der Sklaverei. Deutschlandfunk. Archiv. https://www.deutschlandfunkkultur.de/das-ende-der-sklaverei-104.html (retrieved at 28.02.2024).

Lutz, Ronald (2018): Tanzende Verhältnisse. In: Lutz, Ronald/Preuschoff, Sarah (Hrsg.): Tanzende Verhältnisse. Zur Soziologie politischer Krisen. Weinheim/Basel: Beltz Juventa, 9–49.

Maurer, Susanne (2019): Soziale Bewegung. In: Kessl, Fabian/Reutlinger, Christian (eds.): Handbuch Sozialraum. Sozialraumforschung und Sozialraumarbeit. Wiesbaden: VS, 359–380.

Neidhardt, Friedhelm (1985): Einige Ideen zu einer allgemeinen Theorie sozialer Bewegungen. In: Hradil, Stefan (Hrsg.): Sozialstruktur im Umbruch. Wiesbaden: VS, 193–204.

Peters, Alina (2019): Frieden – (k)ein Thema Sozialer Arbeit? In: neue praxis. Zeitschrift für Sozialarbeit, Sozialpädagogik und Sozialpolitik 49, H. 6, 556–567.

Roth, Roland/Rucht, Dieter (2002): Neue soziale Bewegungen. In: Greiffenhagen, Martin/Greiffenhagen, Sylvia/Neller, Katja (eds.): Handwörterbuch zur politischen Kultur der Bundesrepublik Deutschland. Opladen: Westdeutscher Verlag, 296–303.

Schutzbach, Katharina (2021): Die Erschöpfung der Frauen. Wider die weibliche Verfügbarkeit. München: Droemer.

Stövesand, Sabine (2014): Soziale Arbeit und Soziale Bewegungen. In: Benz, Benjamin et al. (eds.): Politik Sozialer Arbeit. Weinheim: Beltz Juventa, 22–42.

Stein-Hinrichsen, Kristina (2022): Tanzen als Widerstand. Bielefeld: transcript.

Terkessides, Mark (2015): Kollaboration. Berlin: edition suhrkamp.

Tilly, Charles/Tarrow, Sidney (2015): Contentious Politic (second revised edition). Oxford: Oxford University Press.

Zimmer, Annette (2021): Zivilgesellschaft. In: Andersen, Uwe/Bogumil, Jörg/Marschall, Stefan/Woyke, Wichard (eds.): Handwörterbuch des politischen Systems der Bundesrepublik Deutschland. Wiesbaden: Springer VS, 1053–1059.

I.2 (Re-)Visions and Challenges: International Social Work and Social Movements

Ute Straub

> Annually on the third Tuesday in March – World Social Work Day
>
> 17th April – The International Day of Peasants' Struggle

Summary

To introduce the topic of this textbook, this chapter provides an overview of International Social Work and the current professional debates, the development of social movements and the interplay between these two actors. A central question is: Regarding its positioning outside the welfare state framework – which in many countries is non-existent or only rudimentary –, could international social work with its commitment to human rights and social justice and with its efforts to exert political influence be called a movement itself?

Two portraits illustrate the chapter: For International Social Work stands Vishantie Sewpaul from South Africa, who has contributed significantly to the further development of the various global standards for social work. For the social movements, Mentona Moser, a social worker from Switzerland, is presented, who anticipated much of what is important for social movements today.

Introduction: Let's dance!

What connects International Social Work (ISW) and social movements (SM)? There is a lot on the move in this question, almost like the dance steps in the cha-cha-cha: back, forward, chachacha, turn-turn, chachacha. The questions in this chapter are correspondingly:

- Backwards: What role did social movements play in the professionalisation of social work a good 100 years ago?
- Forwards: What will cooperation look like in the future? What research questions need to be asked?
- Chachacha: On the international/transnational level across national borders and continents: How do social movements and social work cooperate and where do they overlap? What can we learn from each other?
- Turn-turn: How have social movements and the profession influenced each other in their development? How does their communication, connection and delineation look like?
- Chachacha: Internationally and in the global federation: What role do SMs play in the concepts and the debates of ISW?
- And finally: Is social work itself a movement?

First of all, it is about definitions: What is international social work? What are social movements?

1. Definition of International Social Work (ISW)

"International social work concerns all issues that go beyond the national framework: organisation in global umbrella organisations, overarching discourses on topics such as ethics, standards for professional education and indigenous and local approaches, as well as fields of practice that are particularly relevant in an international context" (Straub 2020).

1.1 The importance of ISW

Why is ISW important? Aren't there enough problems to solve locally? In principle, yes, but the fact is that it is no longer sufficient to tackle problems only "on the ground":

- Global interdependencies lead to the emergence of new significant areas of international accountability, changing the tasks and (working) environment of social work.
- The demands on nation-state social work and the problems for which it is responsible increasingly arise outside its own borders.
- Social problems are having a greater impact than before in both industrialised and developing countries. In addition, innovations in social work practice are emerging in the Global South with target groups that are also relevant in the North, especially street children, the elderly and families whose structures are changing.
- Jointly acquired knowledge and networking through practical projects, teaching and research, i.e. global professional literacy, strengthen the profile with regard to the professional contribution to dealing with global social problems (Healy 2014: 378).
- Social work is developed in different ways; in some countries professional social work has existed for over 100 years, in some it is just beginning and local and indigenous approaches are included. ISW must therefore ask itself self-critically which voices were/are involved in defining social work.
- The global social upheavals, the consequences of climate change, war, flight and migration are changing social work on the ground and require competences in new fields of practice such as disaster prevention and management (Dominelli 2014; Mathbor/Bourassa 2012), peacebuilding (cf. Peterlini's contribution in this volume) and ecologically oriented approaches (cf. Schmelz's contribution in this volume).
- Neoliberalism as an increasingly widespread political guideline makes it necessary to defend the profession as a politically independent entity on a global level (Abramowitz 2012; Ferguson 2008).
- Global governance and policy co-creation with non-state actors has become an important dimension of international social work (Bähr et al. 2014: 15).
- Policy practice is the effort to influence policy in legislation, agencies and communities and is considered an integral part of social work practice at the

international level with increasing importance as transnational linkage processes progress (Pawar 2019).
- New communication technologies enable rapid exchange, which can be used to support civil society action in the sense of global advocacy (Healy 2014).
- The self-definition as a human rights profession (IASSW/ IFSW 2014; Staub-Bernasconi 2008; UN 1992) cannot be limited to nation-state borders.
- Through the international umbrella organisations and various global initiatives, most recently through the Global Agenda for Social Work and Social Development (cf. section 3.1), the profession has set itself global tasks.

1.2 International umbrella organisations

The three large international umbrella organisations – the International Association of Schools of Social Work (IASSW, member for Germany: Fachbereichstag Soziale Arbeit), the International Federation of Social Workers (IFSW, member for Germany: DBSH – Deutscher Berufsverband Soziale Arbeit) and the – in Germany largely unknown – International Council on Social Welfare (ICSW, member for Germany: DV – Deutscher Verein für öffentliche und private Fürsorge) – form the umbrella for social work at global level and are in close cooperation with their regional associations: Africa, Asia/Pacific, Europe, Latin America/Caribbean and North America. They all have their origins in the first International Conference of Social Work held in Paris in 1928 (Healy/Hall 2009; Kruse 2009). The role played by committed women in internationalisation cannot be overestimated: merging closely in national and international women's movements and women's federations and especially in the International Council of Women (ICW), founded as early as 1888, formed the basis for an influential transnational network. In part, it were the same women who were involved in the women's and peace movements as well as in the development of social work as a women's profession (Kruse 2009; Kniephoff-Knebel 2006).

After the interruption of global exchange by the Second World War, the international dimension of social work and the commitment to human rights and social justice could be resumed in the 1950s. The focus on Europe and North America gave way over time to a "real internationalisation" that included the Global South, which was finally reflected, among other things, in the new global definition of the social work profession in 2014 (Hall 2013; Cox/Pawar 2012: 55–64; Healy/Hall 2009)[7].

1.3 Basic papers and global agenda

In addition to the definition, the most important basic documents of the umbrella organisations are the "Ethics in Social Work, Statement of Principles" and the "Global Standards for Social Work Education and Training of the Social Work Profession", whose respective updates reflect paradigm shifts in professional theory as well as debates about conflicts in the context of postcolonialism and

---

[7] For a comparison of the 2004 and 2014 definitions, cf. Straub 2015

globalisation (e.g. Gray et al. 2010; Rehklau/Lutz 2001; Midgley 2010). Concepts such as social cohesion and social development were newly included in the global definition, and indigenous knowledge was recognised as an essential component of social work (Straub 2014).

The "Global Standards for Social Work Education and Training" describe the guidelines and goals for the (higher) schools, for the curriculum including internships, for the teachers, the students as well as for the administration and management of the educational institutions. The appendix emphasises how important the process of elaboration was for the exchange among the higher education institutions; it shows the course of discussion, and minority opinions are presented. A second appendix refers to the fact that the standards are to be handled with care and caution, that it is not a matter of paternalism (by the countries in which the profession is more developed) but rather, among other things, an argumentation aid for better equipment of the universities.

Ethical standards are part of every profession. For social work, the "Ethics in Social Work, Statement of Principles" are all the more important because in everyday practice social workers have to resolve conflicts between advocacy in the interest of clients and socio-political demands for effectiveness and efficiency (dual mandate). Their own human rights-based claims (triple mandate) are often incompatible with restrictive measures taken by governments against marginalised and/or vulnerable groups. Therefore, reference is made to various UN conventions, and human rights and human dignity as well as social justice are highlighted as central principles. Further explanations concern professional behaviour, on the one hand of course in relation to the target groups, but on the other hand also in relation to one's own wellbeing in the sense of self-care.

The most recent joint commitment is the project "Global Agenda for Social Work and Social Development", a long-term action plan. It was launched for the period 2010–2020, and the follow-up agenda 2020–2030 is in the works. Monitoring (reporting) is intended to make the activities of practitioners, teachers and researchers in the field of social development visible in the political arena and to expand the possibilities for influence. This monitoring tool is fed by information from members on good practices in practice and teaching. A major focus is on the involvement of practitioners in research or clients in teaching and development of concepts in social institutions (service user involvement). The agenda is in line with the Social Development Goals (SDGs), highlighting the proximity of ISW to global social development. Unfortunately, the continuous and established activities of NGOs and other non-professional social activists have not been sufficiently included.

1.4 Points of Criticism and further development

Critical voices doubt that these standards (as well as a global definition) can bridge the wide range of social, political, economic, geographical and cultural differences and the global/local divide (Gray/Webb 2008; Straub 2018: 29–31) – which is difficult enough at the national level.

But much has changed in recent years: In the beginning, the focus was on the global unification of (ethical) norms and professional standards in order to create a common basis for all the different members and to make the concerns of social work more heard at the political level, but now the focus is increasingly on the diversity within the globally active profession.

The demand for "decolonisation" of social work should also be seen in this context (Tamburro 2013). An increasingly important area of ISW is therefore the Social Work of the South, i.e. the view of those countries where, on the one hand, the social system is still little/not at all developed and, on the other hand, their own regional and local approaches are being developed in rejection of, or adaptation to, the concepts/methods of social work in the Global North. At the same time, this perspective "raises questions about the power, recognition and diversity of social work knowledge and possibilities for action in the Global North due to postcolonial developments and global migration movements and questions their claim to hegemony [...]. In particular, the focus is on the implementation of human rights with the simultaneous recognition of difference and global power hierarchies" (author's translation, Lutz et al. 2021). This also includes indigenous knowledge systems. These proven traditional ways of thinking and acting, transmitted over many generations, have always addressed today's urgent problems of food supply, health and human-animal relations, education, environment and natural resource management. Community-oriented processes of gathering, consensus-building and healing (also related to community cohesion) are characteristic of indigenous peoples' traditional support systems and problem-solving strategies. These approaches provide impulses for the further development of social work (Straub et al. 2020; cf. the contribution by Pfaller-Rott/Straub in this volume).

Portrait: Vishantie Sewpaul

Vishantie Sewpaul, born on 11th January 1956 in Durban, of Indian descent, grows up in apartheid South Africa. Her father commits suicide when she is five months old; she and her six siblings are raised alone by their mother, a domestic servant and illiterate. She spends her childhood and adolescence in various segregated Indian communities in Durban. At first, she does not question the "racial segregation" prescribed by the apartheid regime, as it is something she takes for granted. She only experiences conscious discrimination when she leaves the "protected" Indian environment and at the same time begins to understand the hierarchy associated with privilege: Whites at the top, followed by Indian/Asian, then Coloured and at the end African Black. She also comes to terms with the fact that in such a structure the oppressed can be oppressors at the same time.

She is allowed to go to secondary school and manages to get a scholarship to study. She enrols in social work at an "ethnic" university, the University of Durban-Westville (UDW), which is exclusively for Indian students. All teaching is done by white professors and is based on Eurocentric theories with a focus on individual case work and on pathology and dysfunction. In their second year of study, 1976, the Soweto Riots break out in Soweto, Johannesburg's largest township, mainly among young blacks. They protest is against the introduction of the Boer language Afrikaans in the school curriculum, which only a few African Blacks know and which is perceived as a language of oppression. This is a move by the government to invoke the crumbling Boer identity, accompanied by an expansion of the security and police state. The uprising is bloodily put down, but it is seen as the beginning of the end of apartheid.

Vishantie Sewpaul takes an active part in the protests that are increasingly directed against the racist and discriminatory education system and against "racial segregation" in general. She becomes part of the Black Consciousness Movement (BCM), develops a positive "identity of black". She takes her Master's in Social Work with a focus on Medical Science at the UDW, which has to do with her commitment to HIV/AIDS, among other things. In this context, she is developing various (training) programmes for affected mothers and children for social work as community work. Her dissertation deals with feminist, ethical and religious aspects of infertility and the new reproductive technologies; the background is her own childlessness. She teaches, after a few stops in between, at the University KwaZulu Natal, which was founded in 2004 through the merger of a "white" and a "black" university. As Head of the Social Work Discipline, she has the difficult task of constructively addressing curricular, ethnic, ideological and historical tensions.

In her academic career, two themes are important to her: on the one hand, there is the criticism of the increasingly neoliberal structures at universities, which are geared towards pure efficiency, and of the neglect of teaching, students and practical relevance in favour of research due to the pressure to publish. Secondly, for Vishanti Sewpaul, practice, especially community work, and biographical work with her students including all their experiences of oppression are indispensable for good teaching. When she had to recognise that both were no longer guaranteed, she took early retirement in 2015, but only to continue her international commitment. During her teaching career and with the end of apartheid, she devotes herself more and more to international activities. As (Vice) President of the Association of South African Social Work Education Institutions (ASASWEI) and the National Association of Social Workers, South Africa (NASW, SA), the first united, non-racial professional association for social workers in South Africa, she organises many international congresses, both within Africa (Africa alone has 54 nations!) and worldwide. Her international reputation is outstanding: she has taught at numerous foreign universities and has been awarded honorary doctorates by a Swedish, a Norwegian and a Chilean university. As Vice-President of the IASSW (2010–2015) she has always defended the position of critical social work and has addressed issues such as racism and (neo-)colonialism. Particularly noteworthy is her commitment to the Global Standards for Social Work Education and Training, although she initially had great reservations: "It smacks of colonialism" (Sewpaul 2021: 131). But then she took over the co-chairmanship of the task force, because "most colleagues wanted global standards, with a tall order that they be broad enough to apply to any context, but specific enough to have salience. Thus began our four years of global consultations, which called for active listening, understanding and humility in responding to a wide range of disparate interests and worldviews" (Sewpaul 2021: 131).

With her understanding of contradictions and ambiguities, she contributed a great deal to the unanimous adoption of a result acceptable to all members of the *IASSW* and the *IFSW*. The same applies to her commitment to the revision

> of the Global Definition for the Social Work Profession and the Global Social Work Statement of Ethical Principles (IASSW).
> Vishantie Sewpaul's path from an Indian community in apartheid South Africa to the international stage of social work was not preordained. Her commitment, especially to the further development of global standards for social work, in which she often mediated between highly divergent positions with the necessary tact, has contributed to advance international social work a good deal.
> Sources: V. Sewpaul's autobiography and many conversations during our collaboration in the IASSW and in the Training and Teaching Standards Task Force.

2. Definition of social movements

So far, social movements (SMs) have hardly been considered in the context of social work but mainly from a sociological perspective, e.g. in the standard work "Oxford Handbook of Social Movements" (Della Porta/Diani 2015). One definition that is still used today is that of Raschke (1991): Movements are collective actors who want to mobilise. They act "with a certain continuity on the basis of high symbolic integration and low role specification by means of variable forms of organisation and work. Their aim is [...] to bring about, prevent or reverse more fundamental social change" (author's translation, Raschke 1991: 32).

"Translated", this means that those who are committed to an issue jointly try to get others, as many people as possible, to join in. Until their concern is heard and in order to become publicly effective (to be noticed by the media, for example), it takes time, which is why a movement must persist over a certain period of time. The necessary "symbolic integration" shows itself in a strong sense of "we" in terms of a common opinion ("being for or against something"), but also in manners, language and symbols up to the style of dress. You can join a social movement without having to formally become a member (unlike in an association). Of course, there are also hierarchies, e.g. through the degree of commitment between initiators, activists and sympathisers. But the roles are not specific, not fixed, but rather flexible. Where and how one gets involved in the organisation (of meetings, public relations, etc.) and activities (e.g. participation in demonstrations, designing posters ...) is open. How far-reaching the project of social change is formulated depends on the objective. It can be global, as in the Global Justice Movement, or local, such as the resistance of indigenous peoples against the construction of dams on the Xingu River in Brazil. However, these local movements can also attain a national or even global scale. The Fridays for Future movement can be taken as an example of the transnationalisation process. Here, transnational mobilisation can be illustrated on three levels: (1) its actors are networking transnationally, (2) their protests address transnational issues, (3) they address international organisations (cf. the contribution by Schmelz in this volume).

Until the early 2000s, SMs were primarily seen as approaches to democratisation and normative and cultural opening, as a counterweight to neoliberalisation and the conventional class and gender order; in any case, they stand for emancipatory alternatives. In the meantime, it has become clear through the analysis of developments that SM also partly support norm regress-tendencies and that there are definitely (international) activities of anti-liberal, exclusionary and reactionary actors in civil society (Davies/Peña 2021: 55f.), e.g. the right-wing extremist Proud Boys, who want to (re-)establish a social order oriented towards traditional, male-dominated Western norms and white supremacy (e.g. their leading role in the storming of the Capitol in Washington in January 2021 in connection with the presidential election in the USA).

Since SMs represent a counter-design to formalised and institutionalised systems such as parties or organisations and, in contrast to the ideal type of an organisation, are not thoroughly formalised, they are to be understood more as networks (Rucht 2016: 29). Nevertheless, they have a "minimum of organisational structure that gives them permanence and a certain leadership structure that enables them to act strategically" (author's translation, Brand et al. 1986: 36), which distinguishes them from revolts and unrest. Maintaining a balance here is one of the great challenges for SMs. If explicit, openly disclosed responsibilities are replaced by informal hierarchies and arbitrariness, it is not possible to guarantee bottom-up decision-making and thus the inclusion of internal minorities. The result: the movement freezes. Rammstedt (1978) has worked out the regularity of the movement process. According to this, crises, commonly shared experiences of injustice that affect many people or the solidarity among those not directly affected are the conditions for the emergence of an SM. The propagation of these consequences of crises leads to the formation of a consensus among the members. The ideology that develops from this, i.e. a commonly shared point of view, is made public in order to gain further members or supporters outside the inner circle. For the movement to keep moving, it is vital that it continues to spread. Despite the priority of horizontal communication and interaction, the movement becomes a quasi-profession for some members out of the need to coordinate the ever-growing number of followers, and a leadership group is formed. "With the quasi-professionalisation of the participants at the centre of the social movement, the interactionist structure transforms into a formal organisation [...] is at the same time the ideal-typical end of every social movement" (author's translation, Rammstedt 1978: 168). Often non-governmental organisations (NGOs, see section 3.5) emerge to continue to represent the concerns and to give them an institutionalised framework. Other reasons for the dissolution of an SM can also be failure, declining interest or – in the best case – the fact that the goal has been achieved or – in the worst case – that authoritarian regimes obstruct and prohibit a movement (Roth/Rucht 2016: 35).

In order to implement the desired social changes, SMs use various forms of protest, networking and communication actions (Herbers/Zobel 2022).

2.1 Forms of protest and media networking

A "protest event" is defined as a public, collective action that goes beyond routine action to articulate dissent or to assert a social or political concern. What is important is the action character that arises when the boundaries of routine communication are transgressed. This ranges from open letters, leaflets, resolutions and press conferences, political cultural events or legal actions to blockades, strikes, damage to property, burglary or even hunger strikes. Online petitions and campaigns or hacking are becoming increasingly important (Institute for Protest and Movement Research 2022). However, there are also critical tendencies: "Various academic studies have noted a trend towards more specialised and personalised protests in the context of digital 'clicktivism', fun protest, professionalisation and NGOisation" (Daphi/Deitelhoff 2017: 311), i.e. developments that (can) lead to a depoliticisation of protest.

How can attention be generated in a time when information overflow has made it a scarce commodity? Rucht (2016) summarises the possibilities as follows: A spectacle has high news or surprise value and provokes. Dramatisation and scandalisation emphasise an unacceptable, outrageous or dangerous issue. Personalisation and symbolisation are used to make complex facts vivid. Narratives place the issues in historical or traditional contexts. With the help of framing strategies, interpretations are suggested, positive or negative associations are evoked, conceivable solution perspectives and responsible bearers of reform approaches are named. Boundaries are drawn and identities asserted to create a sense of unity and a sense of "we" (Rucht 2016: 7–10).

To generate mass attention, as many people as possible must proclaim the message. Networks are therefore the veins of SMs, networking is its survival strategy. Yet the nature of communication is very specific, because it "unfolds in that elusive intermediate zone of private and public, spontaneous and organised, informal and regulated, of cultural innovation and political intervention, of self-transformation and social critique" (author's translation, Roth/Roland 1991: 263).

Whereas in the 1970s the interaction network was formed via self-organised pubs, bookshops or alternative media such as "counter newspapers" or "pirate radio stations", today internal and external networking is no longer conceivable without the internet. Although physical presence at demonstrations, meetings or tent camps are important for the feeling of togetherness – the affective side of protest –, digital networking and the use of the virtual protest space via websites, press mobile phones and, above all, social media is just as relevant. Thus, when considering networking, the following questions must be asked: In which places did the protests take place and in which ways were spaces appropriated? To what extent have digital and analogue spaces been connected to each other? The worldwide protests between 2009 and 2011 (more on this in section 3.3) usually begin in the digital networks and thus become transnational. At the same time, activists occupy public spaces through demonstrations and rallies and are thus also anchored locally and regionally. The SMs have a viral character but can also be experienced locally and physically. More recently, campaign organisations have emerged that predominantly use the internet, for example for digitally distributed petitions (at the international level avaaz.org and change.org are active). In this way, they offer the possibility to start campaigns individually: the platforms are open to all, anyone can join in (Daphi/Deitelhoff 2018). Movements are changing and trying out new dance steps and choreographies with innovative protest and mobilisation actions.

Having defined international social work and social movements, the next sections will look at how their relationship has developed over the last more or less 120 years.

3. Social movements and social work

The attribution "social" is found in the movements as well as in the profession/discipline, and both are concerned with social relations. Both have been networking on an international level from the beginning and are in transnational exchange. If the SMs bring social problems and social contradictions into the public sphere, social work takes on the task of taking them up and working on them (Wagner 2010: 9). This interaction has decisively promoted the dissemination of ideas, knowledge and concepts across national and continental borders (Köngeter 2013). At the same time, social work is embedded in national traditions and discourses. Lorenz sees this seemingly contradictory relationship "as a central element of its historical character and as such as the very starting point for its further scientific and professional elaboration" (author's translation, Lorenz 2015: 1437). It is important to note: Social work has its origins not exclusively in charity and benevolence/welfare but also in the politically active society-changing SMs. "Social change" and "social development" are also currently defined as central tasks of the profession and discipline.

3.1 "Old" social movements

Social work is a relatively young profession and discipline that only begins to emerge in the late 19th century and the first third of the 20th century. A multitude of previously unknown social problems, caused by industrialisation and its consequences and then by the First World War, require new socio-political measures. At the same time – and also in this context – the first social movements develop: the workers' movement, the two women's movements (the bourgeois and the proletarian), later also the social reform movements, the youth movements and the peace movement. Many pioneers of social work are also active in the various movements at the same time, especially in the women's movement.

From a historical perspective, social work and social movements are not only connected through their shared critique of social, political or economic conditions but also through professional and personal networks of relationships. It is true that there are tensions: The women's movement criticises the lack of professionalism in social work, which is done more out of charitable motives than out of social responsibility. For the workers' movement, social work is too much on the side of repressive politics, and it criticises the pressure with which attempts are made to enforce bourgeois norms (cf. Wagner 2010: 14–16); for the workers, the class struggle is in the foreground. The bourgeois women's movement, on the other hand, from which the majority of social workers come, strives for the reconciliation of classes and wants to achieve more social justice through measures of family welfare and health and youth care.

I.2 (Re-)Visions and Challenges: International Social Work and Social Movements

With regard to pacifism, brought into public consciousness internationally by the World Peace Congress of Glasgow in 1901, in the period before the First World War the first professional women social workers split into those who were nationalistically minded and shared enthusiasm for war and those who were internationalist in outlook and joined an international peace movement (mostly) with the socialist and communist-oriented women's movement.

But it remains to be said that the common criticism of societal, social and political conditions leads to mutual inspiration. "Thus, the women's movement [...] contributed significantly to the establishment of vocational training and the professionalisation of social work, the youth movement pioneered social education after the First World War, and the working-class movement contributed at least indirectly to the creation of a differentiated socio-political system" (author's translation, Wagner 2010: 9). The internationalist and co-educational labour youth movement influenced the methods of political education and international youth work, the bourgeois youth movement those of social education. The peace movement has contributed to the fact that social work has (currently) opened up a new field of practice with peacebuilding in post-conflict societies and can fall back on proven approaches and strategies such as civil conflict transformation and non-violent intervention.

Portrait: Mentona Moser

Mentona Moser is a pioneer of social work, not only as a co-founder of the first social work training in Switzerland but especially in terms of her activities related to internationalism and her political engagement as a social worker and activist (Schmelz 2021).

She was born on 9th October 1874 in Badenweiler/Switzerland as the daughter of Baroness Fanny Louise von Sulzer-Wart and the watch manufacturer Heinrich Moser, one of the richest families in Switzerland. She distanced herself early on and used the fortune she inherited in later years for social purposes. First, however, she studied social work from 1898 to 1901 at the Women's University in Cambridge, England, which had a settlement in Southwark, a London poor district. This brought her into contact with the settlement movement and through it to the workers' and women's movement. When she returned to Switzerland, she tried to integrate the approaches of the settlement movement into the newly emerging social work training: no adaptation to the norms of the bourgeois class but support based on the real living conditions and needs of the workers and overcoming class antagonisms, i.e. partnership instead of paternalism. When she could not assert herself in this way, she resigned from her leading function. A quotation from her autobiography makes her attitude drastically clear: "Never is the bourgeoisie so repulsive as where it engages in charity, stinking welfare" (author's translation, Schiel 1987: 250, quoted in Schmelz 2021: 338).

The ideas of the cooperative movement, in which she is active for a while as a social democrat, correspond to her attitude: to achieve the improvement of precarious living conditions through self-help in solidarity. After she converted from social democracy to communism, she found her final "ideological home" in the International Red Help (IRH). This was founded in the aftermath of the First World War, after various revolutions had failed and waves of refugees of communists persecuted by the police and military made their support necessary. At its peak in 1932, the IRH was a world organisation with national sections in 68 countries and nearly 12 million members, many of them non-party members. In the course of her life, Moser became involved also on an international level, both ideally and financially: for women's rights, sexual counselling and the right to abortion, in refugee aid, as a producer of records with workers' songs, for political education in the countryside, for a prisoners' library, for children's homes in the Soviet Union, for the children of political emigrants or prisoners – always in accordance with her maxim that activation, ownership and participation are the foundations of politically understood and socially relevant social work. When Hitler rose to power, her remaining inheritance was confiscated and she fled back to Switzerland.

Due to illness and age, she lived in precarious circumstances in the 1940s until she accepted citizenship of the German Democratic Republic (GDR) in 1950 at the invitation of the Socialist Unity Party of Germany (SED). There she died in 1971. Because of her dedication to communism and development of social programs she was awarded both the Clara Zetkin Medal and the Patriotic Order of Merit by the GDR.

What connects Mentona Moser and the topic of this chapter?

Mentona Moser has always seen the relevance of social work only in the connection with internationalism and political interference. In this respect, she can be considered an early representative and protagonist of anti-oppressive social work (AOSW) and popular social work – even if the Red Help as a party-affiliated movement cannot be assigned to SMs as defined above. Both approaches are close to social movements and see themselves as part of radical social work.

AOSW is an umbrella term in Canada and Great Britain for different practice approaches of anti-racist, feminist and other social movements and criticises the established social work as an "oppressive caring profession". "Private" problems are to be evaluated as a social matter, from which a critical relationship between social structure and the consciousness of individuals is derived. Awareness and analysis of oppression are necessary but not sufficient components of AOSW; equally important is the impetus to change society (Straub 2006). Popular social work also explicitly refers to social movements, also known as "popular classes". The approach assumes that professional engagement with innovative and "popular", movement-oriented forms of (mutual) support that emerge outside the self-imposed boundaries of the profession enriches and politicises social work (Lavalette 2019).

Mentona Moser's thoughts, convictions and activities are reflecting these ideas, and she anticipated, propagated and lived many of the things that are now (re-)entering the professional discussion.

> **Recommended reading**
> Lavalette, Michael (2019): Popular social work. In: Webb, Steven A (ed.): The Routledge Handbook of Critical Social Work, London: Routledge: 536–548
> Morgaine, Karen/Capous-Desyllas, Moshoula: Anti-Oppressive Social Work Practice – Putting Theory into Action (2015): London:Sage
> Schilling, Sigrid (2015): Mentona Moser (1874–1971): the battle for a more just society. https://bristoluniversitypressdigital.com/view/journals/crsw/3/3/article-p 433.xml?tab_body=contributor%20notes (retrieved at 28.02.2024).

3.2 New social movements (from the 1970s)

Social movements can only re-emerge in the Federal Republic after the end of National Socialism. One of the first is the revival of the peace movement, which was directed against the rearmament of the Federal Republic of Germany (FRG) between 1951 and 1955. Many other movements of the 1970s and 1980s are triggered by the international students' movement. They are not only concerned with changes in politics and exposing the social costs of social modernisation but also with changing lifestyles in the "alternative movements", in which communal forms of living and working are tried out. In the counterculture or subculture, numerous alternative projects and institutions emerged (cf. Wagner 2010: 12), such as cooperative businesses, women's health centres, free clinics for drug counselling, and organic and one-world shops, some of which continue to exist today.

The themes of the New SMs include gender, racism, sexuality, the environment and disarmament. They include the new women's movement, the new peace movement, the ecology movement and the anti-nuclear movement. "Their basic patterns fit modern lifestyles and the increased self-actualisation and creative demands of their sponsors: fluid, network-like forms of cooperation instead of bureaucratic large-scale organisations, an emphasis on thematic and ideological diversity instead of standardisation, rather 'leaderless' structures instead of fixation on prominent leaders, a wide range of civil, creative forms of mobilisation and action instead of a culture of militancy and determination, comprehensive inner democracy and co-creation instead of subordination and discipline" (author's translation, Roth 2012: 3-4). The terms "grassroots movements" or "society from below" point to the civil society significance. On the other hand, SMs are themselves hegemonic projects, i.e., they reproduce social inequalities and are themselves involved in the production of difference (development of structures that create disadvantages). They are often carried by activists from socially well-off milieus. In the 1990s, this analytical gap was filled by the concept of intersectionality (Crenshaw 1991). (Crenshaw 1991) and thus became an explicit object of the political articulation of social movements. It is about the interaction of different forms of social hierarchisation and differentiation, such as class, gender, racial discrimination, disability and body. The roots lie in the environment of Black Feminism, the feminist, anti-racist and anti-capitalist movement of Black women and lesbians in the USA (Ganz 2019).

3.3 "New" new social movements or post-2011 movements

For a long time now, there have been SMs in the Global South, e.g. by women, by smallholders, by indigenous peoples, which are little known beyond national borders. This is changing in 2011, which is considered the starting year of a new wave of protest movements. It is the year of worldwide, transnational (youth) protests against authoritarian regimes and social grievances, banking crises and national debt among other things in the wake of the 2008 banking crisis.

In that year, "The Protester" was named "person of the year" (2011) by the US news magazine "Time" (this award has been given since 1827). This shows how relevant the SMs have become in the social consciousness.

Across national borders, "a mostly colourful movement sector can establish itself in the political space alongside and partly against the dominant institutions (such as parties, parliaments, governments) [...] from which important political impulses emanate. The protests have also made it clear that the national borders of movements have become more open. International impulses, issues and forms of action are being taken up, and approaches to a common agenda are emerging" (author's translation, Roth 2012: 2–3). Examples of this international movement against political paternalism and economic inequality are the Arab Spring in North Africa and the Middle East, followed by occupations of public spaces in Madrid, Athens and other cities by anti-austerity activists explicitly referring to the uprisings in the Arab world. This was followed by the Occupy Wall Street protests with a critical focus on the global financial system, which, starting in New York, were taken up in many metropolises around the world.

An element unifying the protest actors is that these protest movements are predominantly carried by youth and young adults. In addition to criticising the economic and financial systems, they also denounce the expropriation of life opportunities. Most of the protesters have a good education, but in Southern Europe and the Arab countries they are exposed to social deprivation and a lack of job prospects. It is a "revolt of the educated" (Kraushaar 2012), which is gaining in vehemence due to globalisation.

3.4 Globalisation

The transnational movements are comparable to national SMs in terms of structure and goals, but they are characterised by the fact that they drive political and social transformations beyond the borders of individual states.

In addition, they include the activities of the so-called "transnational social movement organisations", e.g., Amnesty International, Attac, Friends of the Earth International (FoEI) and others. In order to shape understanding of global issues and to influence intergovernmental and transnational arenas, it is important to convey the transnational similarities of the causes of protest. Thus, transnational movements help to overcome obstacles to national SMs (in authoritarian societies) and to transport (oppressed) concerns on multiple levels, thus circumventing potential restrictive measures. Another important aspect is global "knowledge empowerment": on the one hand, the empowerment of protest actors through knowledge, on the other hand, the empowerment of knowledge content that is disregarded or stigmatised in political discourse. "A central role is played by different experts who produce, identify and provide knowledge for the movement and act as legitimising references. [...] Counter-knowledge, however, is not only alternative knowledge content but also disparate forms of knowledge and cognition, for example, when expert knowledge, which is perceived as sober and distanced, is countered with allegedly 'holistic', e.g. emotional, evidence and an argumentation based on subjective concern" (author's translation, Pantenburg et al. 2021: 7).

Not only the SMs but also social work has become globalised – also as a result of digitalisation –, which is reflected in publications with international editors and congresses with participants from all over the world. In addition, new social problems are emerging across national borders, while "old" social problems are becoming more and more similar across borders. Topics such as commuter migration and transmigration, reproductive trafficking/surrogate motherhood, transnational family biographies or the care chains require social work not only to expand its knowledge and expertise but also to develop new forms of intervention and advocacy (Diwersy/Köngeter 2022; Schwarzer et al. 2016).

3.5 SMs, non-governmental organisations (NGOs) and social work

Looking at this relationship is highly relevant because social workers are involved in many NGOs. NGOs are often a part of SMs, but they are more of an organisation in structure and sometimes also differentiate themselves from SMs, which often have more radical demands and use civil disobedience. "And while one or the other self-image as a social worker stems from their own protest past, for some activists it is unthinkable to submit to such an institutionalisation. At the same time, the term 'social' and the claim to shape the social express a certain connection between these two phenomena. It should always be borne in mind that social movements are multifaceted, just as social work is not all the same" (author's translation, Bunk 2018: 266).

Whether NGOs represent an institutional core or a transnational leg for the SMs, whether they are their social and political basis or whether the SMs form the avant-garde of international NGOs or both together are the bearers of a "world civil society" (cf. Roth 2001: 51) – whatever pattern of interpretation is considered, one thing is certain: in the countries of the Global South, professional and para-social work, political activism and one's own concern are often difficult to separate. The continuing impacts of sexism, anti-Semitism, colonialism and racism, unrest and wars, former and current struggles for independence and reform, and the lack of welfare state structures mean that groups and movements outside state organisations both cover the social sphere and at the same time represent and publicise positions critical of society.

This results in a more radical form of social work for which, according to Lutz et al. (2021), the following demand could be made not only on a transnational and international level but also nationally: "It must shed its liberal character of a value-free science and adopt more radical as well as liberating positions in order to be able to detach itself from the institutions and processes that create the social problems that social work is supposed to combat in the first place; it must appear as a political actor and intervene" (https://www.socialnet.de/lexikon/Soziale-Arbeit-des-Suedens).

All this leads back to the question posed at the beginning: Is international social work itself a movement? Is the self-mandate to become a "human rights profession" (Staub-Bernasconi 2008; UN 1992) sufficient?

4. Social work as a movement?

This question divides opinions, not only in the professional policy discussion in the Global North but also in the North/South debate. At the same time, it is also a question of the "Zeitgeist".

In the 1970s, Karam Khella (1982), starting from a Marxist understanding of theory, takes a radical position with his "social work from below", which he sees as an antithesis to the established, officially funded social work supported by the state or 'free' social work providers (inverted commas in the original, ed.). In a 10-phase programme, he sets out a strategy in which steps are developed for mobilising marginalised groups through social work. If this practical guide finds great approval shortly after its publication, this approach disappears in the neoliberal tendencies of the 1980s.

Merten (2001), on the other hand, describes the political mandate as a (self-)misunderstanding of the professional mission of social work, which contributes to misjudging the real possibilities of social work. He argues that social work has no political mandate but ("only") a professional mission. However: "If it wants to fulfil this with the highest degree of competence, then it will help to ensure that its clients receive the rights to which they are entitled, and even better, that it enables them to exercise and realise their rights independently" (author's translation, Merten 2001: 89). But according to Kusche/Krüger, it is precisely this task of gaining resources that is the socio-political mandate. They argue that it does not matter whether this mandate is based on socio-legal regulations, whether it is legitimised socio-politically or whether it is realised through self-appropriation. "What is decisive is the content of this mandate in the exercise of socio-political responsibility and design. This requires politically motivated everyday professional action, support in social movements, influence on professional-political organisations and curricula at universities" (author's translation, Kusche/Krüger 2001: 16). Schröder argues similarly with regard to the transnational interlocking of social work and SMs in the common goal of fighting neoliberalism. Social work, however, "can only occupy a marginal position here. It will always remain linked to its state connection and location [...]. Nevertheless, social work can act as a supporter of such protests" (author's translation, Schröder 2016: 125) and play an important role in the start-up phase of SMs. He derives this position from a comparison of Raschke's definition of SMs (see above) with the characteristics of social work. There are many similarities, but the main difference is that social work is integrated into the organisations of the welfare state, while SMs are qua definition non-organisations that often oppose state measures or interventions.

Questions of political interference by social work have been discussed at the international level since the beginning of the 1990s under the heading of policy practice (cf. Wyers 1991). Jansson was one of the first to conceptualise policy practice as an independent aspect of social work practice. He distinguishes between policy practice and advocacy in the following way: Policy practice is the commitment to influence and change policy in legislation, authorities and municipalities. Advocacy is "only" an aspect of policy practice that represents the more traditional conception of the social, namely the representation of the interests of the recipients of social work who are trying to improve their social and economic living conditions. Thus, advocacy is part of political practice but not the whole of political practice (Jansson 2014; Pawar 2019).

For Healy (2014), it is indisputable that at least international social work (ISW) is a movement. She identifies three directions in which ISW is developing or moving: firstly, as a movement committed to the dissemination of standards for teaching, practice and research; secondly, implementing a form of specific practice globally; and thirdly, as a (professional) political actor with the claim to intervene in global policy development and advocate for worldwide socio-political standards (cf. Healy 2014: 370).

If one searches in various codes of ethics of different national professional associations worldwide where and how political engagement is inscribed, one regularly finds the demand that social workers should engage in political practice in order to promote social change and development. In the global code of ethics (see above), this is formulated as follows: "Social workers recognise the political dimension of the profession as a consequence of the power and authority conferred on them by the State to take action with or on behalf of people, within the boundaries of the profession's ethical principles" (IASSW/IFSW 2018).

5. Outlook and research questions: Is social work dancing out of line?

The question of whether ISW is a movement cannot be answered conclusively here. It should be noted that the extent of integration and participation in SM is different in the Global North than in the South. So the question arises to what extent the theories and perspectives of previous movement research from the North can also capture those movements that have to operate under different conditions. Does it provide an analysis of the conditions in which the boundaries between social security and existential-political struggles are blurred, where the commitment to social justice and against repressive governments on the one hand and social movements on the other are often inseparable? The German Association for Development Policy and Humanitarian Aid (VENRO) warns of the phenomenon of "shrinking spaces", the restriction of civil society actors' scope for action. This is shown by the example of Russia, where NGOs working with international partners are registered on lists of "foreign agents" and thus tend to be suspected of espionage. The same applies to India, which is dependent on civil society services but does not allow any criticism of the government and uses the idea that "the foreign hand" is exerting a harmful influence on Indian politics as a pretext for monitoring social movements and even punishing them. Engagement in movements can become a dance on the volcano for the activists.

Altmann et al. (2017) see a further point of criticism in the bias of northern movement research. They describe the emergence of social movements as having gone hand in hand with political developments in the North, which has led to the "invisibilisation" of movements in the South.

In this context, it is worth recalling the approaches of social development and community development as central focal points of social work in the South, where "community" is not limited to sites but includes the sense of belonging. For social workers engaged in this field, there is often a correspondence between personal conviction and professional activity. In their practice, they are involved in socio-political measures to bring about a change in existing grievances through political influence. Indispensable for this is, among other things, an understanding of historical processes and the prioritisation of socio-political framework conditions in the analysis of social problems, i.e. the shift from focusing on individual problems to concentrating on structural oppression and its many forms and locations (Altmann 2017). Furthermore, it is about developing equal cooperation with service users and using creative approaches from art, music, literature, poetry, storytelling, radio, film, theatre and social media for activation, which can be part of local culture (Goel 2014; Nobel 2015).

How movement-oriented is social work as a profession? This will undoubtedly be one of the exciting research questions for the future, not only with regard to the emancipative movements but also with regard to the "backward-looking" ones.

Social movements and social work, as this chapter points out, have much in common, also historically. This is reinforced by globalisation and transnational problems. Social work in the North could make greater use of the power and influence given to it by the state – as formulated in the global code of ethics. It could as well increase the power to take action for more social justice for and together with people. In doing so, it could learn a lot from the social work of the South and the local movements.

Reflective questions

- Does social work deal with SMs? If so, in what form?
- What do you think are the motivations and attitudes of activists who are also active in social work? What is their influence on social work?
- What responsibility does international social work have in relation to the risk of endangering activists from its own ranks in repressive regimes?
- In your estimation, will social work as a whole become (re-)politicised and radicalised?
- Would you define international social work as a movement?

I.2 (Re-)Visions and Challenges: International Social Work and Social Movements

- Were/are you yourself active in a social movement/NGO or do you have contact?
- Explore the situation of social movements in a country of your choice.

Introductory Literature

IASSW/IFSW/ICSW: International Social Work: a scholarly refereed journal designed to extend knowledge and promote international exchange in the fields of social work, social welfare, and community development. It aims at examining the meaning of international social work in practice and theory, and exploring how those concerned with social work and community development can engage with international issues. https://us.sagepub.com/en-us/nam/journal/international-social-work#description (retrieved at 28.02.2024).

Nobel, Carolyn (2015): Social Protest Movements and Social Work Practice. www.researchgate.net/publication/304193330_Social_Protest_Movements_and_Social_Work_Practice (retrieved at 28.02.2024).

Altmann, Philipp/Demirhisar, Deniz Günce /Mwathi Mati, Jacob (2017): Social Movements in the Global South, www.researchgate.net/publication/327856967_Social_Movements_in_the_Global_South (retrieved at 28.02.2024).

Further Literature

Abramowitz, Mimi (2012): Theorising the Neoliberal Welfare State for Social Work. In: Sage Handbook of Social Work. Thousand Oaks: Sage, 33–50.

Almeida, Paul/ Cordero Ulate, Allen (2015): Social Movements Across Latin America. In: Dies. (Hrsg): Handbook of Social Movements across Latin America. Wiesbaden: Springer VS, 3–10.

Alston, Margaret/Besthorn, Fred H. (2012): Environment and Sustainability. In: Lyons, Karen H./Hokenstad, Terry/Hall, Nigel/Pawar, Manohar S. (eds.) (2012): Sage Handbook of International Social Work. London: Sage, 56–69.

Altmann, Philipp/Demirhisar, Deniz Günce /Mwathi Mati, Jacob (2017): Social Movements in the Global South, www.researchgate.net/publication/327856967_Social_Movements_in_the_Global_South (retrieved at 28.02.2024).

Bähr, Christiane/ Homfeldt, Hans-Günther/ Schröder, Christian/ Schröer, Wolfgang/ Schweppe, Cornelia (2014): Weltatlas Soziale Arbeit. Jenseits aller Vermessungen (Vorwort). In: Dies. (eds.): Weltatlas Soziale Arbeit. Jenseits aller Vermessungen. Weinheim, Basel: Beltz Juventa, 9–30.

Brand, Karl-Werner/Büsser, Detlef/Rucht, Dieter (1986^2): Aufbruch in eine andere Gesellschaft. Neue soziale Bewegungen in der Bundesrepublik. 2. Frankfurt a.M.: Campus.

Bunk, Benjamin (2018): Zur Differenz von Sozialer Arbeit und sozialen Bewegungen. Annäherungen über die brasilianische Movimento dos Sem Terra. In: Franke-Meyer, Diana/Kullmann, Carola (eds.) (2018). Soziale Bewegungen und Soziale Arbeit. Von der Kindergartenbewegung zur Homosexuellenbewegung. Wiesbaden: Springer VS, 265–282.

Cox, David/Pawar, Manohar (2012^2): International Social Work. Issues, Strategies, and Programs. Thousand Oaks: Sage.

Crenshaw, Kimberlé (1991): Mapping the Margins: Intersectionality, Identity Politics, and Violence Against Women of Color. In: Stanford Law Review, Volume 43/6, 1241–1299.

Daphi, Priska/Deitelhoff, Nicole (2018): Protest im Wandel? Jenseits von Transnationalisierung und Entpolitisierung. In: Leviathan, 45. Jg., Sonderband 33/2018, 306–322.

Davies, Thomas R./Peña, Alejandro M. (2021): Social movements and international relations: a relational framework. In: Journal of International Relations and Development, Heft 24, 51–76.

Della Porta, Donatella/Diani, Mario (Hrsg.) (2015): The Oxford Handbook of Social Movements. Oxford: Oxford University Press.

Diwersy, Bettina/Köngeter, Stefan (eds.) (2022): Internationale und Transnationale Soziale Arbeit. Baltmannsweiler: Schneider Verlag Hohengehren.

Dominelli, Lena (2014): Learning from our past: climate change and desaster interventions in practice. In: Noble, Carolyn/Strauss, Helle/Littlechild, Brian (eds.): Global Social Work. Crossing borders, blurring boundaries. Sydney: Sydney University Press, 341–351.

Ferguson, Iain (2008): Reclaiming Social Work. Challenging Neo-liberalism and Promoting Social Justice. London: Sage.

Ganz, Kathrin (2019): Kollektive Identitäten als Koalitionen denken. Intersektionalität in der sozialen Bewegungsforschung. In: Vey, Judith/Leinius, Johanna/Hagemann, Ingmar (eds.): Handbuch Poststrukturalistische Perspektiven auf soziale Bewegungen. Bielefeld: transcript Verlag, 168–183.

Goel, Kalpana (2019[2]): Understanding Community and Community Development - Defining the Concept of Community. In: Goel Kalpana, Pulla Venkat, Francis P. Abraham (ed.): Community Work: Theories, Experiences and Challenges. Niratanka:Niruta Publications, 1–15.

Gray, Mel/ Coates, John (2010): Conclusion. In: Gray, Mel/ Coates, John/ Yellow Bird, Michael: Indigenous Social Work around the World. Towards Culturally Relevant Education and Practice. Southhampton: Ashgate, 271–274.

Gray, Mel/ Webb, Stephen A. (2008): The Myth of Global Social Work – Global double standards in Social Work. In: Journal of Progressive Human Service, June 2008, 19 (1), 61–66. www.researchgate.net/publication/248920653_The_Myth_of_Global_Social_Work_Double_Standards_and_the_Local-Global_Divide (retrieved at 28.02.2024).

Hall, Nigel (2015): International Federation of Social Workers (IFSW). In: Encyclopedia of Social Work. oxfordre.com/socialwork/view/10.1093/acrefore/9780199975839.001.0001/acrefore-9780199975839-e-202 (retrieved at 28.02.2024).

Healy, L. (2014): Global education for social work: old debates and future directions for international social work. In: Noble, C./Strauss, H./Littlechild, B. (eds.) (2014): Global Social Work. Crossing borders, blurring boundaries. Sydney: Sydney University Press, 369–280.

Healy, Lynne/ Hall, Nigel (2009[2]): Internationale Organisationen der Sozialen Arbeit. In: Wagner, Leonie/ Lutz, Ronald (eds.): Internationale Perspektiven Sozialer Arbeit. Wiesbaden: VS-Verlag, 243–260.

Herbers, Lena/Zobel, Mareike (2022): Soziale Bewegung. In: socialnet Lexikon. Bonn: socialnet, https://www.socialnet.de/lexikon/Soziale-Bewegung (retrieved at 28.02.2024).

Hering, Sabine/ Waaldijk, Berteke (Hrsg.) (2002): Die Geschichte der Sozialen Arbeit in Europa (1900-1960). Wichtige Pionierinnen und ihr Einfluss auf die Entwicklung internationaler Organisationen. Opladen: Leske + Budrich.

Homfeldt, H.-G./Reutlinger, C. (Hrsg.) (2009): Soziale Arbeit und Soziale Entwicklung. Baltmannsweiler: Schneider Verlag Hohengehren.

IFSW/IASSW (2018): Global Social Work Statement of Ethical Principles. www.ifsw.org/global-social-work-statement-of-ethical-principles/ (retrieved at 28.02.2024).

IFSW (2014): Global Definition of the Social Work Profession. http://ifsw.org/get-involved/global-definition-of-social-work/ (retrieved at 28.02.2024).

IFSW, IASSW, ICSW (2012): The Global Agenda for Social Work and Social development – committment to action. In: Social Dialogue, 2/2012, 46–49.

Institut für Protest- und Bewegungsforschung (ipb) (2021): Basiscodebuch-Protestereignisanalyse. https://protestinstitut.eu/wp-content/uploads/2021/05/ipb-Basiscodebuch-Protestereignisanalyse.pdf (retrieved at 28.02.2024).

Jansson, Bruce S. (2014). Becoming an Effective Policy Advocate: From Policy Practice to Social Justice. Belmont, CA: Brooks/Cole.

Kniephoff-Knebel, Anette/Seibel, Friedrich W. (2008): Establishing international cooperation in social work education: the first decade of the „International Committee of

Schools for Social Work" (ICSSW). In: International Social Work, November 2008 (51), 790–812.

Khella, Karam (1982): Sozialarbeit von unten. Praktische Methoden der fortschrittlichen Sozialarbeit. Einführung in die Sozialarbeit und Sozialpädagogik, vol. 1, part 3. Hamburg: Theorie und Praxisverlag.

Köngeter, Stefan (2013): Transnationales Wissen in der Geschichte der Sozialen Arbeit. Zur Bedeutung religiöser Verbindungen für die grenzüberschreitende Verbreitung der Settlement-Bewegung. In: Bender, Desireé/Duscha, Annemarie/Huber, Lena/Klein-Zimmer, Kathrin (eds.): Transnationales Wissen und Soziale Arbeit. Weinheim: Beltz Juventa, 80–97.

Kraushaar, Wolfgang (2012): Aufruhr der Ausgebildeten. Vom Arabischen Frühling zur Occupy-Bewegung. Hamburger Edition: Hamburg.

Kruse, Elke (2009): Zur Geschichte der internationalen Dimension in der Sozialen Arbeit: In: Wagner, Leonie/ Lutz, Ronald (eds.): Internationale Perspektiven Sozialer Arbeit. Wiesbaden: VS-Verlag, 15–32.

Kusche, Christoph/Krüger, Rolf (2001): Sozialarbeit muss sich endlich zu ihrem politischen Mandat bekennen! In: Merten, Roland (ed.): Hat Soziale Arbeit ein politisches Mandat? Positionen zu einem strittigen Thema. VS Verlag für Sozialwissenschaften: Wiesbaden, 15–25.

Lorenz, Walter (2015): Soziale Arbeit in Europa. In: Otto, Hans-Uwe/Thiersch, Hans (ed.): Handbuch Soziale Arbeit. München und Basel: Reinhardt, 1436–1443.

Lutz, Ronald/Kleibl, Tanja/Neureither, Franziska (2021): Soziale Arbeit des Südens. socialnet Lexikon. Bonn: socialnet. www.socialnet.de/lexikon/Soziale-Arbeit-des-Suedens (retrieved at 28.02.2024).

Mathbor, Golam M./ Bourassa, Jennifer (2012): Desaster Management and Humanitarian Action. In: Lyons, Karen H./ Hokenstad, Terry/ Hall, Nigel/ Pawar, Manohar S. (eds.): Sage Handbook of International Social Work. London: Sage, 294–310.

Merten, Roland (2001). Politisches Mandat als (Selbst-)Missverständnis des professionellen Auftrags Sozialer Arbeit. In: ders. (ed.): Hat Soziale Arbeit ein politisches Mandat? Wiesbaden: VS Verlag, 89–10.

Midgley, James (2010): Promoting Reciprocal International Social Work Exchanges: Professional Imperialism Revisited. In: Gray, Mel/ Coates, John/ Yellow Bird, Michael: Indigenous Social Work around the World. Towards Culturally Relevant Education and Practice. Southhampton: Ashgate, 31–45.

Nobel, Carolyn (2015): Social Protest Movements and Social Work Practice www.researchgate.net/publication/304193330_Social_Protest_Movements_and_Social_Work_Practice (retrieved at 28.02.2024).

Pantenburg, Johannes/Reichardt, Sven/Sepp, Benedikt (2021): Corona-Proteste und das (Gegen-)Wissen sozialer Bewegungen. In: Aus Politik und Zeitgeschichte (ApuZ 15.1.2021), Bundeszentrale für politische Bildung. www.bpb.de/apuz/wissen-2021/325605/corona-proteste-und-das-gegen-wissen-sozialer-bewegungen (retrieved at 28.02.2024).

Pawar, Manhar (2019): Social Work and Social Policy Practice: Imperatives for Political Engagement https://doi.org/10.1177%2F2516602619833219 (retrieved at 28.02.2024).

Rammstedt, Otthein (1978): Soziale Bewegung. Frankfurt: Suhrkamp.

Raschke, Joachim (1991): Zum Begriff der sozialen Bewegung. In: Roth, Roland/Rucht, Dieter (Hrsg.): Neue Soziale Bewegungen in der Bundesrepublik Deutschland. Bonn: Bundeszentrale für Politische Bildung, 31–39.

Rehklau, Christine/Lutz, Ronald (2010): Partnerschaft oder Kolonisation? In: Wagner, Leonie/ Lutz, Ronald (eds.): Internationale Perspektiven Sozialer Arbeit, Wiesbaden: VS-Verlag, 33–53.

Roth, Roland (2012): Occupy und Acampada: Vorboten einer neuen Protestgeneration? In: Aus Politik und Zeitgeschichte (APuZ) Bundeszentrale für politische Bildung,

11.06.2012 https://www.bpb.de/shop/zeitschriften/apuz/138286/occupy-und-acampada-vorboten-einer-neuen-protestgeneration/ (retrieved at 28.02.2024).

Roth, Roland (2001): NGO und transnationale soziale Bewegungen: Akteure einer „Weltzivilgesellschaft". In: Brand, Ulrich/Demirovic, Alex/Görg, Christoph/Hirsch, Joachim (eds.): Nichtregierungsorganisationen in der Transformation des Staates, Münster: Westfälisches Dampfboot, 43–63.

Roth, Roland (1991²): Kommunikationsstrukturen und Vernetzungen in den neuen sozialen Bewegungen. In: Roth, Roland/Rucht, Dieter (eds.): Neue soziale Bewegungen in der Bundesrepublik Deutschland. Bonn: Bundeszentrale für politische Bildung (bpb).

Roth, Roland/Rucht, Dieter (2008): Einleitung. In: Roth, Roland/Rucht, Dieter (ed.): Die sozialen Bewegungen in Deutschland seit 1945. Ein Handbuch. Frankfurt/Main, New York: Campus, 9–38.

Rucht, Dieter (2016a): Die medienorientierte Inszenierung von Protest. APUZ 09.12.2016, bpb bpb.de/themen/medien-journalismus/medienpolitik/236953/die-medienorientierte-inszenierung-von-protest/ (retrieved at 28.02.2024).

Rucht, Dieter (2016b): "Protest Cultures in Social Movements. Dimensions and Functions". In: Kathrin Fahlenbrach/Martin Klimke/Joachim Scharloth (Eds.): Protest Cultures. A Companion. Protest, Culture & Society, Vol. 17. New York, NY/Oxford: Berghahn Books, 26–32.

Rucht, Dieter (1994): Öffentlichkeit als Mobilisierungsfaktor für soziale Bewegungen, In: Neidhardt, Friedhelm eds.): Öffentlichkeit, öffentliche Meinung, soziale Bewegungen, Opladen: Westdeutscher Verlag, 337–358.

Schmelz, Andrea (2021): Rebellin gegen Klassenverhältnisse: Mentona Moser (1874-1971). Eine Pionierin der internationalen Sozialen Arbeit. In: Soziale Arbeit, 9/2021, pp. 337–334.

Schwarzer, Beatrix/Kämmerer-Rütten, Ursula/Schleyer-Lindenmann, Alexandra/Wang, Yafang (2016) (eds.): Transnational Social Work and Social Welfare: Challenges for the Social Work Profession. London, New York: Routledge.

Staub-Bernasconi, Silvia (2008): Menschenrechte in ihrer Relevanz für die Theorie und Praxis Sozialer Arbeit. Oder: Was haben Menschenrechte überhaupt in der Sozialen Arbeit zu suchen? In: Widersprüche, Vol. 107. Bielefeld: Kleine Verlag, 9–32.

Straub, Ute (2020a): Internationale Soziale Arbeit. socialnet Lexikon. Bonn: socialnet. www.socialnet.de/lexikon/Internationale-Soziale-Arbeit (retrieved at 28.02.2024).

Straub, Ute/ Rott, Gerhard/ Lutz, Ronald (eds.) (2020b): Indigenous and Local Knowledge. Vol. IX Soziale Arbeit des Südens. Opladen: Paulo Freire-Verlag.

Straub, Ute (2018): Definitionen Sozialer Arbeit. In: Wagner, Leonie/Lutz, Ronald/Rehklau, Christine /Friso Ross (eds.): Handbuch Internationale Soziale Arbeit. Weinheim, Basel: Beltz Juventa, 22–34.

Straub, Ute (2016): „All my relations" – indigene Ansätze und Relationalität in der Sozialen Arbeit. In Früchtel, Frank/ Strassner, Mischa/ Schwarzloos, Christian (eds.) (2016): Relationale Sozialarbeit - versammelnde, vernetzende und kooperative Hilfeformen. Weinheim, Basel: Beltz-Juventa, 54–74.

Straub, Ute (2015) Machtungleichgewichte - Konflikte in der Internationalen Sozialen Arbeit. Die neue Globale Definition und indigene Soziale Arbeit. In: Stövesand, Sabine/ Röh, Dieter Eds.) 2015: Konflikte – theoretische und praktische Herausforderungen für die Soziale Arbeit. Opladen, Berlin &Toronto: Verlag Barbara Budrich, 58–68.

Tamburro, Andrea (2013): Including Decolonization in Social Work Education and Practice. In: Journal of Indigenous Social Development, Heft 3 (1), 1–16.

Wagner, Leonie (2010) (Hrsg.): Soziale Arbeit und soziale Bewegungen - Einleitung. In: Dies. (ed.): Soziale Arbeit und Soziale Bewegungen. Wiesbaden: VS Verlag, 9–19.

II. International Social Work in Social Movements

II.1 "Your Body Is a Battleground"[1]
Women's Movements, Queer Feminism and Gender Justice

Claudia Lohrenscheit

> 8th May – International Women's Day/Women's Strike Day
>
> 17th May – International Day for LGBTIQ+ Human Rights
>
> 26th October – International Intersex Awareness Day
>
> 25th November – International Day against Violence against Women

Summary

Critical contributions and interventions against sexism and violence against women and LGBTIQ+ are among the core topics of social movements in numerous countries around the globe. However, it is not self-evident that these topics are anchored in curricula and teaching practices at universities. The following chapter therefore provides a basic introduction to questions of gender justice in Social Work and then looks at three current examples of international social movements that advocate for gender justice and queer feminist goals; these are the social struggles (1) against femicide (murders of women), (2) for reproductive rights and the decriminalisation of abortion and (3) for the dignity and the human rights of intersex people.

1. Introduction

"That's gender gaga"; "Boys don't cry"; "Lesbians (or feminists) are frustrated man-haters" – many readers will have heard and been annoyed by these or similar comments. Others are familiar with women's rights and queer feminist issues because they are directly or indirectly affected, e.g. because they know the fear of being out alone at night or because they have to hide and deny themselves for fear of violence against their sexual orientation or gender identity. Laurie Penny (2022) speaks of a culture of violence in this context that she calls *rape culture*. With this term she refers to a society where sexual violence and rape is not only commonplace but part of a culture where rape happens and is *normal*; where especially women and LGBTIQ+ grow up knowing that rape is a fact that is affecting them as kind of a *normal* routine.

Against this, millions of people participate in strikes, campaigns and political action worldwide. At the beginning of the 21st century, the queer and feminist

---

[1] *Your body is a battleground* – this title refers to an iconic work by the US artist and feminist Barbara Kruger for the Women's March on Washington in 1989.

movements are stronger and more diverse than ever. They inspire and link up with other social movements and repeatedly lead to asking critical questions of power (cf. Wolff et al. 2015: 109). They encompass the human rights concerns of heterosexual, lesbian or bisexual women[2] and girls, differently abled, with and without disabilities, non-binary, intersex and trans women. They link the human rights of black and *white* women, migrant and refugee women with different faiths or worldviews.

At the same time and on the contrary, opposite tendencies and developments expand in many places: In Poland, for example, abortions were recently completely banned. Turkey has withdrawn from the Istanbul Convention[3]. In countries like Bulgaria or Hungary, queer feminist movements, lesbians, gays and transgender people are violently attacked, and many conservative, populist or right-wing parties call for the defence of "Christian values" or the so-called "natural" family. In doing so, they actively politicise against sexual self-determination rights and increasingly form transnational alliances. For the Social Work profession this is not new. Gender relations and gender justice have been a core topic for Social Work since its beginnings in Germany, Europe or the US (cf. Hering 2002). Pioneers like Jane Addams, for example, were both at the same time: protagonists for developing the profession and activists of the international women's and peace movements before the beginning of the First World War (cf. Franger 2015; see also Straub in this volume). This must be understood in context: Social Work is as a field in itself structured according to gender roles. The historical roots of Social Work in reproductive, educational as well as health and care-oriented professions are found in female connoted, poorly paid or undervalued *care* work of women who still have to struggle for social and financial recognition today. "They call it love, we call it unpaid work" – this is how Silvia Federici comments it (quoted from Tsomou 2018).

Progress in gender justice is never assured. On the contrary, especially in times of crisis, regressions and continuing injustice are evident. The COVID-19 pandemic, for example, was also a crisis of care work, which in many cases pushed women out of paid work and back into unpaid care work. And while paid care work received a lot of appreciation on the symbolic level as "system-relevant", the poor working conditions remained, especially for precarious workers. Also, the war in Ukraine currently shows in a very brutal way, despite all progress, how traditional gender roles are coming back with force. As the two German journalists Anne Fromm and Sophie Fichtner put it:

> *„Männer erschießen, Frauen kümmern sich um die Leichen. Männer ziehen an die Front, Frauen tragen ihre Kinder über die Grenze. In Talkshows und auf Zeitungsseiten erklären Männer Militärstrategien. Und hinter den Grenzen verteilen polnische und slowakische Frauen Tee und Salamibrote*

---

2 Women*: In this text, I do not use the asterisk when referring to women, but the term "women" refers to all those who (want to) identify themselves as such, regardless of other categories such as the gender entry in the birth certificate or civil status of a person.
3 The Council of Europe Convention on preventing and combating violence against women and domestic violence (2011); see below.

an geflüchtete Ukrainer:innen" ("Men shoot, women take care of the corpses. Men go to the front, women carry their children across the border. Men explain military strategies in talk shows and on newspaper pages. And behind the borders, Polish and Slovakian women distribute tea and salami sandwiches to Ukrainians who have fled") (Fromm/Fichtner 2022).[4]

The social movements around the topic of gender justice include the feminist and women's rights movements, which have existed (with interruptions) since the end of the 19th century, as well as the queer-feminist movements since the middle of the 20th century, which today are differentiated into LGBTIQ+ = Lesbian, Gay, Bisexual, Trans*, Intersex, Queer. Together, these political initiatives and social movements are comprehensive, and they are among the most dynamic drivers of social and democratic developments worldwide. In the following, after a brief reference to current professional and political foundations and a general introduction to the queer feminist movements, the following questions will be in focus:

1. What are femicides; and what (new) forms for resistance, education and solidarity have been developed in the struggle against femicides?
2. *"My Body my Choice"* – Sexual self-determination and the fight against the criminalisation of abortion
3. Global queer feminist movements for the rights of intersex people

What is gender?

Gender is a multidimensional category that has been developed and differentiated over the past decades. Usually, a distinction is made between the biological sexes *(sex)* and the social sexes *(gender)*. These definitions can be further differentiated into gender expression (how we show ourselves) and gender identity (how we feel). There are people who identify with the gender entered in the birth register *(cisgender)*, people who don't and who transform in the course of life *(transgender)* and people who do not want to (let themselves) be identified either or not at all *(non-binary)*. Gender must be understood as a construct; it can be perceived as fixed or as fluid. Societies as well as individual people change over time with regard to gender roles and identities. Gender relations do not only describe the relationship between individuals but also encompass structural categories whereby social structure analyses reveals where disadvantages persist on the grounds of gender (e.g. gender pay gap). At the global level, current data on this can be found in the assessment of *Goal 5 "Achieve gender equality and empower all women and girls"* of the *Sustainable Development Goals* by the United Nations (see below).

The somatic (also biological) sex is composed of chromosomes (e.g. XX or XY or XXY), the gonads, hormones and the external and internal sex organs. The mental (cerebral) sphere includes the perception of one's own sex or gender identity. The social dimension includes the ascribed gender, which is registered with the birth certificate, and gender as a significant legal category (cf. Plett 2021). Furthermore, social gender norms imply diverse social, historical and

---

[4] It is not quite that simple, of course, but Fromm and Fichtner point out that various conflicts around the world have shown that peace is more stable where women are involved in the negotiations. For this purpose, the UN Resolution 1325 on "Women, Peace and Security" was created.

> cultural aspects that allow for different variants of gender identity. Thus, the former dual gender norm, which only knew two sexes and only one sexual orientation (heteronormativity), is increasingly breaking down. More and more, fluid concepts transform strict gender norms and include (biologically and socially) third options (e.g. inter*, diverse or non-binary) or gender diversity.
> This also increasingly changes patriarchal structures in which gender relations are shaped by power, domination and hierarchical boundaries that place the heterosexual, *white* cis man at the top of the social order and oppress women and LGBTIQ+. However, this cannot hide how stable gender remains as a structural category – especially with regard to family structures and the labour market including Social Work and the health sector: gender is inscribed in the segregated labour market, in which women, often also migrants, work in precarious situations, often paid less than men (gender *pay gap*) and with the prospect of being less secure in old age (*gender pension gap*).
> To explore further: A well-known graphic representation of this diversity of gender dimensions can be found online under the title *"genderbread person"*, because it is shaped like the famous gingerbread.

2. Professional and political foundations for International Social Work in the field of gender justice

The *International Federation of Social Work* (IFSW) and the *International Association of Schools of Social Work* (IASSW) jointly publish the *Global Standards for Social Work Education and Training* since 2004 (last update in 2020).[5] These standards are intended to establish a certain degree of consistency and uniformity in the study, education and training of Social Workers. Gender justice plays a central role as (1) an ethical basis, (2) an objective and (3) the content of the curriculum (cf. in particular the fourth chapter, *Core Curriculum*). Their recommendation is that basic knowledge about human rights, social movements and their connection with class issues, gender issues and anti-racist issues be taught in the study of Social Work. The study programme should also have a clear focus on gender justice and a deeper understanding of the structural conditions for gender-based violence.

At the global level, the United Nations advocate for seventeen *Sustainable Development Goals* (SDGs) as a political agenda for the world community up to the year 2030. The goals are aimed at everyone: states, civil society, the economy, science and (higher) education in general and Social Work in particular. The IFSW is a registered group at the UN and supports the work on the SDGs and accordingly develops its own *policy papers*. At the same time, it also sees itself as a critical companion for the analysis of opportunities and obstacles in the implementation of the goals.[6] Gender equality is included in the goals both implicitly as a cross-cutting issue (e.g. in Goal No. 4 on education) and explicitly

---

5　The 2020 version of the *Global Standards for Social Work Education and Training* was developed through a global consultation with experts from 125 countries, five regional social work associations and more than 400 higher education institutions and training institutes; see: https://www.iassw-aiets.org/global-standards-for-social-work-education-and-training (retrieved at 28.02.2024).

6　See on this: Social Work and the United Nations Sustainable Development Goals (SDGs, Policy Topic: IFSW, UN, April 1, 2021, https://www.ifsw.org/social-work-and-the-united-nations-sustainable-development-goals-sdgs/ (retrieved at 28.02.2024)).

as Goal No. 5 on *gender equality*. Here, gender is understood as a structural category that refers to inequality between the social groups of women and men. The UN justifies this with the persisting inequalities between the sexes, which still massively disadvantage women as a social group and which exist in all societies worldwide, albeit to varying degrees. To give a brief snapshot, the UN (2022) refers to the following data as examples:

- Up to 200 million girls and women in 30 countries worldwide are affected by FGM – *Female Genital Mutilation/Cutting*;
- In 18 states, men can still prohibit their wives from working; in 39 states, sons and daughters do not have equal access to inheritance rights, and 49 states have not established legal foundations that protect women from domestic violence;
- Worldwide, one in five women or girls has experienced physical and/or sexual violence in the last twelve months, often by an intimate partner;
- Only one in two women can freely decide on her sexual relations and contraceptive methods within the framework of her marriage or intimate partnership;
- Only 13% of the world's agricultural land is owned by women;
- In political decision-making bodies, women won 30% of parliamentary seats in 46 states, giving them a global percentage of 23.7 in national parliaments.

3. The diversity of queer feminist movements against patriarchal violence and sexism

(Queer) feminist movements have always existed as a plurality. In retrospect, these movements for women's rights, emancipation and liberation from gender norms and violence are divided (roughly) into three waves or phases, i.e. a first phase from the Enlightenment onwards, a second phase after WWII (1950s with peaks in the 1970s) and a third wave until today (1990s to the present).[7] In particular the first wave, advocating for women's suffrage and peace politics, was closely interwoven with the history of Social Work and the establishment of the first training institutions and curricula about 100 years ago. Rita Braches-Chyrek (2013) and Gaby Franger (2015) point out that German students of Social Work today know its founders, but they don't know the commitment of these founders as international peace activists and feminists. The lives and work of women like Alice Salomon and Jane Addams exemplify the fact that Social Work has been constitutively linked with the peace movement and the social movements for women's and human rights internationally since the beginning. With the second wave, the right to one's own body and sexual and reproductive justice came into focus. Many of today's lecturers at colleges and universities still remember the slogan *"Mein Bauch gehört mir"* (My belly belongs to me) or the campaign *"Ich habe abgetrieben"* (I had an abortion), which caused a furore for example in Germany and France in the late 1970s. But these campaigns alone do not describe the breadth of the feminist movements of the time. For example, the issues of

---

7 A detailed history of women's movements can be found elsewhere; e.g. Gerhard 2009, 2020; Wichterich 2000.

women in the Global North differed significantly from those of the Global South, who repeatedly emphasised that feminism must also be a struggle against racism and poverty (cf. Frey 2003). Even today, in Germany, for example, many people are not aware of the fact that there has been a strong Black German women's movement since the mid-1980s, with its own associations and organs and with important activists such as May Ayim and Audre Lorde, who also coined the term "Afro-German" for the first time (cf. the contribution by Arndt/Scalisi in this volume).

Current movements are trying to build bridges and act in a conceptually inclusive way (e.g. "The Feminism of the 99%", Arruzza et al. (2019). This is exemplified by the strike call published by Nancy Fraser, Angela Davis and others in the English *Guardian* in January 2018 (cited in Wiedemann 2021: 105; translated by the author) and characterising the so-called third wave: "The new international feminist movement is anti-racist, anti-imperialist, anti-heterosexist and anti-neoliberal", because violence against women cannot be separated from the "violence of the market, of debt, of capitalist property relations and of the state; of the violence of state criminalisation of migration movements; of the violence of mass incarceration and institutional violence against women through abortion bans and lack of access to free health care."

Although this call may sound negative ("anti"), the current women's and queer feminist movements are progressive and strengthen the resilience of societies and democracy. A new global anti-patriarchal mass movement is growing out of the interplay of #metoo, international strike days and new creative, pop-cultural and artistic initiatives such as the Chilean collective *Las Tesis* (see below). Critical men as well as queer people and transgender people have long since shown solidarity here. This new transnational feminism is multi-voiced, diverse and, through its connection to social networks and digital information channels, partly popular. An example of this is the TED Talk *We should all be feminists* by Chimamanda Ngozi Adichie, which went viral and has been seen by more than 7.9 million people around the globe.[8]

4. Femicide: *Justicia para nuestras hijas* – Justice for our daughters

Gender-based violence is directed against a person because of their biological or social sex/gender. It disproportionately affects women worldwide. Femicides, i.e. murders of women, are only the "tip of the iceberg". Gender-based violence includes sexualised violence but also psychological, economic or social violence, and even warfare. The most dangerous place for a woman is her own home; the most dangerous person is often her own (ex-)partner. *Rape culture* and violence against women are spreading in pandemic proportions. In many countries, a woman's life is worth nothing. Yet this violence is often not characterised as a serious crime and human rights violation but is trivialised or made invisible. Politicians and the media often regard the phenomenon of domestic violence as a private problem.

---

[8] If you enter the title on YouTube, you will be taken directly to the link of the approximately thirty-minute speech that Adichie gave in the TED series in 2013.

Accordingly, when a man murders his (ex-)partner, journalists still trivially report it as a "relationship act", a "family drama" or an "act of jealousy". But the available figures and data are alarming: in Germany, every fourth woman experiences sexual violence at least once in her life. Every day women are beaten up, locked up, controlled or insulted by their partners. Every second or third day, a woman dies from so-called intimate partner violence, and the number of unreported cases is probably much higher. 95% of the reported perpetrators are male; 95% of the victims are female (cf. Clemm 2020: 19)[9], whereby trans or intersex persons are not explicitly recorded by the official statistics. Globally, the WHO, World Health Organisation of the UN, states that sexualised violence in particular against women and violence in partnerships are among the greatest risks and problems in the public health sector. According to WHO estimates (2021), 30% of all women worldwide are affected by sexualised violence at least once in their lives. The majority of these acts of violence take place in the context of intimate couple relationships. The consequences for the victims of violence and society are serious. Gender-based violence can seriously affect physical, psychological, sexual and reproductive health and can also significantly increase the risk of contracting HIV/AIDS.

#NousToutes, #metoo, #NiUnaMenos – these hashtags stand for new transnational queer-feminist movements around the world that stand up against violence and vehemently fight to publicly scandalise gender-based violence. They are largely fed by initiatives from the Global South, especially Latin America. They have coined the term femicide to specifically describe gender-based violence against women.

Femicide

As early as 1976, at the first international tribunal on violence against women the term femicide was introduced by the South African sociologist Diana Russel, in distinction to the gender-neutral term homicide. She defined femicide as a hate crime and the murder of a woman because she is a woman (*the intentional killing of women or girls because they are female*). This usually happens in the domestic sphere as well as in connection with sexualised violence (cf. Backes/Bettoni 2021).

Marcela Lagarde, Mexican activist, professor and author, later expands the term to highlight the lack of prosecution and frequent impunity for perpetrators which she coins as part of the institutional violence against women and LGBTIQ* (see Lateinamerika Nachrichten 2020). She also defines the term *transfemicide* to indicate that violence against trans women combines the hatred of people who deviate from binary gender norms with misogynistic hatred of women. Murders of trans women often remain invisible because in many countries they continue to be listed as men in the civil status.

However, the term femicide is not uniformly defined, as it is embedded in specific historical, political or regional contexts and shaped by joint efforts and discus-

---

9 Only in the case of children and adolescents do these figures differ: in the case of sexual abuse of children, 20% of the victims are male (cf. Clemm 2021: 19).

sions of activists, academics and lawyers (Dyroff et al. 2020: 4). The authors refer to the 1992 anthology edited by Diane Russel and Jill Radford, *Femicide. The Politics of Women Killing*, in which Radford proposed to also speak of femicide in situations in which women die due to social practices (for example forced marriages, illegalised abortions or intentional abortions of female foetuses). The World Health Organisation (WHO, 2012) further distinguishes between different types of femicide, such as intimate or non-intimate femicide. The WHO further argues that femicides have a prevalence of 35%, i.e., more than one in three murders of women is committed by their (ex-)partners, while this figure for murders of men is only about 5% in comparison (ibid.). Globally the figures on violence against women remain constantly high. They multiply when also digital violence and hatred in social media and networks are taken into account. From a Social Work perspective, the resources for the protection of victims are restricted and the available space for example in women's shelters and violence protection centres is insufficient (cf. Clemm 2021). At the same time, developments at the international legal level can give hope; the most recent and comprehensive document is the so-called *Istanbul Convention*, but also the *UN-Women's Rights Convention CEDAW* is a central institution as well as the *UN-Special Rapporteur on Violence against Women*.

Istanbul Convention – Council of Europe Convention on preventing and combating violence against Women and Domestic Violence (2011/2014)

The Istanbul Convention is a treaty under international human rights law which, after ratification, creates binding legal standards for the member states of the Council of Europe to protect women from violence. The Convention pursues the goal (cf. Art. 1) of protecting victims from violence, contributing to the elimination of all forms of discrimination against women and improving the possibilities of effective prosecution. It covers a wide range of areas such as education and prevention, ensuring access to help and protection facilities, and punishing perpetrators. The Convention also aims to strengthen research in the field of gender-based violence in order to collect data on the forms, causes and effects of gender-based violence. The Convention also obliges member states to establish a national coordinating body responsible for the implementation, monitoring and evaluation of all measures. (Council of Europe Convention on preventing and combating violence against women and domestic violence, https://www.coe.int/en/web/istanbul-convention/home, 28.02.2024).

CEDAW – UN-Convention on the Elimination of all forms of Discrimination Against Women (1979/1981)

The United Nations Convention on the Elimination of All Forms of Discrimination against Women is the most important international human rights instrument for women's rights and entered into force in 1981. Since then, 189 states, including Germany in 1985, have ratified the Convention. The provisions thus have the status of federal law. The current CEDAW State Report was adopted by the Federal Cabinet in 2021 and forwarded to the CEDAW Committee in Geneva. Further information can be found on the websites of the ministry with core-responsibility for the implementation of CEDAW (BMFSFJ), the National Human Rights Institution (German Institute for Human Rights) and the CE-

DAW Committee, the monitoring body of the Women's Rights Convention (see: https://www.ohchr.org/en/treaty-bodies/cedaw, (retrieved at 28.02.2024)).

UN Special Rapporteur on Violence against Women

The mandate was established by the UN Human Rights Council in 1994 and belongs to the UN-*Special Procedures*. These are mandates for selected topics or countries which report regularly to the Human Rights Council. The aim is to establish an understanding of violence against women as a human rights violation within the UN system and in cooperation with member states.
Further information: https://www.ohchr.org/en/special-procedures/sr-violence-against-women, (retrieved at 28.02.2024).

Linking theory, practice and activism: the performance "A rapist in your path" (*Las Tesis*) and "Fearless Song" (Vivir Quintana)

Feminist movements in many places are calling for the introduction of a specific legal mechanism for the offence of femicide in the respective penal codes of states worldwide. This has already been implemented for example in Spain, Mexico, Brazil and Argentina in recent years. The feminist movements – especially in Latin America – are radical, innovative and vocal in their protests against sexualised violence (cf. Dyhoff et al. 2020). One group that inspired the social movements internationally in this context is the Chilean collective *Las Tesis*, following the goal of making feminist theory accessible and available through art and activism. *Las Tesis* are: Dafne Valdés, Paula Cometa, Sibila Sotomayor and Lea Cáceres. Their performance *"Un violador en tu camino"* – a choreography with blindfold and chorally recited text – became famous since 2019/2020. It scandalises patriarchal violence as a combination of domestic and state, individual and structural violence. The lyrics say:

> „Das Patriarchat ist wie ein Richter, der uns verurteilt für unsere Geburt. [...] Und es war nicht meine Schuld, wo ich war oder was ich trug. Der Vergewaltiger bist Du" ("Patriarchy is like a judge who condemns us for our birth. [...] It wasn't my fault, where I was or what I wore. The rapist is you") (cf. Wiedemann 2021: 99ff).[10]

After its premiere in Chile in November 2020, the performance went viral and spread like wildfire in numerous Latin American cities, in the USA, Germany, France, India, Spain or Turkey. Through the performance, rape is defined as a strategic means of male power maintenance. This culture of violence against women begins with the depiction of women (bodies) as objects of male lust, in advertising and everyday culture. It is aggressively displayed by men in public positions of power, such as Donald Trump in the USA.[11] This attitude leads to the

---

10 The performance of Las Tesis "Un violador en tu camino" in Chile as well as countless performances inspired by it can be watched on YouTube (enter the name of the collective or the performance as a search term).
11 He expressed his misogynist attitude in the 2005 election campaign with his statement *"Grab 'em by the pussy"*, which led to numerous artistic and activist resistance actions (online search via image or video search).

oppression of women, to the control of their sexual self-determination and finally to femicide, the deadly end of this spiral of violence.

Almost at the same time as Las Tesis, a second feminist "anthem" went viral in Mexico: *Cancion sin miedo* – Song without Fear/Fearless Song by *Vivir Quintara*. Mexico is one of the countries with the highest murder rates of femicide on the globe. In recent years, a broad protest movement has developed against this, and on 8th March 2020, an impressive 80,000 people took to the streets of Mexico City to protest against violence against women. The Fearless Song (quoted in the translation by Daphne Karina on https://lyricstranslate.com, (retrieved at 28.02.2024)) portrays the spirit of the queer-feminist movement *Justicia para nuestras hijas* (Justice for our daughters) in Chile, Mexico – and internationally.

Vivir Quintana: Fearless Song/Song Without Fear

May the State, the sky, the streets tremble,
may the judges and policemen be afraid.
Today, peace is taken away from us women.
They sowed fear in us, we grew wings

Every minute of every week,
they steal friends from us, they kill our sisters.
They tear their bodies apart, they disappear them
Don't forget their names, please, Mr. President

[...]

We sing fearless, we ask for justice
We shout for every missing woman
Let it resound strongly: "We want us alive!"
The murderer will fall fiercely!

I will burn everything, I will destroy everything
if one day some nobody turns off your eyes.
Nothing will shut me up anymore, it's enough.
If they touch one of us, we all will answer.

I'm Claudia, I'm Esther, and I'm Teresa.
I'm Ingrid, I'm Fabiola, and I'm Valeria
I'm the girl that you took by force
I'm the mother that now cries for her dead daughters.
And I'm also the one who will make you pay.
Justice! Justice! Justice!

5. "My body, my choice: raise your voice!" – Sexual self-determination, reproductive rights and the decriminalisation of abortion

Sexual self-determination and reproductive rights have been core issues of struggle since the second wave of feminist movements. Everyone should be able to freely self-determine the own body and sexuality. This includes issues of sexual and reproductive health, contraception and family planning as well as making one's own decisions about whether or not I want to have children, with whom, when and how many. In order to be able to make such decisions in an informed way, appropriate means, knowledge and information are necessary. This of course applies to all girls and women regardless of whether they have a disability, for example, or not. The state must also offer protection against (sexualised) violence and distress in every field of reproductive health, i.e. pregnancy, contraception and abortions, birth and motherhood or parenthood. These human rights obligations of the state also include the destigmatisation of women who are single parents or who have consciously decided against pregnancy and children, as well as the equality of rainbow families.[12]

For over a century, women's movements around the world have been fighting for the right to self-determination over their own bodies. That's why you can frequently read on the banners on feminist marches *"I can't believe I still have to protest this shit"*.

As early as 1916, Margaret Sanger opened the first birth control clinic in the USA with the conviction:

> „Keine Frau, die nicht selbst über ihren Körper bestimmt, kann sich selbst als frei bezeichnen" ("A woman who does not have control over her own body cannot call herself free") (originally quoted from Gerhard/Tucker 2020: 50).

But Margret Sanger was also a eugenicist and is today a controversial figure, rightly so, who exemplifies that historically the social struggles for reproductive rights, on the one hand, stand for recognising them as human rights but, on the other hand, denied granting them equally to all people, including mixed-abled women or women with disabilities. Such contradictions, divisions and exclusions run like a thread through the history of women's rights movements because also neo-colonial, classist and racist structures are linked to the field of reproductive rights. That's why reproductive rights in many countries are also a core topic for mobilisation of right wing and populist movements.

Anti-feminism, right-wing extremism and racism

"It's the birth rates. It's the birth rates. It's the birth rates" – with these words begins the 74-page manifesto of the racist terrorist who attacked two mosques in Christchurch, New Zealand, in 2019 (Agena et al. 2022: 17). Numerous right-wing extremist acts around the globe are based not only on racist but also decidedly anti-feminist motives. In their view, feminism is to blame for the so called "great population replacement", because *white* women have too few children and *non-white* women too many. This is why the supporters of right-wing populist and extremist movements are vehemently opposed to reproductive rights and the decriminalisation of abortion. Sexism and contempt for women

---

12 The term rainbow families is used to describe the fact of children growing up in a diversity of family constellations including LGBTIQ+ parents and broader inclusive family structures.

are decisive driving forces of right-wing and racist movements worldwide and also extend into the so-called *Incel scene – Involuntarily Celibate*, i.e. unintentionally celibate men (Wiedemann 2021). Such argumentation is not new, by the way. *Hedwig Dohm*'s radical book "Die Anti-Feministen" (The Anti-Feminists) was published as early as 1902, and its analyses are still valid today.

Can feminism also be racist?

Time and again, black women and lesbians have analysed the lack of consciousness of *white* feminist movements, which regularly ignored intersectional perspectives such as the intersection of racism, classism and sexism. This is also true from a historical perspective, because mostly white Europeans decided "which women owned wombs that are profitable for whites and which women had the right to be mothers of the children they bore […], whose babies were born free and whose babies were born enslaved (original quote in German: Meist entschieden weiße Europäer:innen, „welche Frauen für *Weiße* profitable Gebärmütter besaßen, und welche Frauen das Recht hatten, Mütter der von ihnen geborenen Kinder zu sein […], wessen Babys frei und wessen Babys versklavt geboren wurden") (Ross/Loretta, cited in Agena et al. 2022: 29f.). The consequences of this racist-reproductive policy stretches into the present, for example when the remains of over 1,000 indigenous children are found in Canada 2021 (ibid: 47).

Already in the first wave of the women's movements, white women fought for their right to vote but did not explicitly include black women. Some of the *suffragettes* did not see it as a contradiction to continue supporting the slave trade. A famous counter speech in this regard is from **Sojourner Truth (1851)**, the women's rights activist and abolitionist, entitled *"Ain't I a Woman"* (enter her name or the title as a search term for online image and video search to find the full speech).

The safety of women undergoing abortions is a crucial issue for International Social Work, whereby positive and negative reports in this regard overlap almost daily. Amnesty International reports, for example, about Ireland, which voted to lift the ban on abortion in 2018, as well as Argentina and Slovakia in 2020. At the same time, the law in Poland is restricted since 2021, so that it de facto bans all abortions. The same applies to the USA, where currently extremely strict laws are re-implemented so that abortions are practically impossible in every case (cf. Amnesty Switzerland 2022).[13] Decriminalisation and safety in abortion remain central demands of international feminist movements. Their symbol is the coat hanger, which stands for the fact that many women risk their lives by such means when they have to end an unwanted pregnancy illegally. In any case, when a woman is forced to carry a pregnancy to term, it is a coercive context that can lead to death. The WHO reports 73 million abortions annually worldwide, more than half of which take place under unsafe conditions. Most women die on the African continent (cf. Agena et al. 2022: 76ff.). But even in the wealthy countries

---

13 The background is that the landmark 1973 Roe v. Wade decision decriminalising abortion was overturned by the US Supreme Court in 2022. Since then, more and more states are re-criminalising women who want to end a pregnancy.

of the Global North, such as the USA, there are differences due to poverty, racism and class. As Angela Davis writes:

> "While women of colour are urged at every turn to become permanently infertile, the same forces urge affluent white women to procreate" (original quoted in German; ibid.: 48: „*Während Frauen of Colour auf Schritt und Tritt aufgefordert sind, dauerhaft unfruchtbar zu werden, drängen die gleichen Kräfte wohlhabende weiße Frauen, sich fortzupflanzen*").

Reproductive justice therefore means that any decision not to get pregnant is to be respected just as much as any decision to get pregnant.

Bans and criminalisation: The alleged pro-life movement

Legal bans never result in the absence of abortions or better health conditions for women and children. Nevertheless, conservative groups and governments continue to push legislative initiatives that restrict access to safe abortions – even after rape or when the life and health of the pregnant woman is at risk. Agena et al. (2022: 76; translated by the author/by AI) document a particularly drastic case:

> "In August 2020, Catholics, Evangelicals and right-wing extremists attempt to storm a clinic in Brazil. The reason: a ten-year-old girl who has been repeatedly raped by her uncle since she was six years old. But it is not this crime that is the reason for the demonstration but the fact that the ten-year-old needs an abortion because of it."

This example unmistakably portrays the double standards and hostility to life of the anti-abortionists. They are not pro-life but pro-control, because they are explicitly not concerned with protecting a girl who would risk her life by not terminating the pregnancy. However, in many countries the alleged pro-life movements are strong, so that the medical professions withdraw from the medical care of abortions. Furthermore, basic education and training in this field is often not a compulsory part of health professions studies and training courses in various countries. *Medical Students for Choice* are therefore working in a global network to ensure that medical professionals receive adequate training.[14] In the meantime, they practice on papayas, which are similar in size and shape to the uterus. Looking at the situation in Germany, many Social Work students believe that abortions are legal. However, this is not the case: pregnant women are obliged to carry the pregnancy to term. Only under narrowly defined conditions is an abortion exempt from punishment (cf. Piesche 2018).

For international Social Work, the issue of abortion is once again in focus. In the face of increasingly restrictive tendencies, critical academics and professional associations are calling on Social Work to take a stand for its clients' right to self-determination (Beddoe 2022). Regardless of whether and how morally charged the issue of reproductive self-determination is, and regardless of where

---

14   See for example the Berlin group of Medical Students for Choice: https://msfcberlin.com/ (retrieved at 28.02.2024).

each Social Worker stands on the issue, their role is not to take decisions but to support clients in their own decisions about sexuality, contraception, childbearing or abortion. Maggie Rosenbloom, founder of the US initiative *Social Workers for Reproductive Justice* expresses this as follows, based on the US-American Code of Ethics for Social Workers:

> "For me the issue has always come down to self-determination. The National Association of Social Workers Code of Ethics (2008) states that Social Workers are ethically obligated to respect their clients' right to self-determination in decision-making. This means that when in practice a Social Worker should support a client who has chosen to engage in sex, use contraception or have an abortion" (cited in West/Rachel 2013).

Amnesty International defines a human rights-based approach and access to legal and safe abortion as follows: Abortion must be carried out under safe, low-threshold and non-discriminatory conditions. The decriminalisation of abortions serves as a first step towards this: neither the pregnant person nor the person performing the abortion should be prosecuted after an abortion. Preventive measures include that every pregnant person must have access to information about sexuality and to safe methods of contraception (original quote in German, translated by the author/by AI; Amnesty Switzerland 2022: „*Ein Schwangerschaftsabbruch muss unter sicheren, niederschwelligen und diskriminierungsfreien Bedingungen durchgeführt werden können. Die Entkriminalisierung von Schwangerschaftsabbrüchen dient dazu als erster Schritt: Weder die schwangere Person noch die Person, die den Abbruch vornimmt, soll nach einem Schwangerschaftsabbruch strafrechtlich verfolgt werden. Wichtig sind zudem präventive Maßnahmen: Jede schwangere Person muss zu Informationen über Sexualität und zu sicheren Methoden der Schwangerschaftsverhütung Zugang haben*"). Since the mid-1990s, more than 50 countries have liberalised their legislations. This does not necessarily mean that reproductive rights and self-determination are fully granted. But it does in any case represent an important step towards legal and safe access to abortion (Agena et al. 2022: 105). Canada is considered an example of good practice. In Canada, abortions are a health service that is recognised as medically necessary. Incidentally, this has not led to an increase in the numbers. Since decriminalisation in the late 1980s, the numbers of abortions in Canada have remained constant (ibid.: 104).

6. Queer feminist movements for the rights of intersex people

The international social movements for the human rights of intersex people spread globally since the beginning of the new millennium. The rights of intersex people are included in the LGBTIQ+ groups. What unites these groups is that they share the experience of discrimination, exclusion and violence in relation to their *sexual orientation* and/or *gender identity*, both in terms of legal and medical definition and in terms of social and political representation. However, in addition to the common concerns and experiences captured by the acronym LGBTIQ+ there are many factors that distinguish these groups, such as their different levels of visibility and safety. This is especially true for intersex people, which is why their social movements and human rights concerns are the focus of the following.

Intersex human rights claims show that human gender – including biological gender – is complex. Variations within gender identity are a natural expression of this complexity; i.e., in the vast majority of cases, people born intersex are neither sick nor abnormal but simply an expression of the gender diversity and variety of "Mother Nature" (cf. Lohrenscheit 2009). This complexity must still find its way into critical thinking and acting in the medical and legal professions as well as in Social Work. As Konstanze Plett, lawyer and legal activist of the intersex human rights movement in Germany, puts it:

> „Aber eine Zweigeschlechtlichkeit des Menschen (wird) vorausgesetzt: mensch ist entweder männlich oder weiblich, etwas anderes gibt es nicht. Dies ist so tief in unserer Kultur verankert, dass man meinen könnte, das Recht greift hier nur eine unbestreitbar gegebene Realität auf. Und doch findet gerade in Bezug auf Geschlecht eine Normierung des Menschen auch durch das Recht statt" (Plett 2021: 111; translated by the author/by AI: "But a two-gendered human being is presupposed: human beings are either male or female, there is nothing else. This is so deeply anchored in our culture that one could think that the law is only referring to an indisputably given reality. And yet it is precisely in relation to gender that a standardisation of the human being also takes place through the law").

What is intersex?

What is it, girl or boy? – The question of sex/gender is often the first question asked during pregnancy, even before asking if mother and child are well and healthy. Intersex people do not fit into the usual definitions and categorisations of male and female. At all times and probably in all regions and cultures of the world, there have always been people going beyond the prevailing binary male-female model. Terms and stories such as the ancient myth of the Greek son of Gods, Hermaphrodite/Hermaphroditos, are centuries old. Today, such terms do no longer define people, as they are considered offensive. The self-designation is intersex (sometimes also intersexy) or intergender, whereby these terms are to be understood as umbrella terms encompassing a multitude of different variations. In some cases, intersex characteristics become visible at birth, in others they do not or do only later at puberty or when pregnancy becomes an option. It is estimated that up to about 1.7% of the population worldwide are intersex (cf. UNHCHR 2015; Jones et al. 2016: 12).

The social movements and self-advocacy organisations of intersex people defend themselves against the pathologisation of gender identity, for which the medical and legal professions claim the power of definition. In the ICD-10, the tenth edition of the *International Classification of Diseases and Related Health Problems* of the WHO, intersex was listed as *Disorder of Sex Development* (DSD), which was creatively renamed *Differences of Sex Development* by the movements. In the current ICD-11, these forms of pathologisation are not withdrawn but – on the contrary – further specified. Many intersex organisations around the globe are fighting against this classification (see for example: Intersex Human Rights Australia 2019).

At this point, common concerns but also difference in the human rights concerns of the groups subsumed under LGBTIQ+ must be taken into account. The ICD-11 is a disaster for intersex people because it can be used to justify medically unnecessary interventions.

> „[Dagegen] sprechen sich Inter*-Aktivist*innen gegen eine medizinische Behandlungspraxis aus, die die körperliche Integrität und die Menschenrechte von intergeschlechtlichen Menschen verletzt. Bis heute kritisieren sie diese Behandlungspraxis als Genitalverstümmelung an inter*Menschen bzw. Intersex Genital Mutilation (IGM)" (Haller et al. 2022: 15; translated by the author/by AI: "[In contrast] inter* activists speak out against medical treatment practices that violate the bodily integrity and human rights of intersex people. To this day, they criticise this treatment practice as genital mutilation of intersex people or Intersex Genital Mutilation (IGM)").

For transgender people, the ICD-11 is a (partial) success, because the index no longer lists transgender or trans-identity as a mental disorder but includes it in the chapter on sexual health.

Principally it should be noted: Intersex and transgender are not the same, although they are often confused. The most important distinction lies in the self-determination of physical integrity: while intersex children are subjected to medically unnecessary surgical procedures to clarify their sex without their explicit consent, transgender people are forced to fight to be allowed to receive medical treatment without discrimination; they are systematically denied or prevented from doing so. Another gap in the understanding of the human rights of intersex people is also the confusion of gender identity and sexual orientation: the social movements of intersex people fight for the recognition of their self-determined sex/gender identity, for their physical integrity and freedom from any form of degrading, humiliating or hurtful treatment and stigmatisation. This is explicitly not about their sexual orientation.

In this context, Wahl (2022) documents how social movements around the globe have used the human rights protection system (especially CEDAW, see above) to advance their causes. In many countries, for example, they have successfully fought for personal status laws that include a third (or non-binary) gender as well as for the prohibition of surgical interventions on children without their informed consent. The following portrait provides an exemplary insight into this important work.

Born Julia and Julius: Portrait of Julius Kaggwa, intersex activist, and the *Support Initiative for People with Atypical Sex Development* from Uganda.

Intersex/Intergender is the term for people who are born outside the typical characteristics of "female" and "male". Sometimes this is not noticed until

puberty, and sometimes already at birth – as in the case of Julius Kaggwa from Uganda, who today heads the NGO SIDP, the *Support Initiative for People with Atypical Sex development*. He campaigns for the human rights of intersex people as well as for sexual health and social support for the LGBTIQ+ community. "In our culture, being inter* is seen as a curse – something to get rid of. Some families isolate the child at home, often the babies are even killed. Sometimes they are genitally mutilated to 'normalise' them" (Kaggwa, quoted in Ausserer 2021: 51; translated by the author/by AI; original quote: „*In unserer Kultur wird das Inter*-Sein als Fluch betrachtet – als etwas, das man loswerden muss. Manche Familien isolieren das Kind zuhause, oft werden die Babys sogar getötet. Manchmal werden sie genital verstümmelt, um sie zu ‚normalisieren'*").
Julius describes his childhood as very complicated. His parents raised him as Julia and tried to hide his status. But Julius always knew he was not a girl and felt alien at the girls' boarding school his parents sent him to. With puberty, "Julia" grew whiskers and his voice became deeper. He could no longer hide his true identity and left his country. On his return, he initially passed himself as "Julia's brother", but people recognised him. He was outed – at first against his will – and fled to South Africa. However, when he follows the story of an intersex boy on the radio there, he comes back to Uganda to support him. Now he tells his story publicly and receives a lot of encouragement for it, even though it can still be life-threatening to publicly stand up for the rights of intersex children and LGBTIQ+ in Uganda. In 2010, he received the Human Rights Award from *Human Rights First*, a US-based human rights organisation, for his commitment.
Today Julius Kaggwa and SIDP focus "on strategic local partnerships and rely on both community education and capacity building to raise awareness of the particular rights and health issues of intersex children" (ibid.: 52). SIDP also works with midwives in the communities and in this way is able to gradually combat stigma and discrimination. Julius Kaggwa is today married and lives with his wife and four children. His faith and commitment give him strength and allow him to hold on to his vision that LGBTIQ+ and intersex children do not have to be "corrected" but can lead a happy life just as they are and want to be.
Julius Kaggwa's story is available as an animated graphic novel under the title *"Born Julia and Julius"* on YouTube. His portrait is also documented by Carolin Ausserer in the Hirschfeld-Eddy Foundation's publication „,*Es ist ein täglicher Kampf!'* 15 Porträts von LSBTI-Menschenrechtsverteidiger*innen aus vier Kontinenten" (Berlin 2021). Further information about SIDP can be found on the website: https://sipdug.org/ (retrieved at 28.02.2024).

"Being proud of being intersex is ... perceived as radical, because society sees intersex as something you should be ashamed of and something you should hide. [...] We show that being intersex is great and that it is the human rights violations that are bad" (Anonymous, cited in Haller et al. 2022; translated by the author/by AI; originally in German: „*Darauf stolz zu sein, intergeschlechtlich zu sein, wird ... als radikal wahrgenommen, da die Gesellschaft Intergeschlechtlichkeit als etwas ansieht, wofür du dich schämen und was du verstecken solltest. [...] Wir zeigen, dass es toll ist, intergeschlechtlich zu sein, und dass es die Menschenrechtsverletzungen sind, die schlecht sind*").

For Social Work, this means critical thinking about gender is as important as acknowledging the given plurality of gender identities in every case. Social Workers can, in every encounter, in every contact with children, young people and adults, create an open, gender-just space in which intersex people can develop their dignity just like everyone else.

Social Work and social movements are linked in their commitment to gender justice and queer feminist goals which was exemplified in this chapter through the social struggles presented here against femicide, for reproductive rights and the human rights of intersex people. In studies and teaching, in research and practice, it is therefore always necessary to link up with queer feminist movements; conversely, Social Workers find a place where they feel "at home" in the movements – whether in harmony with or in opposition to the politics of the institutions and organisations for which they work. Sexism, as Susan Arndt puts it, is powerful. To overcome it, equality before the law, the recognition of difference, "love and responsibility instead of hate and violence" are needed – "in short, a right to self-determination while respecting the very right of others" (Arndt 2021: 353, translated by the author/by AI; original quote in German: „*Sexismus ist wirkmächtig. Um ihn zu überwinden braucht es die Gleichheit vor dem Gesetz, die Anerkennung von Differenz, ‚Liebe und Verantwortung statt Hass und Gewalt – kurzum ein Recht auf Selbstbestimmung bei Wahrung ebendieses Rechtes anderer'*").

Reflection questions

- Why are gender justice issues important for (international) Social Work?
- With which topics, concerns, demands of the international queer feminist movements can you identify, with which ones rather not?
- What thoughts and feelings arise when you watch the video of the performance by *Las Tesis "Un violador en tu camino"?*
- Regardless of how you personally feel about reproductive rights and the legalisation of abortion, what protection must Social Work guarantee for all those who need/want to terminate a pregnancy?
- How can and must Social Work contribute in theory and practice to protect gender justice and the rights of intersex people?
- What can (International) Social Workers learn from women's and queer feminist movements?

References

Agena, Gesine/Hecht, Patricia/Riese, Dinah (2022): Frauenrechte bei Fortpflanzung: Kinder oder keine; Die Tageszeitung, 13.3.2022, https://taz.de/Frauenrechte-bei-Fortpflanzung/!5838230/, (retrieved at 28.02.2024).

Agena, Gesine/Hecht, Patricia/Riese, Dinah (2022): Selbstbestimmt. Für reproduktive Rechte. Berlin

Arndt, Susan (2020): Sexismus. Geschichte einer Unterdrückung. München.

Amnesty International Schweiz (2022): Schwangerschaftsabbruch Das Recht auf eine selbstbestimmte Entscheidung und auf Entkriminalisierung – weltweit; https://www.amnesty.c

h/de/themen/frauenrechte/schwangerschaftsabbruch/das-recht-auf-eine-selbstbestimmte-entscheidung-und-auf-entkriminalisierung-weltweit (retrieved at 28.02.2024).

Arruzza, Cinzia/Bhattacharya, Tithi/Fraser, Nancy (2019): Feminismus für die 99%. Ein Manifest. Berlin: matthes & seitz.

Backes, Laura/Bettoni, Margherita (2021): Alle drei Tage. Warum Männer Frauen töten und was wir dagegen tun müssen. München.

Beddoe, Liz (2022) Reproductive justice, abortion rights and social work. Critical and radical Social Work, vol 10, no 1, 7–22, DOI: 10.1332/204986021X16355170868404 (retrieved at 28.02.2024).

Braches-Chyrek, Rita (2013): Jane Addams, Mary Richmond und Alice Salomon. Professionalisierung und Disziplinbildung Sozialer Arbeit. Opladen, Berlin, Toronto, Verlag Barbara Budrich.

Clemm, Christina (2020): Akteneinsicht. Geschichten von Frauen und Gewalt. München.

Commission International Association of Schools of Social Work, International Federation of Social Workers- Interim Education (Hrsg.) (2020): Global Standards for Social Work Education and Training.

Digitales Deutschs Frauenarchiv (Hrsg.) (2021): Dossier § 218 und die Deutsche Frauenbewegung. Akteurinnen, Debatten, Kämpfe. Berlin 2021; siehe: https://www.digitales-deutsches-frauenarchiv.de/angebote/dossiers/218-und-die-frauenbewegung (retrieved at 28.02.2024).

Dyhoff, Merle/Pardeller, Marlene/Wischnewski, Alex (2020): #keinemehr. Femizide in Deutschland. Berlin, Rosa Luxemburg Stiftung.

Franger, Gaby (2015): Women's Peace Movements and Pioneers of Social Work at the Dawn of World War I. In: Franger, Gaby/Lohrnscheit, Claudia (Hrsg.): Peacebuilding-Gender-Social Work: International Human rights Dialogue: Celebrating the 100th Anniversary of the Women's Peace Congress. Oldenburg: Paulo Freire Verlag, 31–48.

Frey, Regina (2002): Gender im Mainstreaming. Geschlechtertheorie und -praxis im internationalen Diskurs. Ulrike Helmer Verlag. Königstein/Taunus.

Fromm, Anne/Fichtner, Sophie (2022): Weibliche Solidarität. Care Arbeit im Krieg. In: Die Tageszeitung, Schwerpunkt Frauentag. Berlin; siehe: https://taz.de/Weibliche-Solidaritaet/!5838894/ (retrieved at 28.02.2024).

Gerhard, Jane/Tucker, Dan (2020): Feminismus. Die illustrierte Geschichte der weltweiten Frauenbewegung. Prestel Verlag, München, London, New York.

Gerhard, Ute (2009): Frauenbewegung und Feminismus. Eine Geschichte seit 1789. München.

Haller, Paul/Pertl, Luan/Ponzer, Tinou (Hrsg.) (2022): Inter*Pride. Perspektiven einer weltweiten Menschenrechtsbewegung. Hiddensee: w_orten & meer.

Hering, Sabine (2002): Die Geschichte der Sozialen Arbeit in Europa (1900-1960). Wichtige Pionierinnen und ihr Einfluss auf die Entwicklung internationaler Organisationen. Leske und Budrich, Opladen.

Hirschfeld-Eddy-Stiftung (Hrsg.) (2021): „Es ist ein täglicher Kampf!" 15 Porträts von LSBTI-Menschenrechtsverteidiger:innen aus vier Kontinenten, Schriftenreihe der Hirschfeld-Eddy-Stiftung, Band 6. Berlin.

IFSW/IASSW - Commission International Association of Schools of Social Work/ International Federation of Social Workers- Interim Education (ed.) (2020): Global Standards for Social work Education and Training; https://www.iassw-aiets.org/global-standards-for-social-work-education-and-training-archive/ (retrieved at 28.02.2024).

Intersex Human Rights Australia (2019): Media statement – International Classification of Diseases 11 and intersex people; https://ihra.org.au/35321/media-statement-icd11-intersex/ (retrieved at 28.02.2024).

Jones, Tiffany/Hart, Bonnie/Carpenter, Morgan/Ansara, Gavi/Leonard, William/Lucke, Jayne (2016). Intersex: Stories and Statistics from Australia. Cambridge, UK: Open Book Publishers.

Keller, Henriette (2021): Gewalt gegen Frauen. Lied ohne Furcht, Hymne der mexikanischen Frauenbewegung; https://www.graswurzel.net/gwr/2021/10/lied-ohne-furcht/ (retrieved at 28.02.2024).

Lateinamerika Nachrichten e.V. (Hrsg.) (2020): Vivas nos queremos! Perspektiven auf und gegen patriarchale Gewalt (Dossier Nr. 18). Berlin.

Lohrenscheit, Claudia/ Deutsches Institut für Menschenrechte (Hrsg.) (2009): Sexuelle Selbstbestimmung als Menschenrecht. Baden-Baden: Nomos Verlag.

Penny, Laurie (2022): Sexuelle Revolution. Rechter Backlash und feministische Zukunft, Hamburg: Edition Nautilus.

Piesche, Peggy (2018): Einführung: Reproduktive Rechte - Definition und Debatten; siehe https://www.boell.de/de/2018/02/28/reproduktive-rechte (retrieved at 28.02.2024).

Plett, Konstanze (2021); Hrsg. von Hulverscheidt, Marion: Geschlechtergerechtigkeit. Aufsätze zu Recht und Geschlecht – vom Tabu der Intersexualiät zur Dritten Option. Bielefeld: transcript.

Wichterich, Christa (2000): Strategische Verschwisterung, multiple Feminismen und die Glokalisierung von Frauenbewegungen; in Lenz, Ilse/Mae, Michiko/Klose, Karin (Hg.): Frauenbewegungen weltweit. Aufbrüche, Kontinuitäten, Veränderungen, Opladen, 233–257.

UN, Department of Economic and Social Affairs (2022): Goal 5. Achieve Gender Equality and empower all women and girls, https://sdgs.un.org/topics/gender-equality-and-womens-empowerment (retrieved at 28.02.2024).

UNHCHR (United Nations Office of the High Commissioner for Human Rights (2015). "Free & Equal Campaign Fact Sheet: Intersex".

WHO (2012): Understanding and Addressing Violence Against Women. Femicide. (WHO/RHR/12.38).

WHO (2020): Fact Sheet: Preventing unsafe abortion; https://www.who.int/news-room/fact-sheets/detail/preventing-unsafe-abortion (retrieved at 28.02.2024).

WHO (2021): Fact Sheet on Violence against Women; https://www.who.int/news-room/fact-sheets/detail/violence-against-women (retrieved at 28.02.2024).

Wahl, Angelika von (2022): From Private Wrongs to Public Rights: The Politics of Intersex Activism in the Merkel Era. In: German Politics, Volume 31, 2022 - Issue 1: Special Issue: Leading from Behind: Gender Equality in Germany during the Merkel Era.

West, Rachel (2013): Interview with Social Workers for Reproductive Justice, Maggie Rosenbloom; https://swhelper.org/2013/03/21/interview-with-social-workers-for-reproductive-justice/ (26.5.202)

Wiedemann, Carolin (2022): Zart und frei. Vom Sturz des Patriarchats. Berlin, Mathes & Seitz Verlag.

Wolff, Stephen/Bernstein, Mary/Taylor, Verta (2015): New theoretical Directions from the Study of Gender and Sexuality Movements. In: Della Porta, Donatella, Diani, Mario: The Oxford Handbook of Social Movements. Oxford University Press.

II.2 Racism and Postcolonial Resistance

Susan Arndt & Mario Faust-Scalisi

21st March – International Day against Racism

23rd August – International Day for the Remembrance of the Slave Trade and its Abolition

> **Summary**
>
> The paper provides an insight into definitions and basic understandings of racism, postcolonialism, Black Studies and Critical Whiteness Studies. The starting point is protest and the achievements of social movements, especially with regard to historical and current developments in Germany. The aim is to illustrate, on the basis of activists and their associations, how those affected by racism worked against racism and how *Black Studies* and Critical Whiteness Studies came into being. A central thesis of the contribution is that there is a need for a continuing, society-wide confrontation with racism and the privileges of *white* people. Racism is not a topic of the past and is also highly relevant for social work. Thus, international social work can learn from postcolonial resistance struggles and should always ask itself how it can resist racism in its fields of action and work and how it can and must contribute to strengthening anti-racist perspectives and approaches.

Postcolonialism uses the word 'after' but does not mean that colonialism is over. Rather it is about the question of how colonialism continues to have an effect today, structurally and discursively, and how colonialism is remembered and its present is debated. Accordingly, postcolonialism must also confront the far too long history of racism and debate its impact on the present without reproducing its violent codes. This is also what decolonisation means: striving to combat the still-living toxic legacy of colonialism and racism. Decolonisation does not mean that history is over. Decolonisation demands that we confront it. Racism as *white supremacy* has a power potential that wrote world history. Conversely, however, there is also power for intervention in resistance. This resistance is above all something that *Black, Indigenous and People of Colour (BIPoC)* achieve. *Whites*, on the other hand, often reduce racism to its extreme forms (such as slavery, apartheid and right-wing extremism) and to being history. However, any refusal to talk about racism is a decidedly political positioning. From this opening thesis, we would like to frame and define racism, and from the history of racism and the resistance against it, as it is done by social movements, we would also like to derive the genesis of postcoloniality and decoloniality with regard to Germany.

1. Racism – a definition

Racism is an ideologically based form of domination that manifests itself as *white supremacy*. Racism claims that there are '~~races~~ of people' and that the "white ~~race~~" is superior to all others. In our contribution, we visually distinguish the term '~~race~~'

from other concepts in order to point out the constructional nature of '~~races~~', i.e. to make clear that '~~races~~' are an invention of racism. For racism constructs body and corresponding differences and charges them with statements about antithetical, i.e. about supposedly contradictory abilities and affiliations. Racism thus not only establishes groups but contrasts them and devalues one of the groups. In essence, it is about *white* people setting themselves up as the norm and normality from a position of power. We deliberately write *"whites"* and *"white"* in italics in our text, because we understand *"white"* as a social position which is based on an ideological construction that makes a difference and which differs from the social position of BIPoC significantly. Initially, the *white* position sought to justify colonialism and its attendant conquests and violence, and all BIPoC were denied (full) humanity. This in turn resulted in privileges for *whites*. Until today, colonialism has hardly been dealt with, especially in Germany. Its legacy continues to have an effect, and *whiteness* is still one of the most powerful currencies in Germany and worldwide. Corresponding power and domination structures and privileges are accessible to all *whites*; thus, *whiteness* means access to privileges. Those who are racially discriminated against and thus excluded from *whiteness* are denied these privileges. This manifests itself as discrimination. Racism as the interaction of privilege and discrimination manifests itself on the one hand structurally and institutionally. Examples of this are *racial profiling* or the lack of equal opportunities when looking for a job or a place to live. At the same time, racism is also expressed and also manifests itself in knowledge or moral concepts. This includes racist stereotypes in the media or textbooks as well as the hyperpresence of *whites* in the reading canon or in textbook illustrations. Both levels affect representations: Who is set as the norm/reality and is hyperpresent (for example in the professoriate or in governing bodies) – *white* people. And who is narrated or portrayed in what way – as 'invisibly ruling normality' (Wachendorfer 2001: 87) with a right to individuality (this applies to *whites*) or stereotypically and pejoratively generalised and absolutised (this applies to BIPoC)? From this framework, racism appears every day and in a systemic way. This means that there are structurally conditioned repetitions of racist acts. These are indeed practiced and experienced individually. However, this does not mean that racism can be reduced to individual cases or even individual experiences. Racism is not an opinion but domination and violence which is repeated in a systemic way. Not naming this divides societies. Conversely, it is precisely the core business of racism to segregate people and to ascribe different values to their lives and aspirations. In this way racism creates social positions. This must – according to the thesis of the article – be named and recognised. For those who deny racism reproduce it.

It is true that it is a racist lie that there are biological '~~races~~' (cf. Cavalli-Sforza/Cavalli-Sforza 1994). But insofar as racism is still effective today, it creates social positions that must be named. For these biologistic '~~race~~ constructions' have become permanently inscribed in patterns of thought and behaviour, which constitute social, cultural and political processes and hegemonies and have irreversibly produced racialised identities and positions. Collette Guillaumin summed this up in the polemical formula: *"Race does not exist. But it does kill people"* (1995: 107).

For this reason, there is a need for a deconstructive movement away from '~~race~~' as a biological construct and towards *race* as a social position and critical category of analysis and knowledge. Shankar Raman (2006) calls this the *'racial turn'*. This correlates with terms such as *white*, white-positioned people or *white* persons on the one hand and terms of resistance such as Black,[15] *People of Colour* or Indigenous people on the other, also summarised as BIPoC. These terms show that there are different forms of racism, such as antisemitism, racism towards black people, ziganist racism or orientalist racism, which is directed inwards and against Muslims or people from Southeast Asia or the corresponding diasporas. These racisms, both inward-looking and colonialist, go hand in hand and have always given each other structural justice and ideological support, despite the differences.

2. Racism fuelled and fought. A brief historical outline with a view on Germany and anti-racist movements

2.1 Early developments

Racism was invented to legitimise European conquests of non-European spaces and resources, including the enslavement and exploitation of BIPoC. They are not considered full human beings, which – and this is racism in a nutshell – only the *whites* are, who were supposedly superior to all others. In return, art and science created a narrative that served racism ideologically.

Colonialism met with resistance from the very beginning. This resistance came from the colonised and the racially discriminated against. These were individuals or small groups, but there were also uprisings and revolutions. Resistance had to be led by force of arms and physically but was always also carried discursively and through knowledge-saturated rhetoric and narratives, which also struggled for a discrimination-sensitive representation in and through language (cf. Arndt 2021).

Among *whites*, there was always isolated support for anti-colonial protests. However, at no time before the end of the 20th century did these protestors take a firm and fundamental stand against colonialism and racism. Above all, however, they were limited to individual aspects. Racism was a murderous machine that was always scientifically fuelled or fought in parallel.

During the Enlightenment, however, abolitionism led to structural support in the fight against the European enslavement of Africans. This moved above all the Kingdom of Great Britain, then the United Kingdom of Great Britain and Ireland, the initially still young USA or France; in Germany, abolitionist opposition was almost completely absent. On the contrary, Enlightenment thinkers such as Immanuel Kant were among the most important advocates of slavery and architects of racism (cf. Kant 1775). This was not contradicted by the fact that there were already Blacks in German kingdoms or principalities at this time and that they also

---

15 The adjectival capitalisation marks both that 'Black' is a construct and resists processes of racism responsible for it.

critically examined racism. The most famous example for Germany is probably Anton Wilhelm Amo.

> **Portrait: Anton Wilhelm Amo**
>
> The boy, of whom only the name Anton Wilhelm Amo has survived, was born in 1703. He was first deported from what is now Ghana to Amsterdam in 1707. From there he arrived at the court of the Dukes of Brunswick-Wolfenbüttel. They subjected him to the racist experiment that investigated the question of whether Black people were capable of learning. Amo attended the Knights' Academy from 1717 and studied at the University of Helmstedt from 1721 to 1727. In 1727 he began studying philosophy and law at the University of Halle as the first, and at the same time for centuries the last, Black. In 1729 he published *De jure Maurorum*, presumably, as it can be reconstructed, a critical examination of the lack of rights of Black people in Europe. In 1734, he finally earned his doctorate and began teaching in Halle and Jena. Presumably due to massive experiences of discrimination, he returned to West Africa and died there in the 1750s (cf. Ette 2014). Amos' actions and work are to be understood as resistant, as a counter-discourse to racist discourses of his time (cf. Kant 1923). But because he endangered the central narrative of racism, he was made forgotten. Blacks were denied access to German universities. That is why Amo remained an exception for a long time.

To the negation of Black *agency* and the justification of racism and slavery Georg Wilhelm Friedrich Hegel made a direct contribution. Even after the successful Haitian Revolution he claimed that Black people had no concept of freedom and that their resistance stemmed from an emotional "inability" to recognise their own inferiority. He attributed the revolution to "the great bravery of the n., supported by tremendous physical strength",[16] which, however, did not follow a striving for freedom but rather a "disregard for life", since Blacks in Haiti "let themselves be shot down by the thousands in the war against the Europeans. For life has value only where it has a worthy to its end" (Hegel 1837/1961: 159). It was all the more striking that Germany in its imperial phase staged itself as a 'protectorate', pretending to protect Africans from 'Arab enslavement' (cf. Anton 2022). During the German participation in the European enslavement of Africans and the German imperial colonial phase from circa 1884 to 1914, colonialism or racism were only occasionally addressed. German-born US migrants, for example, stood for one of the first anti-enslavement documents of the later USA, the *Germantown Petition Against Slavery* of 1688. In contrast, there was hardly any corresponding resolute positioning in German states. Towards the end of the 19th century, a certain albeit not particularly strong or even majority scientific anti-racism developed. This is exemplified by the German ethnologist Adolf Bastian (1826–1905), who scientifically attempted to postulate and prove the equality, or rather equality of origin, of all human beings – and thus clearly spoke out against postulates of racist differences – though he remained in racist thoughts (cf. Köpping 2005).

---

16 Written out in full in the original. Abbreviated here because the article deliberately uses the n-word as it does not want to reproduce racist language but to criticise it.

II.2 Racism and Postcolonial Resistance

Comparable problem lines also appeared in communist circles. Initially, communist resistance meant the sole emphasis on classism as the basic problem of inequality and the driving force of history, with teleological assumptions analogous to scientific observations being the guiding principle. This clearly included '~~race~~ theory' assumptions, which on the one hand dismissed racism as a mere symptom, whereas, on the other, the corresponding basic assumptions of binarity and inequality guided the struggle. This clearly included racist thoughts and concepts. The communist tradition of anti-imperialism and a Communist International did not and does not stand against this, because it remained paternalistically *white* in its nominal support of Black or BIPoC resistance (cf. Adi 2013).

So far, there has been and still is hardly any resistance to racism from within the *white* German majority society. An exception is the ecumenical anti-racism program of 1969, which opposed apartheid in South Africa and was also highly controversial within the churches – especially along the question of whether churches should get involved in this field at all. A reflection back on Germany only took place insofar as cooperation with 'racist states' was rejected, but racism was not seen and criticised in Germany (cf. Fuchs/Karner 1979).

2.2 Resistance and activists from the 1980s onwards

For the establishment and stabilisation of BIPoC-resistance to racism and its institutionalisation, the 1980s, West Berlin and Black women were of particular importance. Katharina Oguntoye was born in Zwickau in 1959 but moved with her family to Nigeria in 1965, where her father was from. After the outbreak of the Biafra war she moved to Heidelberg with her mother. In 1982 she went to Berlin and graduated from the Kreuzberg School for Adult Education. There, two years later, she met the poet, scholar and activist Audre Lorde, who held a guest professorship at the FU Berlin in 1984.

> **Portrait: Audre Lorde, May Ayim and the *Initiative Black People in Germany* (ISD = Initiative Schwarze Menschen in Deutschland)**
>
> As a global beacon, Audre Lorde was able to focus the seething flames in Germany. When she came to Germany, she was already a proven and well-known player in the Black civil-rights movement as well as the early LGBTIQ* movement in the USA. In Germany, the Afro-German movement was formed with her support. May Ayim, who was born in Hamburg in 1960, was also part of this movement. After a violent childhood, May Ayim studied in Regensburg and moved from there to West Berlin in 1984 (cf. Piesche 2019). These developments reached new culmination points in late 1985, early 1986. Firstly, at the end of 1985, the *Initiative Schwarze Menschen in Deutschland* (ISD) was founded, initially still as the *Initiative Schwarze Deutsche* (Initiative Black Germans), which went back to a first federal meeting of Black Germans in Wiesbaden in November 1985. Regional groups were quickly formed, in which Theodor Wonja Michael – a German actor and Afro-German contemporary witness of the Weimar Republic and National Socialism – became involved. From the very beginning, the ISD was committed to countering racism and to create racism-free spaces as an island for and of empowerment. This was done through

> educational offers but also networking in an intersectional understanding. Until today, the ISD is a central actor of Black resistance in Germany (cf. ISD 2022).

In parallel, *ADEFRA – Schwarze Frauen in Deutschland* (Black Women in Germany) was founded, initially as *Initiative Schwarze Deutsche Frauen* (Initiative of Black German Women). ADEFRA also focused on empowerment and educational work, on networking and an intersectional understanding of racism. International contacts were particularly important from the beginning (cf. ADEFRA 2016).

These developments then experienced a clear break at the end of the 1980s with the East German revolution and the subsequent 'reunification' as well as the encounter with activists from the GDR. For BIPoC, the fall of the Wall also meant the end of state repression in the GDR, but by no means an end to experiences of racism. Quite a few were verbally excluded from 'the people' who were calling for freedom, and at the latest when 'We are the people' became 'We are one people', the *white*-nationalist character of the protests was clear and could no longer be denied. Rather, racism soon became even more visible than before (cf. Piesche 2019). At the same time, the Black women already mentioned who were active in West Berlin met Black activists from the then soon-to-be former GDR, for example Peggy Piesche, who had already been active in the GDR and now became a central figure in the Afro-German movement. Some contacts already existed before 1989, for example when Raja Lubinetzki left for West Berlin, who was active as a poet and painter and is still active today. In addition to these new networks and mobilisations, especially within the framework of ADEFRA and the ISD, these years were also traumatic for Black resistance. Audre Lorde died in 1992. May Ayim analysed the increase in nationalism and violence with reference to the murder of Amadeu Antonio in Eberswalde in December 1990, for example, as the first victim of 'reunified' racism. In these years there was an increasing escalation of violence of racism especially in the former GDR, but also in the former West (cf. Begrich 2016). These experiences also made further resistance more difficult and possibly also had an influence on May Ayim's suicide in mid-1996. Before that, however, May Ayim – along with other BIPoC-scholars – played a significant role in the emergence of Critical Whiteness Studies in Germany, building on international developments, and the establishment of *Black Studies* out of postcolonial research.

From the 1990s onwards, a new generation of Black women scholars and activists shaped racism research in Germany. Peggy Piesche (see above), among others, was instrumental in this. A decisive step was her coordination of the externally funded project *'Black European Studies'* at the Johannes Gutenberg University Mainz (2004–2007). Later, diaspora research and *Critical Race/Whiteness Studies* became her focal points. Peggy Piesche's work overlapped with that of Maisha Auma, who studied social pedagogy in Kiel in the early 1990s and then added psychology and sociology. After her doctorate she worked in the field of Gender Studies at the Humboldt University in Berlin in the mid-2000s before becoming a professor of Diversity Studies in 2008. Both of them had made racism a central theme of their work and also sought publicity for it. In this way, they both helped to create a certain, albeit still very limited, awareness of racism in Germany for the first time. Katja Kinder also played an important role in this context. She was a co-founder of ADEFRA and works as an educationalist with a critical approach to racism. All three worked on their own, but time and again also together, to combat racism in society and especially in the field of education (cf. Auma et al. 2020).

2.3 New social movements and initiatives from the 1990s onwards

It was not until the 1990s that the first broader debates on racism in Germany were established among *whites*, but the focus was mostly on right-wing extremism. In the meantime, the institutions of Blacks and BIPoC developed further and beyond those of the 1980s. This took place within the framework of a differentiation of resistance, also in order to achieve more awareness of the existence of multiple racism in Germany. This is what the NGO *Neue Deutsche Medienmacher*innen (New German Media Makers)*, founded in Berlin in 2008, stands for. The declared goal of this NGO is to give diversity and variety a voice in society. Understanding Germany as a country of immigration, the NGO also tries to reflect this in the media. To this end, media professionals in particular are networked. Clearly this went beyond Black resistance and was intersectional, while at the same time concentrating on a specific area (cf. Neue Deutsche Medienmacher*innen 2022). The association *Der Braune Mob* (The Brown Mob), founded by Noah Sow in 2001, was also active in a comparable field. It pursued the goal of changing the representation of Black people in public and to problematise existing structures of discrimination. Noah Sow is also active beyond the association, both in relation to the media and media representations, but also as an author, musician or speaker (cf. Der Braune Mob 2014). More clearly, in 2012, *Each One Teach One* (EOTO) was founded in Berlin out of the movement of Black people in Germany as a library of Black literature for empowerment and shared exchange and learning. The aim is to strengthen Black perspectives and create a more diverse catalogue of knowledge. These are just three examples of the institutionalisation of BIPoC resistance in Germany, as it has increasingly differentiated and established itself since the 1990s, partly with local or regional, partly with nationwide initiatives and institutions.

This also included an increasingly broad understanding of racism, including, for example, antisemitism or antiziganism. In this way, links are also increasingly strengthened with institutions that have existed in part for significantly longer but have not yet been seen in the common resistance against racism. This more networked understanding of racism is also reflected in the corresponding research and activism. In this context, action was also repeatedly demanded and initiated from research. Examples of this are various initiatives for a decolonial approach to urban spaces, such as Berlin or Hamburg Dekolonial. The initiative *Dekoloniale Erinnerungskultur in der Stadt (*Decolonial Remembrance Culture in the City) in Berlin problematises the materialisation of racism and aims to decolonise space. This includes city tours critical of racism, but also initiatives to rename streets. In this framework, science, culture and activism combine in different ways (cf. Decolonial 2022).

Nevertheless, there is still a tendency among *whites* to deny racism. This includes not positioning oneself as *white* and placing racism only with other *whites*.

3. Black Studies as a site of resistance

Revolutions and uprisings of BIPoC were thus always fought out rhetorically and with corresponding knowledge, i.e. knowledge about colonial modes of rule, about racism and its modes of action, about power and resistance. Generations of African and African-diasporic writers, among them W.E.B. Du Bois, Ida B. Wells, James Baldwin and Toni Morrison, have concretised and questioned *white* racialised positions. Oral literature, too, as an important social authority, stood in the way of racism. For BIPoC, having knowledge about *whites/whiteness* and colonialism was essential to life and to surviving (cf. Roediger 1998). The feminist African American theorist bell hooks writes: "[B]lack folks have from slavery on shared in conversations with one another 'special knowledge' of whiteness gleaned from close scrutiny of white people" (hooks 1992: 165). One of the main aims was to support each other "to [...] cope and survive in a white supremacist society" (hooks 1992: 165).

Theorists of racism such as Frantz Fanon (1952) and Albert Memmi (1957) have dealt with the subject of this domination in the context of their analyses of colonialism and racism and thus addressed *whiteness*, knowing full well that knowledge about *whites/whiteness* in the context of slavery and colonialism was vital for people of colour. But the actual focus of the research was on Black people and their experiences under colonialism and racism.. Moreover, the focus on *whiteness* primarily implied describing *white* patterns of behaviour in the context of colonialism and racism. What began as a prism that dissected colonialism and racism developed into a branch of research in the wake of the growing decolonial and the civil rights movements in the USA from the 1950s onwards. However, this initially took shape mainly as *Black Studies*. The *focus* was on experiences of colonised societies and diasporas intertwined with them in the Global North. From the 1960s onwards, 'race' and racism were theorised within the framework of the sociology of '*race relations*'. The publication of Michael Banton's book *Race Relations* (1967) and John Rex's *Race Relations in Sociological Theory* (1970) can be seen as paradigmatic of broader social trends and their influence on academic research and debate. These debates were most fundamentally shaped out of gender studies and/or by neo-Marxist, cultural studies and postcolonial approaches with their offshoots of Critical Whiteness Studies and Critical Occidentalism (cf. Couze 2000). In close methodological and theoretical kinship with *Cultural Studies*, Black Feminism has also contributed to the recognition of the dynamics and complexity of the category of *race*. Black Studies had remained patriarchally shaped. In the context of colonial history, scholars such as Ania Loomba (1998) and Oyèrónké Oyewúmí (1997) have shown that seminal racism theorists such as Frantz Fanon and Albert Memmi ultimately discussed only the situation and experiences of men, reproducing existing gender hierarchies and completely neglecting the category of gender. Insofar as these studies date back to the 1950s and 1960s, this is by no means surprising, but it must nevertheless be stated that these theorists had to come up against analytical limits in their analysis of colonialism. Oyèrónké Oyewúmí emphasises: "The two radically distinct and hierarchical categories of the colonizer and the native should be expanded to four, incorporating the gender factor" (1997: 122).

At the same time, however, feminism of colour showed that mainstream feminism almost exclusively championed the interests of *white* women of the Global North and systematically ignored those of women of colour (cf. Lohrenscheit's contribution in this volume). The feminism of women of colour challenged *Black Studies* as well as *white* traditional feminism. In this way, decisive steps were taken to open up the academic debate along the category of *race* to a consideration of other differences (cf. Frankenberg 1993; Hill Collins 1990).

In Germany, *Farbe bekennen. Afro-deutsche Frauen auf den Spuren ihrer Geschichte*, edited by May Ayim (still under the name May Opitz), Dagmar Schultz and Katharina Oguntoye (1986), is seen as a caesura. It contained, among other things, May Ayim's thesis, *Afro-Deutsche: Ihre Kultur- und Sozialgeschichte auf dem Hintergrund gesellschaftlicher Veränderungen*, which had previously been rejected by the Regensburg professor in charge, claiming that there was no racism in Germany. Conversely, this work remains the first academic book in German language with a certain reach that described everyday racism as an experience and further fuelled the politicisation of Black resistance in Germany. The work mobilised BIPoC in Germany, but it was hardly noticed in *white* feminist circles, for example, even though it was decidedly feminist.

4. Critical Whiteness Studies

In the early 1990s, bell hooks and the African-American writer Toni Morrison went beyond the approaches of early racism research. The innovative aspect of hooks' and Morrison's approaches was and is that they argued for *whiteness* as a cultural and social science category of analysis and placed *whiteness* as subject and motor of racialisation processes at the centre of deconstruction processes.

4.1 Whiteness as a category of analysis

In this context, the African-American writer Toni Morrison points out in her volume of essays *Playing in the Dark* (1992) that critical research on *race*, which began in the early 20th century and has been theoretically formed since the 1960s, has presented itself primarily as *Black Studies* and with a focus on Black experiences, identities and cultures. This quickly gives the impression that racism is (solely) a matter for Black people or BIPoC – and *white* people are 'neutral' in this regard, as if they were uninvolved. However, any analysis of patterns of domination must reach its limits if it concentrates solely on the objects. Only when the subjects of the production processes (in a sense the inventors and beneficiaries of '~~race~~ theories') and their myths are included in a complementary and supplementary way, a more complex and dynamic understanding of the mechanisms and effects of domination processes can develop. For this reason it is necessary to place *whiteness* relationally, i.e. in addition to Blackness and in its complex relationship to Blackness, at the centre of the analysis of social and political processes as well as their linguistic, fictional and media representation. In doing so, Morrison is not concerned with denigrating *whiteness* (*vilify*) but with concretising it (*reify*). In this way, *race* as a social position and as a critical category of knowledge is contoured relationally and symmetrically, and the analytical view of representations of Blackness is complemented by that of *whiteness*.

Catalysed by the award of the Nobel Prize to Toni Morrison in 1992, which led to the popularisation of her essay collection *Playing in the Dark*, as well as by the works of bell hooks (1992), the early 1990s saw the formation of the research direction for which the term *Critical Whiteness Studies*, raised by David Stowe (1996), has become established in the Anglo-American world. Soon after, Rosi Braidotti and Gabriele Griffin (2002) examined the transfer potential and limitations of Critical Whiteness Studies to the European context. Initially taken up in the United Kingdom, this Anglo-American theory formation then also found a fruitful resonance in other parts of Europe, especially the former colonial societies. In Germany and with a view to German society, the examination of *whiteness* gained increasing weight, too, whereby it is obvious that the first impulses for this approach came, and probably had to come, from Black German researchers who had been academically and politically socialised in or from the USA. For this stand especially Peggy Piesche and Maisha Auma and their co-edited book *Mythen, Masken und Subjekte. Kritische Weißseinsforschung in Deutschland* (2005), which brought together for the first time the work of all researchers critical of racism and dissected racism as *white supremacy*. In this way, Critical Whiteness Studies found its way to Germany via critical approaches in English/American studies or African studies.

4.2 Engagements with whiteness. Historical perspectives

A substantive focus of early Critical Whiteness Studies was the tendency for *white* people in the USA or Germany to find it impossible to give information about their *whiteness* and their share in the existence of Blackness. For example, when *white* Germans describe themselves – as Ursula Wachendorfer (2001) points out –, they mention things like occupation, age, gender, religious orientation and marital status. All of these descriptions are presumably mentioned because the persons in question see these categories as important for themselves and also want others to do so. *Whiteness* is usually not consciously present as a self-concept. When *white* people are confronted with this gap, they often explain that *whiteness* says nothing about their 'own' life. They also like to add that they do not find 'race' important at all and that they do not perceive Black people as Black people at all. This shows that *whiteness*, especially in Germany, remains "structurally invisible" and at the same time presents itself as the "invisibly prevailing normality" (Wachendorfer 2001: 87). bell hooks speaks of the *"myth of sameness"* (1992: 338) and Toni Morrison (1992: 342) of "evasion". Morrison emphasises that this attitude of refusal is complicated by the fact that "the habit of ignoring race is understood to be a graceful, even generous, liberal gesture". Problematic is not to name an existing difference but to "deny" it. For this prevents an "adult discourse" (in the sense of a responsible discussion), which imposes on the "black body a shadowless participation in the dominant cultural body" (all Morrison 1992: 9–10).

Social, political and cultural formation processes are based on a historical racialisation process in which *whiteness* has a hegemonic role. These hegemonies and the differences cannot be overcome simply by negating or ignoring them. On the contrary, when *whiteness* is 'denominated', the social positions, privileges, hegemonies and rhetoric attached to *whiteness* are also denied, and no account is taken of the experiences of exclusion and violence that Black people, or more generally BIPoC, experience in real by *whites*. As a result, *whiteness is* not only reinforced and naturalised, but its status as an "unmarked marker" (Stowe 1996: 68) remains unshaken.

5. Postcoloniality

While colonialism studies strives to depict the 'obvious material sides of colonial rule', postcolonial theory strives to develop theoretical and methodological foundations for historically tracing the interplay of ideas, structures and institutions and to identify and restitute the violent power of the representation of colonialism and racism in their complex interactions (cf. Castro Varela/Dhawan 2015). Postcoloniality is defined by a potential for resistance that has the immanent goal of not only identifying the current presence of discursive processes of colonialism and racism but also of resituating them (cf. Castro Varela/Dhawan 2015). Established knowledge archives, however, have always met postcolonial approaches with reserved rejection. Academic code words carry at their core the message that postcoloniality is inherently scientifically incompetent, indeed lacking scientific character. At the same time it is accused of an overly political approach and emotionality that allows for a subjectivity that obscures objective perspectives.

These defence mechanisms are increasingly extended to include an inflation and depoliticisation of postcoloniality, which drives it into crisis. Often, 'postcolonial' is woven into a text as a keyword without actually working postcolonially in a saturated way. On the other hand, postcolonial research has achieved a plurality that pursues partially divergent paths in the context of migration and diaspora research, globalisation and digitalisation, technology and ethics, transcending traditional subject boundaries in a trans- and postdisciplinary manner. Postcolonial research has just reached a point where it is indispensable to allow for new parameters of *Ecocriticism*, *Posthumanism* or *Digital Studies*, for example. In concrete terms, this means that postcolonial research must differentiate itself along diversely pursued traces, aspects and theorems in order to strengthen the foundation that supports it.

6. Conclusion

Postcolonial Studies in Germany are just as stuck in their infancy as the decolonial debate as a whole. An adequate reappraisal of colonialism is missing, as is the recognition of racism as structural. Just as science and art supported colonialism, science, understood as research and teaching, but also as an intervention in society as a whole, must now frame a culture of debate that moves Germany and other countries and regions of the world in a decolonial sense.

> **Reflective questions**
>
> - What is meant by a decolonial perspective?
> - How are racism and Critical Whiteness Studies connected?
> - What role do social movements and activists play in decolonial struggles?
> - Where does racism play a role in social work fields, too?
> - How can a racism-critical international social work look like? What ideas do you have on how a critique of racism can be implemented and shaped in your fields of work and internships?

Introductory literature

Arndt, Susan (2021): Rassismus begreifen. München: C.H. Beck.
Banton, Michael (1967): Race Relations. New York: Basic Books.
Eggers, Maisha/Kilomba, Grada/Piesche Peggy/Arndt, Susan (2005): *Mythen, Masken und Subjekte. Kritische Weißseinsforschung in Deutschland.* Münster: Unrast.
Fanon, Frantz (1952): Peau noire, masques blancs. Paris: Éditions du seuil.
Hill Collins, Patricia (1990): Black Feminist Thought. Knowledge, consciousness, and the politics of empowerment. Boston: Hyman.
Jones, Robert Patrick (2023): The hidden roots of white supremacy and the path to a shared American future, New York: Simon & Schuster.
Kant, Immanuel (1775): Von den Verschiedenen Racen Der Menschen. Zur Ankündigung der Vorlesungen der physischen Geographie im Sommerhalbjahre 1775. Königsberg: Hartung.
Loomba, Ania (1998): Colonialism/Postcolonialism. London: Routledge.
Morrison, Toni (1992): Playing in the Dark. Whiteness and the Literary Imagination. Cambridge: Harvard University Press.
Oguntoye, Katharina/Opitz, May/Schultz, Dagmar (Hrsg.) (1986): Farbe Bekennen. Afrodeutsche Frauen auf den Spuren ihrer Geschichte. Berlin: Orlanda.
Oyewùmí, Oyèrónké (1997): The Invention of Women. Making an African Sense of Western Gender Discourses. Minneapolis: University of Minnesota Press.
Piesche, Peggy (2019): Labor 89. Intersektionale Bewegungsgeschichte*n aus West und Ost. Berlin: Yilmaz-Günay.
Rath, Anna von (2022): Afropolitan encounters. Literature and activism in London and Berlin. Oxford: Peter Lang.
Rex, John (1970): Race Relations in Sociological Theory. London: Weidelfeld&Nicolson.
Veracini, Lorenzo (2023): Colonialism. A global history. New York: Routledge.

Further reading

ADEFRA (2016): That's us. adefra.com/index.php/about/3-ueber-uns, (retrieved at 28.02.2024).
Adi, Hakim (2013): Pan-Africanism and Communism. The Communist International, Africa and the Diaspora, 1919-1939. Trenton: Africa World Press.
Anton, Ralph (2018): Großfriedrichsburg. www.deutsche-schutzgebiete.de/grossfriedrichsburg.htm (retrieved at 28.02.2024).
Auma, Maisha/Kinder, Katja/Piesche, Peggy (2020): Generation ADEFRA. www.adefra.com/index.php/blog (retrieved at 28.02.2024).

Begrich, David (2016): Hoyerswerda und Lichtenhagen. Urszenen rassistischer Gewalt in Ostdeutschland. In: Kleffer, Heike/Spangenberg, Anna (Hrsg.): Generation Hoyerswerda: Das Netzwerk militanter Neonazis in Brandenburg. Berlin: be.bra, 32–44.

Braidotti, Rosi/ Griffin, Gabriele (2002): Whiteness and European Situatedness. In: Dies. (Hrsg.): Thinking Differently. A Reader in European Women's Studies. London/New York: Zed Books, 221–236.

Castro Varela, María do Mar/Dhawan, Nikita (2015): Postkoloniale Theorie. Eine kritische Einführung. 2. Auflg., Bielefeld: transcript.

Cavalli-Sforza, Lucio/ Cavalli-Sforza, Francesco (1994): Verschieden und doch gleich. Ein Genetiker entzieht dem Rassismus die Grundlage. München: dtv.

Couze, Venn (2000): Occidentalism. Modernity and Subjectivity. London: SAGE.

Dekoloniale (2022): Über uns. www.dekoloniale.de/de/about (retrieved at 28.02.2024).

Der Braune Mob (2014): Homepage. Über Uns. web.archive.org/web/20200721051152/https://www.derbraunemob.de/uber-uns/ (retrieved at 28.02.2024).

Frankenberg, Ruth (1993): White Women, Race Matters. The Social Construction of Whiteness. Minneapolis: University of Minnesota Press.

Fuchs, Erika/Karner, Peter (Hrsg.) (1979): Antirassismus-Programm: 1969-1979. Eine Dokumentation. Wien: Evangelischer Oberkirchenrat.

Guillaumin, Collette (1995): Racism, Sexism, Power and Ideology. London: Routledge.

Hegel, Georg Friedrich Wilhelm (1837/1961): Vorlesungen über die Philosophie der Geschichte. Stuttgart: Universal Bibliothek.

hooks, bell (1992): Representations of Whiteness. In: Dies: Black Looks. Race and Representation. Boston: South End Press, 165–178.

ISD (2022): Über uns. Geschichte. 2022. isdonline.de/ueber-uns/#geschichte (retrieved at 28.02.2024).

Kant, Immanuel (1923): Reflexionen zur Anthropologie. In: Ders.: Kants Gesammelte Schriften. Bd. XV. Berlin/Leipzig: Walter de Gruyter, 877–879.

Köpping Klaus Peter (2005): Adolf Bastian and the Psychic Unity of Mankind. The Foundations of Anthropology in Nineteenth Century Germany. Münster: LIT.

Memmi, Albert (1957): Portrait du colonisé; précédé du portrait du colonisateur. Paris: Buchet-Chastel/Corrêa.

Neue Deutsche Medienmacher*innen (2022): Das Volle Programm. neuemedienmacher.de/#DasVolleProgramm (retrieved at 28.02.2024).

Raman, Shankar (1995): The Racial Turn: 'Race', Postkolonialität, Literaturwissenschaft. In: Pechlivanos, Miltos/ Rieger, Stefan/ Struck, Wolfgan/Weitz, Michael (Hrsg.): Einführung in die Literaturwissenschaft. Stuttgart: Metzler, 241–255.

Roediger, David R. (1998): Black on White. Black Writers on What it Means to be White. New York: Schocken.

Stowe, David (1996): Uncolored People. The Rise of Whiteness Studies. In: Lingua Franca, September/October, 68–77.

Wachendorfer, Ursula (2001): Weiß-Sein in Deutschland. Zur Unsichtbarkeit einer herrschenden Normalität. In: Arndt, Susan (Hrsg.): AfrikaBilder. Studien zu Rassismus in Deutschland. Münster: Unrast, 87–101.

II.3 The Global Movements for Children's Rights - with an Interview with Manfred Liebel

Claudia Lohrenscheit

20th November – International Children's Rights Day

> **Summary**
>
> The following chapter focuses on the United Nations Convention on the Rights of the Child, which is one of the best-known human rights treaties and recognised worldwide. This also applies to Social Work, but in the curricula at German-speaking universities, for example, the focus is mostly on national child and youth welfare law. Here, a look at the global movements for children's rights can be helpful in discovering new perspectives and critically questioning dominant, even *adultist* attitudes. For generations, child rights activists, social educators and not least children and young people themselves have been campaigning for their human rights to be respected. In this context, some important figures such as Janusz Korczak will be introduced from a historical perspective. A current example for activism in this field is Malala Yousafzai, fighting for the right to education for girls and boys. A highlight of this chapter is the interview with *Manfred Liebel*, sociologist, social scientist and international expert of the human rights of children and young people. He critically reflects on children's rights and the global movements for children's rights.

1. Introduction

Children's rights are "normal" human rights. They specify human rights from the perspective of children and young people. As the former Human Rights Commissioner of the Council of Europe, Thomas Hammarberg puts it:

> "It has a very special meaning to accept children as bearers of rights. It is not enough to be nice and kind to children or to care for them in a welfare sense. Children have rights, and these rights can sometimes come into conflict with the interests of adults" (quoted from Kerber-Ganse 2009: 11, translation by the author/by AI; original quote in German: „*Es hat eine sehr besondere Bedeutung, Kinder als Träger von Rechten zu akzeptieren. Es ist nicht ausreichend, nett und freundlich zu Kindern zu sein oder sich im Sinne der Wohlfahrt um sie zu sorgen. Kinder haben Rechte und diese Rechte können manchmal mit den Interessen von Erwachsenen in Konflikt geraten*").

For children's rights, which according to the definition of the UN Convention on the Rights of the Child (UN CRC) cover the life span of 0–18 years, the same structural characteristics apply as for all human rights: they are rights that we have solely due to the fact that we are human beings. They are neither tied to any particular status of a person, nor to *age*. The universality of children's and human rights is linked solely to the category of being human, and as human beings, as enshrined in Article 1 of the *Universal Declaration of Human Rights*, we are endowed with equal dignity and rights.

Internationally, the need to provide specific protection for children and young people was firstly expressed in the *Geneva Declaration* of 1924. The author of this first declaration for children's rights was a "smart lobbyist" for children (Kittel 2008: 17): Eglantyne Jebb, born in England in 1876, had founded a lobby organisation for children's rights and charity after the end of the First World War, which is still one of the most important children's rights organisations worldwide today.[17] The aim of founding *Save the Children* was above all to help the countless war-affected children all over Europe who had been made orphans by the war. Eglantyne Jebb was convinced (see Kittel ibid.) that certain rights of children must be claimed and recognised and that children need support no matter where they are or where they are from. Her *Declaration on the Rights of the Child* includes five rights or groups of rights. It is still remarkably relevant from today's perspective:

(1) the right to life and development,
(2) the right to comprehensive social, material and medical care,
(3) protection from exploitation,
(4) protection in times of war and crisis, and
(5) the right to develop one's talents in the service of the community.[18]

However, these rights were not defined as enforceable rights but rather as appeals to states and governments. Eglantyne Jebb was a contemporary of Janusz Korczak and like him is considered one of the most important pioneers of children's rights. Korczak himself, however, as will become clear in the following, takes a fundamentally different perspective, which he developed from his own practice as a doctor, educator and director of a children's orphanage for Jewish children during the time of the Nazi terror in Poland.

2. Portrait of Janusz Korczak: the child's right to respect

"Children have a right to today."

Janusz Korczak was born in 1879 under the civil name Henryk Goldschmidt into a wealthy family of assimilated Jews in Warsaw, Poland. The educator and author first studied medicine and became a respected paediatrician. He later began writing children's novels under the pseudonym Janusz Korczak and kept this name throughout his life. During the First World War he worked as a military doctor in a Russian military hospital. He gained his first educational experience in various holiday colonies for poor children before he took over the management of the Jewish orphanage in Warsaw in 1912, which was designed according to his plans, and gave up his private medical practice. In 1919 he then took over the

---

17 *Save the Children* Thailand has produced an animated film that is worth seeing. It can be viewed on YouTube under the search term *"The life of Eglantyne Jebb – Animation"*.
18 See Museum of Cambridge, UK; see: https://www.museumofcambridge.org.uk/resources/family-fun/story-time-with-cambridge-characters/eglantyne-jebb-founder-of-save-the-children/ (retrieved at 28.02.2024).

management of an orphanage for Polish workers' children together with Maria Falska. In 1929 he published one of his best-known writings, "The Child's Right to Respect" (cf. Coellen 2013).

Waltraud Kerber-Ganse describes Korczak as a passionate, practical educator, who worked with, and lobbied for, children with all his power, spelling out for adults how to coexist with children based on respect for the equal dignity of every child (Kerber-Ganse 2009: 42). Korczak tirelessly wrote reports and stories for children and adults, published children's books, gave lectures, trained educators and arranged for a newspaper to produce a weekly children's supplement (cf. Korczak 1998). An indispensable prerequisite for understanding Korczak is the fact that he did not develop his ideas through theory but through his practice. He once described himself as "a doctor by training, a pedagogue by chance, a writer by passion, and a psychologist by necessity" (Hammarberg 2019: 5). Hammerberg has no doubts that Korczak also had an influence when the UN Convention on the Rights of the Child was drafted in the 1980s. But still he would deserve much more attention: "Korczak was one of those thinkers who was ahead of his time. Some of his ideas are still not fully understood, and they are absolutely relevant to the work for children's rights today" (ibid).

In the orphanages that Korczak helped to run, children and young people were extensively involved in shaping everyday life. For example, there were newspapers, which were published independently, and self-governing bodies, which, like courts, settled disputes among the children and young people in a highly constructive way. Korczak was convinced that in the future there would be no more schools or educational institutions that could do without such self-governing bodies. For him, the pedagogical relationship was an encounter, a relationship between the young person and an older one, aiming at dialogue and partnership. Central elements of his pedagogy are: the role of the educator, the specifics of the pedagogical place and the three dimensions of rights, which Korczak defines as follows: "the child's right to die", "the child's right to the present day" and "the child's right to be what he or she is" (cf. Kerber-Ganse 2009). In comparison with the five rights of Eglantyne Jebb's *Declaration on the Rights of the Child*, Korczak's fundamentally different approach becomes clear. What these formulations have in common is the unconditional insistence on the child's self-determination – over their own body, their own life and personality, their own time. Quite contrary to the talk about children as "our future", Korczak insists on their right to be present. Hammarberg sees him as "the first and most radical campaigner for children's rights", quoting Korczak as follows:

> "He wanted rights – not charity – and rights now, not in the far future. *Children are not the people of tomorrow, but are people of today. They have a right to be taken seriously, and to be treated with tenderness and respect. They should be allowed to grow into whoever they were meant to be – the unknown person inside each of them is our hope for the future* (Hammarberg 2019: 8).

In the 1930s, Korczak became famous through the "Old Doctor's Radio Talks", but due to Nazi terror and anti-Semitism the name of the Jewish doctor Korczak was no longer allowed to be mentioned. Today, streets and squares in many places bear Korczak's name, memorials and monuments keep his memory alive: they often show him as a man surrounded by children on his way to the death camp. Kerber-Ganse emphasises the unconditional consistency of his decision to live with the children entrusted to him in the Warsaw Ghetto and not to leave them when they were sent to gas deaths in Treblinka in 1942. In doing so, he by no means saw himself as a martyr (Kerber-Ganse 2009: 40).

Janusz Korczak's ideas are still ground-breaking today, and below they also will be taken up and elaborated on at various points in the interview with Manfred Liebel. First, after this brief insight into the developmental histories of children's rights, the focus is on the UN Convention on the Rights of the Child.

3. The UN Convention on the Rights of the Child (UNCRC)

The idea that children need special protection, especially in emergency, war and crisis situations, was still relatively new at the beginning of the 20th century, and it was a long way until the UN Convention on the Rights of the Child was adopted by the United Nations in 1989. As the first legally binding document in this field, it is considered a milestone in the development of children's rights. The UNCRC adds two further important dimensions to the idea of protection of the rights of children and adolescents: promotion rights and participation rights (also called the 3 Ps: protect, promote, participate). Children do not only need protection, care and support, but they are fundamentally rights holders, bearers of their own rights. This principle of respecting children as independent legal subjects is considered a decisive paradigm shift. Respect for and protection of their inalienable dignity should be the central guideline for all those who work with children and young people. They are thus not only the objects of protection and care by adults, but they are also subjects of their own development, which they themselves want to, should and can help to determine. Germany ratified the UNCRC in 1992, thereby committing itself to respecting, protecting and guaranteeing the rights of children enshrined in the Convention and its currently three additional protocols.

> **Basic principles of the UN Convention on the Rights of the Child**
>
> The UN Convention on the Rights of the Child includes protection, promotion and participation rights. In 54 articles, it defines civil, political, economic, social and cultural rights of children and adolescents. The UNCRC is divided into three parts: after the preamble, the first part (Art. 1–41) comprises the specific material provisions for children and adolescents, whose life situation is comprehensively taken into account. These include, for example, the rights to education, health and adequate nutrition, freedom of opinion and religion, as well as the right to an identity, the right to have a say, to have contact with their parents, to leisure time, play and recreation, as well as protection against abuse, violence and exploitation of any kind.

The second part (Art. 42–45) refers to the implementation of the UN Convention on the Rights of the Child at national and international level. It explains the composition and functioning of the UN Committee on the Rights of the Child to monitor the Convention, the reporting obligations of the States Parties and the cooperation with other organs of the United Nations, such as the United Nations Children's Fund UNICEF. The third part (Art. 46–54) contains the final provisions on signing, ratification and entry into force of the UNCRC. Here, the States Parties are also given the opportunity to define reservations, which, however, must not contradict the object and purpose of the Convention (Art. 51). However, practice shows that such reservations can lead to the partial exclusion of certain children (e.g. refugee children) from the comprehensive scope of protection of the UNCRC, because national legal regulations such as provisions in the law on foreigners and asylum might be given higher priority.

The individual provisions of the CRC are explained by four basic principles (Art. 2, 3, 6 and 12), which define the standards underlying all rights:

1. *Right to life and personal development* (Art. 6): States parties to the UNCRC are obliged to respect the right to life of the child and to ensure that "to the maximum extent possible, the survival and development of the child" is secured.
2. *Best interests of the child* (Art. 3): The second principle and fundamental guiding principle of the UNCRC is the *best interest of the child*. It should be given priority in all decisions concerning children and adolescents (e.g. in social welfare institutions, courts, authorities or legislation).
3. *Right to participation and co-determination* (Art. 12): Directly related to the best interests of the child, the third principle is the right of participation of children and young people. The best basis for determining the best interests of the child is to give children the opportunity to express their opinions freely and to have their voices heard. The basic idea here is that each child can be involved according to his or her abilities. This requires a safe framework in which children can express themselves free from fear or influence by adults and care givers.
4. *Prohibition of discrimination* (Art. 2): The fourth basic principle of the UNCRC is the duty of States Parties to respect and ensure the equal rights of all children, free from discrimination and without exceptions.

Three Additional Protocols to the UNCRC

The same provisions apply to the three additional protocols of the Convention. As soon as a State Party accedes, it undertakes all necessary means to realise the rights and to submit regular accountability reports. The three additional protocols to the UNCRC explicitly shape the following areas of law:

- the involvement of children in armed conflicts (2000)
- the protection of children from sale, child prostitution and child pornography (2000)
- the individual complaints procedure for children (2011).

Germany brought the three additional protocols into force in 2005, 2009 and 2012.

4 Who monitors compliance with children's rights?

"Everything is wrapped in plastic five times...
There is plastic in plastic everywhere. How am I supposed to reduce it?
And I would like to use less.
It bugs me!"[19] (National Coalition 2019: 32; translated by the author(by AI)

The monitoring of the implementation process of children's rights in each member state is carried out by means of accountability reports, the so-called state reports, which each member state has to submit periodically to the United Nations. The State Reports[20] are examined by the treaty body, in this case the Committee on the Rights of the Child, which submits the so-called concluding observations. These contain praise and criticism, requests for information as well as concrete recommendations to the State Party to improve the realisation of children's rights. For this purpose, the Committee on the Rights of the Child also evaluates parallel or alternative reports which are not submitted by government agencies but by non-governmental organisations and civil society. In Germany, as in other countries, these reports are coordinated by a *National Coalition*, a network for the implementation of the UN Convention on the Rights of the Child. It currently comprises more than 100 organisations and institutions, including some universities and faculties of Social Work.[21] The network is also concerned with involving children and young people as actors for their own rights in the reporting process. For this purpose, they are interviewed or empowered to hold their own workshops and take over the interviews and reporting themselves. The practice of such child and youth reports has already been tested in some countries in Europe as well as on the African continent and in India.[22] In Germany, the second child rights report was prepared in 2019. More than 3,000 children and young people have played a key role in this, including numerous workshops in schools and day-care centres. In addition to their analysis of the living conditions of all children and young people living in Germany, they defined hundreds of concrete ideas, proposals and demands to politicians, of which only a few are mentioned here as examples (quoted from National Coalition 2019: 14ff.; translated by the author/by AI):

---

19 Original quote in German: „Alles wird 5-mal in Plastik verpackt... Überall ist Plastik in Plastik. Wie soll ich es da reduzieren? Dabei würde ich gerne weniger verbrauchen. Es nervt mich!" (National Coalition 2019: 32)
20 In Germany, the Federal Ministry for Family Affairs, Senior Citizens, Women and Youth is in charge of compiling the national reports. In Austria, comprehensive information as well as the national and alternative reports can be found on the website of the Austrian Ombudsperson for Children and Young People: https://www.kija.at/kinderrechte (retrieved at 28.02.2024).
21 National Coalition for the Implementation of the UN Convention on the Rights of the Child in Germany; see: https://netzwerk-kinderrechte.de/ (retrieved at 28.02.2024).
22 All documents on the UNCRC can be downloaded from the homepage of the UN-Office of the High Commissioner for Human Rights: https://www.ohchr.org/en/treaty-bodies/crc (retrieved at 28.02.2024). In Germany, the German Institute for Human Rights (under the keyword/search term "Implementation CRC in Germany") gives the most comprehensive information. The Institute is also the independent monitoring body for the UN Convention on the Rights of the Child; see: https://www.institut-fuer-menschenrechte.de/das-institut/abteilungen/monitoring-stelle-un-kinderrechtskonvention (retrieved at 28.02.2024).

"Politicians should take responsibility for creating political structures, processes and content accessible to children and young people and in understandable language."

"There should be more space in educational institutions where children and young people can talk about their problems and about violations of their rights."

"There should be more and better measures against domestic violence and for violence-free parenting".

"Every student should have barrier-free access to education. Children and young people should have enough free time and no pressure to perform. Money must not be the key to a good education".

"Refugees should quickly get a place to live and their children should be able to access schools quickly. Refugee children should be allowed to feel comfortable and should not have to live in fear".

"Plastic bags should be banned".

In order to promote and critically accompany the development, observance and implementation of children's and human rights, the state reporting procedure with its diverse actors plays a central role. The respective reports and concluding observations should therefore be made known and applied in the relevant fields of Social Work. In addition, individual researchers, young people as well as adults, continue to play a decisive role in the (further) development of children's rights with their own contributions and reflections. From a historical perspective, Janusz Korczak has already been mentioned here. In the direct tradition of Korczak is Manfred Liebel, one of the internationally recognised experts in the field of children's movements and children's rights, who in the following interview takes a critical look at the current state of the debate on children's rights and children's movements.

5. Interview with Manfred Liebel: "It is bonding experiences that lead children to become active, to speak out and protest together."[23]

Manfred Liebel is a passionate initiator, author and campaigner for the human rights of children and young people. His work at universities, in trade unions and social movements, as a social scientist, educator and author is internationally recognised. His research and work focuses are diverse and are characterised above all by his fundamental emancipatory and solidarity-based orientation, which runs through his life's work like a "red thread". His works are a major contribution to the development of a theory of precarious childhood and youth in a global perspective.[24]

---

23 The interview was conducted by Claudia Lohrenscheit and Manfred Liebel in July 2022 via video conference; based on an interview guideline, it was subsequently transcribed, shortened and revised as a text version.
24 Liebel's most recent publications are: Liebel, Manfred (with Rebecca Budde, Urszula Markowska-Manista and Philip Meade): Childhoods of the Global South. Children's Rights and Resistance. Bristol University

Children's rights, conceptions and constructs of childhood

Claudia Lohrenscheit: Important pioneers of children's rights such as Eglantyne Jebb and Janus Korczak were already campaigning for children's rights at the beginning of the 20th century. Were children and adolescents themselves activists at that time? Since when do we have children's (rights) movements?

Manfred Liebel: From a historical perspective, it is always important to remember that young people were active, that they struggled and played a role in the history of children's rights. But this role remained largely invisible because children did not leave any testimonies or they were not noticed. It is a permanent challenge to think about writing history from the perspective of young people. Whenever we refer to children, we think of certain ideas of childhood that are different from being an adult. Yet children who were active in history did not see themselves at all as people who were fundamentally different from adults. If we go back a long way, for example to the Children's Crusade in the Middle Ages, we see: Young people always played an active role, but they did not explicitly see themselves as children. There are interesting testimonies where children, for example, as an active part of strikes and uprising social movements put forward their own demands. That is the central point: They are concerned that they are not treated badly, that they are recognised as human beings, that their human dignity is respected. There is, for example, a petition from 1836 by working children who addressed parliament in Manchester, England, complaining about lousy working conditions. Such or similar testimonies also exist from Denmark or Belgium. Nevertheless, children are not mentioned as the creators of children's rights.

C.L.: Today it makes sense to think of the active participation and initiative of young people as part of the children's rights movement, doesn't it?

M.L.: Yes, we also call it *child-led* (i.e. led or guided by children/young people themselves). *Child-led* means that children stand up for others, in this case also for other children, but in a self-determined way and not only through adults who get involved by proxy. It was adults who invented and introduced the term "children's rights". These rights were explicitly understood as protective rights, e.g. better protection against violence and exploitation. Already at the end of the 19th century, the first international agreements were made that served the protection of children, even if they did not explicitly speak of children's rights. Against this background, it is a great merit of people like Janusz Korczak and others that children should not be seen only in terms of protection; or that protection is also understood in such a way that children have a better chance to find recognition in society and to participate. Today we call this participation rights.

Policy Press, 2023, https://doi.org/10.56687/9781447370437 (retrieved at 28.02.2024); and in German: Liebel, Manfred: Kinderinteressen. Zwischen Paternalismus und Partizipation (Children's Interests. Between Paternalism and Participation; 2015); Postkoloniale Kindheiten. Zwischen Ausgrenzung und Widerstand (Postcolonial Childhoods. Between Exclusion and Resistance; 2017); Unerhört. Kinder und Macht (Unheard. Children and Power; 2020) und Adultismus. Die Macht der Erwachsenen über die Kinder. Eine kritische Einführung (Adultism. The Power of Adults over Children. A Critical Introduction (together with Philip Meade; 2023).

CL: Korczak did not only think radically differently for that time, for example with the "right to death" defined by him, by which he meant: children have the right to self-determination, children have the right to their own voice, don't they?

ML: Yes, he was a pioneer there! Another perspective arises with regard to youth movements. Already in the last 20 to 30 years of the 19th century there were uprisings of young people. These were not necessarily political uprisings, but the youth articulated themselves as an age group and developed their own forms of communication and action. They said, "Something is wrong". They were like a seismograph for problems that existed during the time of the authoritarian state, but also for possible changes. There were also children among the more socially excluded, or proletarian classes, during that time who gave birth to independent movements. They called themselves "wild cliques", for example, and had a significance and influence on the thinking that young people were more likely to be respected, taken seriously and granted a certain autonomy.

Children's rights as a process and a learning story

CL: The UN Convention on the Rights of the Child is unique as an international human rights treaty and is considered a milestone. What is special about the UNCRC, and what do you possibly also see critically?

ML: Clearly, the UNCRC and its predecessors are a great luck. It is indeed amazing that something like this came about at all. It's almost a miracle. But children were not involved at that time. And there was no talk of Korczak either, because he was considered too radical and was kept quiet in this diplomatic context. The main problem with the Convention on the Rights of the Child is that a certain image of childhood is set as absolute, even if it also includes taking note of other cultures. This particular image of childhood makes it difficult to imagine other childhoods, e.g. those in which children do not live so separated from adults but themselves play an active role and are part of society and action. When it comes to children's active participation, the rights to participation are conditioned by maturity and by rationality. Children are not granted participation unconditionally, because adults reserve the right to judge. That is why it is important that we also look at the UNCRC with a critical eye and understand it as part of a process that was fought for in a certain historical context and that must be further developed. We should therefore understand children's rights not only as children's rights but in connection with social movements, struggles and protest actions. The demands and ideas that arise here can be an enrichment of rights, even if this is not always formulated in terms of rights.

CL: Can you give an example?

ML: One example that is very obvious is the African Movement of Working Children and Youth. They defined 12 rights in 1994. One of them says: "We have the right to return to our villages." That is very concrete. It immediately makes it clear that they had to migrate because they could not survive, or because their parents took them away as babies. Even if they grew up outside the villages, they have a bond with the village, the place of their origin. This is not found in the UN

Convention on the Rights of the Child. And further: If a movement of working children defines a right to work with dignity, or dignified work, then this again concerns the fundamental question of which concept of childhood underlies children's rights. The UN Convention on the Rights of the Child assumes that children do not work. And when they do work, it tends to be negative or dangerous. Then they have to be protected, and a minimum age has to be set. This breathes the spirit of the child as a human being who actually leads a departed special existence – as if that is normal, or as if that is a fact of nature. The idea that children have the right to work with dignity is diametrically opposed to this.

Rights and responsibilities in communities

CL: In human rights education on the topic of children's rights, I often come across the statement "Children's rights are important, but so are their duties". What do such statements stand for and how should they be countered?

ML: The question is how children's rights are understood in each case. How are they received, for example, in communities where the separation of being a child and being an adult is not so strict? Or what happens when children take on responsibilities at an early age? The problem is when duties are cited to relativise rights – according to the motto: children only get rights when they fulfil their duties. This must be rejected! But there are many situations and cultures where children take on responsibility and also feel that living together is a life of shared responsibility and shared duties. In the *African Charter on the Rights and Welfare of the Child* this is explicitly included, but not as a condition or prerequisite for children to have rights but as a specific means of the implementation of rights. The challenge here is to balance more precisely how the respective roles are determined. A real danger is the overwhelming of children. The younger they are, the more vulnerable they are and can become the object of violence, manipulation or paternalism. That is why it is so important that we see the interdependence, i.e. the reciprocity, the dependence on each other. Children are human beings; they are social beings in specific concrete living conditions. I think that is also a challenge in social work: not only to ask children what rights are important to them but also to learn with them about their current experiences and their hopes and dreams. Social workers can help to reformulate the ideas that children express into rights.

Pitfalls

CL: As adults, we advocate for children's rights. What pitfalls do we have to be particularly aware of here?

ML: In German, for example, there are already quite a few pitfalls in the language, e.g. the words "minderjährig" (minor) and "Kleinkinder" (small children). That sounds like a problem – with this doubling of "small" and "child" or the word "minor". There is a lot of adultism or discrimination in the language. Also that we constantly think we have to involve children or let them "participate". That's what it says in the law. I came across a criticism of this wording in the first Children's Rights Report for Germany (see above). Children were quoted as saying that this wording is stupid. They don't want to be involved or "be participated", they want to do it themselves.

CL: That is paternalism, or how would you call it?

ML: That is paternalism pure and simple, but we think it is somehow child rights-friendly to give children a voice. We are back in the centre, as it were, and do it from the top: "Bravo, now we'll give it to you." Therefore, it is important that we see our responsibility and create conditions that enable children to act, to act as subjects, and in this way strengthen their position, their recognition in society. But not in the sense that I give children a voice or empower them in a friendly and gracious way. The idea of children's rights is actually opposed to this paternalistic attitude.

Autonomy: Countering the paternalism and disregard for children

CL: I sometimes talk to students about whether they remember the first time they made a self-determined decision as a child that was respected by adults. This question is not harmless at all, because many also remember situations in this framework where adults ignored them.

ML: Yes, that happened to me too, with my children, that they criticised me: you're not listening to me at all or: you keep on talking, although I want to say something. Children simply interrupt you. Nevertheless, at first I didn't hear it or didn't even notice it. I am currently observing this with my granddaughter. I am a grandfather for a few months now, and it's fascinating because I'm now much more aware, from a distance, of what happens in the first months of a child's life. One thing I notice is that the child is constantly being touched and kissed. And even in the first few days the child has signalled that it's too much for her. She has turned away, or I have interpreted the facial expression to mean that somehow she doesn't want it. Even children in the first days and weeks of life have a need for autonomy. They also want to be themselves. They want to be loved and cared for, of course, and they need other people, adult people, but they also need their own space, their autonomy. That is part of what I would call respect. Korczak's wording for this is beautiful: to recognise the child as he/she is. It is already a human being, not just becoming one.

CL: You have been involved in and with social movements for children's rights all your life, especially for working children. What is the current situation, what do they stand up for, how do they express solidarity?

ML: *Fridays for Future* is the current example of an almost worldwide movement of young people, especially young women. However, they do not see themselves as a children's rights movement, although of course they demand rights: ecological rights to which they themselves are entitled to as young people and which are different for them as the present and future generations. The unifying factor in *Fridays for Future* is something generational, a common interest or an empathy and solidarity for future generations. For the working children, the unifying thing is the experience of discrimination, but also that they take responsibility. Their common experiences are bonding them, making the children want to take action now and do something together, protest together or speak out together.

When we talk about movements, we often think of what becomes visible, what stands out. But children and young people also often fight back in their everyday lives, or they try to create their own spaces. Even babies, as described earlier, articulate their desire for autonomy. This resistant action is partly individual, but it also finds expression in informal groups that children form: in friendship groups, sibling groups, trying to resist things and ways of acting that they feel are unjust, that don't suit them. I think this is where social movements begin. And this is one of the biggest challenges in Social Work: how can we relate to it in solidarity?

6. Human rights education and children's rights

> "One child, one teacher, one pen, and one book can change the world."
> *Malala Yousafzai*

Learning processes play a central role in the understanding of children's rights, their realisation, implementation and further development, as unfolded in the previous interview with Manfred Liebel. At the end of this chapter the focus is therefore on education – also as a central field of action for Social Work. Instead of a concrete practical project, Malala Yousafzai is portrayed, who became internationally known as a fighter for every child's human right to education (especially for girls). To set the mood, education and Social Work will be linked as complementary professions that often share common goals (cf. Huxtable et al. 2012). As a children's right and human right, education is an effective means of overcoming poverty and strengthening social cohesion, as formulated by the *International Federation of Social Workers*:

> "Education is not only a right, but also one of the more proven ways to overcome poverty and enhance social cohesion. As is evident in many affluent countries, educated and well-trained populations, far more than raw materials, are the safest source of their wealth. Therefore, the right of every person to education directed to the full development of the human personality not only lays obligations on State Parties to the Covenant on Economic, Social and Political Rights, but constitutes one of the surest means to further the progress of those States" (IFSW 2005).

Social Work intervenes and operates both directly in educational processes and institutions (e.g. as School Social Work) and indirectly or outside the traditional educational systems, e.g. as non-formal or informal education, and this across the whole span of human life and learning, i.e. from early childhood and school education, to vocational training and lifelong learning, to educational processes in old age. Despite the enormous importance of education for individual and collective development, it usually appears only marginally, if at all, in the relevant

German-language literature on international Social Work (cf. Wagner et al. 2018; Graßhoff et al. 2016). The human-rights-based perspective on education, which underlies the following, shares with Social Work the focus on marginalised children and youth who are discriminated against or disadvantaged or excluded from education altogether (Lohrenscheit 2021; Niendorf/Reitz 2016). There are many exclusions. From a global perspective, these include, for example, poor children who have to work, girls and pregnant young women, Sinti and Roma, disabled children and young people, or refugee children – with or without their families.

Education for all – just a dream!?

In too many countries today education still means: outdated and broken school buildings, overcrowded classrooms, high costs for school fees, uniforms and books, missing or broken sanitary facilities and lack of access to clean water. "Education for all" has been the promise of the international community for many years, so that every child can go to school in any place (cf. Brock-Utne 2000; Lohrenscheit 2013). Behind this is the insight that education is a key to personal fulfilment, development and democracy, even if the fact of attending school alone says nothing about the quality of education or about the conditions in the schools, whether, for example, children are beaten, the curriculum is outdated and geared to colonial content, or teaching staff are so poorly paid and badly treated that the profession degenerates into a part-time and undervalued job. After all, the vast majority of children, especially the younger ones of primary school age, can go to school worldwide, even if most of them have probably never heard that it is their human right to education that is at stake, and that they should also be able to enjoy this right, or that education may be fun. For many children and young people lack of access to schooling results in massive further disadvantages, for example in terms of nutrition and health, due to the lack of healthy drinking water and regular school meals. This is exacerbated by humanitarian disasters, wars and pandemics, as recently experienced worldwide during the Covid-19 pandemic or by the war against Ukraine and in Israel/Palestine. Worldwide, for example, the sudden closure of schools at the beginning of the pandemic deprived or denied access to education for more than 1.5 billion children, adolescents and young adults in 191 countries (UN Human Rights Council 2020: 4). Experiences from previous epidemics, such as the Ebola crisis[25], testify to the massive consequences for students when they are denied access to schools: Children and adolescents are exposed to increased risks because they are not connected to schools, teachers, social workers and classmates. The current UN Special Rapporteur on the Right to Education, Koumbou Boly Barry, explains that millions of girls do not return to school after a lockdown, that more children, especially girls, are forced into marriages as well as harmful child labour and that more children are at risk of being recruited as child soldiers – or into forced prostitution through human trafficking (ibid.: 8). *Save the Children* also points to the increased risks

---

25 Ebola is a life-threatening, extremely contagious viral disease that led to a major epidemic in western Africa in 2014–2016. After infection, the sick usually suffer from flu-like symptoms. As the disease progresses, fever increases and internal bleeding occurs, which without treatment can lead to death (see: www.unicef.de/informieren/aktuelles/blog/ebola-fakten-und-lichtblicke/201558; last accessed on 28.02.2024).

of violence due to the closure of education and care facilities. During the Ebola crisis, the number of teenage pregnancies increased by up to 65% in some regions, and girls and young women in particular were increasingly exposed to sexual violence and violations of sexual self-determination (Save the Children 06/2020; UNESCO 2020). This shows the interconnectedness of children's and human rights, their interdependence. No right can be neglected without having a massive impact on the realisation of other rights. The first Special Rapporteur on the right to education, Katarina Tomasevski, repeatedly pointed out this connection:

> "Leaving seven-year-olds to fend for themselves routinely drives them into child labour, child marriage, or child soldiering. The right to education operates as a multiplier. It enhances all other human rights when guaranteed and forecloses the enjoyment of most, if not all, when denied" (Tomasevski 2003: 1).

7. Portrait: Malala Yousafzai – a child and human rights activist for the right to education

As an *empowerment right*, the right to education is of central importance in enabling (young) people to learn about children's and human rights, to stand up for their own rights and to stand up in solidarity for the human rights of others. The biography of Malala Yousafzai, born 12th July 1997 in Pakistan, stands like no other for the fact that education is a human right and not an unfulfilled dream. That is why this chapter concludes with her story. In addition to her two biographies, there are countless documents about and by Malala, including a documentary film made for cinema as well as numerous films on YouTube, among others, of which the reader is particularly recommended to watch her speech when she accepted the Nobel Peace Prize together with the Indian children's rights and education rights activist Kailash Satyarthi in 2014 – at the age of 17. She was by far the youngest winner of the prize ever.

"Thank God, I am not dead" („Gott sei Dank, ich bin nicht tot"; Yousafzai 2014: 333). This was the first thought Malala remembers when she wakes up in an English hospital on 16 October 2012, a week after Islamist militants had almost assassinated her. They had forced their way onto the school bus and shot her in the head. Emergency surgery in Birmingham saved her life. What had happened?

Malala Yousafzai and her two brothers grew up with their family in the Swat Valley in Pakistan. Her father in particular was committed to education rights, including the rights of Pakistani girls. Already at a young age, Malala followed his example – with a clever head and an alert mind. She was a good speaker. In 2009, at the age of eleven, she started an internet diary at the invitation of the BBC to report on the violence of the Pakistani Taliban in the Swat Valley. She writes:

> "I was ten when the Taliban came to our valley. Moniba and I had read the *Twilight books* and wanted to be vampires so badly. For us it felt like the Taliban had appeared like vampires in the night… armed with knives and Kalashnikovs" (ibid.: 143; translated by the author/by AI; original quote in German: „Ich war zehn, als die Taliban in unser Tal kamen. Moniba

und ich hatten die Twilight-*Bücher gelesen und wollten unbedingt Vampire sein. Für uns fühlte es sich an, als wären die Taliban wie Vampire in der Nacht aufgetaucht ... mit Messern und Kalaschnikows bewaffnet"*).

She blogged about how girls were not allowed to go to school under Taliban rule, that dancing, listening to music or going out without a veil was forbidden and that the Taliban were destroying schools. They did not like Malala's reporting at all. They searched for her until the terrorist attack took place in October 2012. But the Taliban missed their target. Malala was not silenced, but she used her fate and transformed her experience to struggle against oppression and for education rights worldwide. In 2014, she founded the *Malala Fund*, an NGO that supports Pakistani girls. Since then, she has been showered with awards, including the Children's Peace Prize, the EU Parliament Prize for Freedom of Thought and the Nobel Peace Prize.

I am Malala. The girl who stood up for education and was shot by the Taliban – with her biography and her unwavering commitment to this day, Malala Yousafzai is gaining international recognition and respect. The United Nations has declared her birthday, 12th July, as "Malala Day" for the right to education. Her guiding principle from her speech at the United Nations truly stands for her own life and remains an inspiration for all those involved in education, children's rights and human rights: *"One child, one teacher, one pen, and one book can change the world."*

> **Reflective questions**
>
> - In your own education biography, can you remember when you first learned about children's rights and/or children's movements?
> - What thoughts and insights do you have when looking at the history of the development of children's rights and the ideas of significant historical and current figures such as Janusz Korczak or Malala Yousafzai?
> - What role and responsibility do you see in Social Work to create conditions that give children and young people more respect and a voice to be heard?
> - What would need to change for education to become a human right enjoyed by everyone? What role can international Social Work play in this?

References

Brock-Utne, Birgit (2000): Whose Education for All? The Recolonization of the African Mind. New York.
Coellen, Barbara (2013): Janusz Korczak, der Vater der Kinderrechte. Deutsche Welle: https://www.dw.com/de/janusz-korczak-der-vater-der-kinderrechte/a-16547892 (retrieved at 28.02.2024)
Graßhoff, Gunther/Homfeldt, Hans Günther/Schröer, Wolfgang (Hrsg.) (2016): Internationale Soziale Arbeit. Grenzüberschreitende Verflechtungen, globale Herausforderungen und transnationale Perspektiven. Weinheim Base: Beltz Juventa.
Hammarberg, Thomas (2019): Korczak – our teacher on the rights of the child; In: Council of Europe Commissioner for Human Rights (2019): Janusz Korczak - The Child's Right to Respect. Janusz Korczak's legacy; Council of Europe Publishing, Strasbourg.

Huxtable, Marion, Sottie, Cyntia A., Ulzititungalag, Khuajin (2012): Social Work and Education; in: Lyons, Karen, Hokenstad, Terry, Pawar, Manohar, Huegler, Nathalie, Hall, Nigel (Hrsg.): The SAGE Handbook of International Social Work. London.

IFSW (2005): Children's Right to Education, Statement to the 58th session of the Commission on Human Rights, Agenda item 10; https://www.ifsw.org/childrens-right-to-education/ (retrieved at 28.02.2024).

Kittel, Claudia (2008): Kinderrechte. Ein Praxisbuch für Kindertageseinrichtungen, München: Kösel Verlag.

Kerber-Ganse, Waltraud (2009): Die Menschenrechte des Kindes. Die UN-Kinderrechtskonvention und die Pädagogik Janusz Korczaks. Versuch einer Perspektivenverschränkung. Münster: Waxmann.

Korczak, Janusz (1998): Das Recht des Kindes auf Achtung. Göttingen: Vandenbrock & Ruprecht.

Liebel, Manfred (with Rebecca Budde, Urszula Markowska-Manista and Philip Meade), (2023): Childhoods of the Global South. Children's Rights and Resistance. Bristol University Policy Press: https://doi.org/10.56687/9781447370437 (retrieved at 28.02.2024).

Liebel, Manfred (2015): Kinderinteressen. Zwischen Paternalismus und Partizipation. Weinheim und Basel: Beltz Juventa.

Lohrenscheit, Claudia (2021): Das Recht auf Bildung im permanenten Krisenzustand. Zur globalen Bildungssituation. In: APuZ 2/2020, 70. Jahrgang, Bonn, 4–8.

Lohrenscheit, Claudia (2013): Das Recht auf Bildung. In: Wissenschaftszentrum Berlin / Bundeszentrale für politische Bildung (Hrsg.): Dossier Zukunft Bildung; siehe: http://www.bpb.de/gesellschaft/kultur/156819/menschenrecht (retrieved at 28.02.2024).

National Coalition Deutschland – Netzwerk zur Umsetzung der UN-Kinderrechtskonvention (Hrsg.), (2019): Der zweite Kinderrechtereport. Berlin.

Niendorf, Mareike/Reitz, Sandra (2016): Das Menschenrecht auf Bildung im deutschen Schulsystem. Was zum Abbau von Diskriminierung notwendig ist. Berlin: Deutsches Institut für Menschenrechte.

Save the Children (6/2020): Save the Children's written submission to the Special Rapporteur on the Right to Education.

Tomasevski, Katarina (2003): Education Denied: Costs and Remedies. London, Zed Books.

UN Human Rights Council (6/2020): Right to education: impact of the COVID-19 crisis on the right to education; concerns, challenges and opportunities; Report of the Special Rapporteur on the right to education, A/HRC/44/39.

UNESCO (Giannini, Stefania /Albrectsen, Anne-Birgitte), (2020): Covid-19 school closures around the world will hit girls hardest. Paris 2020; siehe: https://en.unesco.org/news/covid-19-school-closures-around-world-will-hit-girls-hardest (retrieved at 28.02.2024).

Wagner, Leonie/Lutz, Ronald/Rehklau, Christine/Ross, Friso (Hrsg.) (2018): Handbuch Internationale Soziale Arbeit. Dimensionen, Konflikte, Positionen. Weinheim Basel: Beltz Juventa.

Yousafzai, Malala (mit Christina Lamb) (2014): Ich bin Malala. München: Knaur.

II.4 Global Migration, Refugees and Protest Movements: International Social Work Approaches

Andrea Schmelz

20th June – World Refugee Day

18th December – International Migrants Day

> **Summary**
>
> Flight and migration are a very significant field of action in international social work. In Europe and on other continents, social work tasks are increasingly characterised by violent, postcolonial borders and the drawing of boundaries towards migrants and refugees. The chapter unfolds the resulting fields of tension between social work and activist movements in four main areas: Firstly, migration and refugee social work are introduced historically and relevant terms are critically considered. Secondly, it will be shown how migration control and border regimes impact on the framework of social work and how protest and solidarity movements have developed that fight for inclusion and human rights of migrants and refugees. Thirdly, selected concepts of action are presented: *social workers without borders*, political social work, human-rights-based and anti-racist social work. Fourthly, the activist resistance of refugee women against gender-based violence and exclusion will be analysed based on the case example of *Women in Exile* (WiE) and the Nobel Peace Prize winner *Nadja Murad*.

1 Introduction to the field of action and key terms

1.1 Development of social work with migrants and refugees

The development of inter- and transnational social work in the 20th and 21st centuries is closely linked to social problems that emerged in the context of cross-border mobility and internal migration. Their root causes of poverty, rural exodus and urbanisation in Europe and worldwide are often linked to marginalisation, exploitation of children, women and men, and especially gender-based violence. A wide spectrum of social work tasks has emerged to protect migrants, refugees and displaced persons in contexts of transnational support, solidarity and human rights work. Selected examples are given below (Schirilla 2016: 81ff.; Gal et al. 2020).

- Dangers of trafficking of women in overseas emigration and the maid question in the 19th and 20th centuries;
- Settlement movement and Hull House in Chicago as the initial phase of community work in immigrant neighbourhoods;
- Refugee social work in the context of Jewish persecution and exile under National Socialism;
- Worldwide expansion of social work in connection with flight, displacement and forced labour, triggered by the Second World War (*UNRRA – United*

Nations Relief and Rehabilitation Administration; relief organisation founded on 9th November 1943 on the initiative of the United States, the Soviet Union, the United Kingdom and China);
- Labour recruitment in the 1950s and 1960s and the emergence of social work with migrants in Germany;
- Worldwide refugee movements under the mandate of the *UNHCR (United Nations High Commissioner for Refugees)*, especially in the 1980s as a result of violent conflicts, and the emergence of social work with refugees.

Today, migrants and refugees are a significant target group of social work all over the world. On the occasion of *International Migrants Day* on 18th December, the *International Federation of Schools of Social Work* (IFSW) declares every year that exclusion shapes the everyday lives of a growing number of migrants and refugees. *The Transnational Platform Europe* (TMP-E), an association of networks for the rights of migrants and refugees, describes the related experiences of exclusion, racism and criminalisation as follows:

> "Despite the fact that we, as migrants and refugees, make an enormous contribution with our work and remittances to the economy and development of our home countries and also to the European economy and society, our working and living conditions have become dramatically worse.
>
> We are confronted with criminalization, racism, discrimination and islamophobia on a daily basis. Especially the undocumented among us are very heavily affected by the daily reality of exclusion, mass raids and deportations."[26]

Social work with migrants and refugees is framed by policies of global migration control and exclusion. In the postcolonial age of migration, according to Samaddar, the *demarcation* of boundaries against "undesirable" migration has emerged as the key question (Samaddar 2020: 5). Inter- and transnational social work in the contexts of migration, flight and mobility is not only interested in the question of 'migration' and mobility or to countries of origin and arrival but also in transit zones and in the borders between countries.

1.2 Key terms and statistics: victimisation through labelling?

The use of language in the context of migration and flight is of far-reaching significance. Terms such as migrant, refugee and asylum seeker go hand in hand with emotionalisations and simplifications, which Zygmunt Bauman has described as 'scaremongering' against migration in its scapegoating function (Bauman 2016). A critical approach to statistics and the danger of labelling people is therefore important for social workers. The definitions of terms and statistical counting are a powerful act. According to Michael Foucault, statistics are used to numerically record populations and make them visible for "ordering and governing" them (Schwenken 2018: 39). From a postcolonial perspective, the categories refugee,

---

[26] https://www.transnationalmigrantplatform.net/about-us/ (retrieved at 28.02.2024).

migrant, asylum seeker are fundamentally criticised as racialised ascriptions because they are associated with *othering*[27] (Schwenken 2018: 39) and the labelling of vulnerability (e.g. Bhimji 2020: 17; Samaddar 2020: 42). "Migrant others" (Mecheril et al. 2010) are determined to a victim status because of an externally assigned vulnerability. In social work, this can promote the ascription of the victim role and lead to a victimisation of people who exercise their right to freedom of movement.

However, sociological attempts to delineate who are refugees and who are migrants cannot be answered unambiguously as either/or, i.e. as either voluntary or involuntary migration. Sociologically a continuum between voluntary and involuntary migration has been assumed (van Hear 1998: 43, cited in Schwenken 2018: 46). Van Hear conceptualises the causes of migration along a line from high to low choice and marks flight and displacement at its lower end. Every migration decision is based on structural constraints and subjective motivations at the same time. This sociological approach differs from a statistical or political categorisation.

Who are migrants, who are refugees?

According to the UN definition, a migrant is a person who leaves, across national borders, their previous place of residence behind for at least one year. However, statistical recording at UN level shows that this varies greatly from country to country, starting with a minimum duration of 3 months (cf. Schwenken 2018: 48). 'Refugee' has been defined as a political category. Who can legally receive refugee status is negotiated and established within the framework of asylum and migration policies. Nation states and political actors develop criteria to distinguish refugees from other migrants.

The basis of international refugee protection is the Geneva Refugee Convention (GRC), which defines a refugee in Article 1 as "a person who is outside the country of his nationality or permanent residence and who, owing to his 'race'[28], religion, nationality, membership of a particular social group or political opinion, has a well-founded fear of being persecuted and is unable to avail himself of the protection of that country or to return there owing to such fear of persecution". Refugees are thus defined internationally, from which legal obligations for reception derive. Recognition of refugee status under the Refugee Convention is linked to persecution as the cause of flight, while civil wars, environmental damage, poverty are excluded. Only those who are recognised as refugees are considered worthy of protection (Scherr 2017: 136). A fundamental protection principle of the Convention is that refugees may not be expelled or returned in situations where life and freedom are threatened (Art. 33 Refugee Convention: *Non-Refoulement*). Once a refugee is recognised, access rights to housing, social benefits, assistance in finding work and integration into society should be guaranteed.

The concepts of flight migration and forced migration take into account the overlapping of forced and voluntary decisions on flight and migration. The

---

27 See also Susan Arndt's chapter in this volume.
28 The use of the term 'race' in legal texts is discussed very critically. The editors distance themselves from a biologistic concept of 'race'. There are no races; what is meant here is racial discrimination. Cf. also the chapter by Susan Arndt in this volume.

> concept of *"mixed migration"* also assumes intersecting factors of (un)voluntary migration decisions. People without a residence permit are referred to as irregular migrants, undocumented or persons without papers. They are not recorded in official statistics and their number is subject to estimates.

The starting point for the political and media discourse on migration and refugees are the published data of the International Organisation for Migration (IOM) and the United Nations High Commissioner for Refugees (UNHCR). These are the result of complex recording systems in more than 150 states worldwide, which are inconsistent at national level, are often the consequence of incomplete registration and contain double counts (Scherr/Scherschel 2019: 65). IOM statistics count 281 million people as migrants in 2020, i.e. 3.6% of the world population (IOM 2021). At the end of the second decade of the 21st century, the scope of forced migration (*"forced displacement"*) in UNHCR's area of responsibility has risen sharply. The total number of people affected grew from 36.4 million (2009) to 86.5 million (2019). The number of refugees has almost doubled, from 10.4 to 20.2 million people. The number of *internally displaced* persons (IDPs) has increased by almost 60%, from 27.1 to 43.5 million (UNHCR 2021). The majority of those affected are victims of persecution, wars and armed conflicts, climate crises and natural disasters, and a wide range of human rights violations. However, even in the year of the European refugee protection crisis of 2015, the vast majority of refugees remained in the neighbouring countries of the crisis areas (2015: 85%). The most important host countries at that time were mainly Turkey, Pakistan, Lebanon and Jordan. In terms of population, Lebanon hosted the highest number of refugees, 232 per 1,000 inhabitants (2015) (Ferguson et al. 2018: 92).

The Russian war of aggression against Ukraine in February 2022 created the largest refugee and displacement crisis in Europe since the Second World War. In the first ten months of the war, UNHCR has registered around 15 million border crossings from Ukraine. Within the country, 6.5 million people are fleeing. However, exact numbers are difficult to ascertain, as Ukrainians can enter the EU visa-free and there are no official border controls within the Schengen area. Under the EU's mass influx directive, 4.7 million people (as of 11/2022) are registered in European states.[29]

2. Global migration control and endless violence

2.1 Policies of migration control versus migrants' agency

Social work and critical migration research both emphasise the agency of migrants and oppose a view that sees them as objects of migration policy. Such a perspective takes up the theoretical concept of the 'autonomy of migration' which sees migration and flight "as a social movement, as resistance, as a flight from exploitation and oppression" (Bojadzijev/Liebelt 2014: 341ff.) and places the wishes and migration projects of the subjects at the centre. Migration is understood as

---

29 https://www.uno-fluechtlingshilfe.de/hilfe-weltweit/ukraine, (retrieved at 28.02.2024).

a dynamic movement that is an expression of social and political struggles. The concept of the 'autonomy of migration' has been criticised because it does not take into account the necessary preconditions for a self-determined *agency* and the actually largely limited scope of action of migrants (Scherr/Scherschel 2019: 39) in view of global migration control politics. The concept is also criticised for the danger of romanticisation and the lack of a gender perspective (Schwenken 2018: 111).

The fact is that the right to freedom of movement is increasingly being made more restrictive or completely undermined by complex migration, border and visa policies. *Shrinking asylum spaces* in the global refugee regime have shaped the framework of action in international social work for more than three decades. At the EU level, migration control policies have been analysed as "*Fortress Europe*". This is symbolically represented by barbed wire, military operations and surveillance technologies in border spaces such as the Mediterranean Sea or the "Jungle" of Calais (Monforte 2020: 46). The accompanying migration management includes, on the one hand, a partial opening of the respective national labour markets based on the desired benefits of migrants and, on the other hand, measures to prevent so-called illegal migration (Scherr/Scherschel 2019: 59).

In order to control and prevent migration, the EU has again tightened border security beyond its own territory since 2014–2016: militarisation of the Mediterranean Sea, increased border security in West Africa, agreements with autocratic and dictatorial regimes to detain people in countries of origin and transit, and, finally, poverty reduction in the classic developmental sense (Bendix 2018: 247; Kasparek/Schmidt-Sembdner 2020: 28). Since legal migration routes are largely lacking, the Mediterranean Sea developed into the most dangerous border in the world. However, it was not until 2014 that the IOM began officially registering the people who die on flight routes and at the borders – although a high number of unreported cases must be assumed. The *Missing Migrant Monitoring Centre* (IOM) counted 22,207 drowned and disappeared migrants in Europe in the years 2014–2020 (Lambert 2020: 32f.). Push-backs at the external borders of the Mediterranean as well as drownings or freezing to death at the Belarusian-Polish border are an expression of intensified and borderless violence. During the Corona pandemic, the defence mechanisms were once again intensified (Autor:innenkollektiv Mutiny 2022).

Similar policies and practices of migration interdiction can be found around the world, most notably at the Mexican-US border or in Australia. Since the early 1990s, the US has installed high fortress-like fences with complex surveillance technology at the border with Mexico and maintains a growing number of *detention centres for* migrants (Ferguson et al. 2018: 93f.). Australia's anti-asylum policy has led to the opening of so-called "*off-shore detention centres*" in faraway Nauru and on the island of Manus, which belong to Papua New Guinea. There are regular reports of violence against asylum seekers from these centres, including sexual abuse of children and the rape of detained women and men (Briskman 2020). Worldwide, this results in demands on social work as a human rights profession in the context of intentional, systematic exclusion and the acceptance of structural violence along migration routes, in the context of deportation and forced immobility, in camps and across borders.

Following the European refugee protection crisis of 2014–2016, social work faces, according to Boccagni and Rughard (2020: 377), complex social protection needs that have to be addressed by a growing number of mobile migrants. Social work with asylum seekers who have been granted international protection status, e.g. after a successful asylum application or as a result of resettlement programmes[30], and who have access to state welfare programmes differs from forms of *popular social work*, in which social workers form alliances with solidarity movements and refugee activists (Lavalette 2019; Briskman 2019). Together they build self-help structures for all and provide social support beyond state social work.

2.2 Borders and Social Work

Borders and boundaries defined by policies of the European Union (EU) and elsewhere impact on the scope of action of social work far beyond a cartographically defined national border. Beyond these externalised borders, the following factors contribute to an internalisation of borders and normalisation of border demarcations in social work:

Omnipresence of borders: Border Studies (in Germany see also: 'Kritische Migrations- und Grenzregimeforschung' / Critical Migration and Border Regime Research) has given us the insight that, in the course of the securitisation[31] and the externalisation of the European policy of migration control, borders cannot be located territorially but are omnipresent. This insight prompted the French social philosopher Balibar to conclude: *"the border is everywhere"* (Balibar 2002: 80). In the process, mechanisms of border *demarcation* have expanded and *border spaces/borderlands/borderscapes* have emerged that no longer correspond to geographically defined territories (Mezzadra/Neilson 2013). Within complex surveillance mechanisms operating at many levels, the EU delegates migration control policies to public service providers such as hospitals, schools, universities, private security companies or airlines to enforce border control throughout society (Monforte 2020: 48). Social workers are involved in these processes as actors who could create, reproduce or overcome borders.

Selective (stratified) rights: Migration management has produced *civic stratification* for different groups of migrants (Morris 2002). A distinction is made between, firstly, migrants with access to citizenship (*citizens*), secondly, migrants with secure residence status (*denizens*), and thirdly, those with no or insecure residence status (*margizins*) (Mohr 2005: 387). This stratification of rights means that migrants' access to rights is partial or non-existent. This formal classification

---

30 In the context of the UNHCR, resettlement means the legal admission of recognised refugees in need of special protection to a third country because adequate protection is not guaranteed in the initial host country.
31 Cf. securitisation: This refers to a political science concept from international relations, i.e. a situation is perceived and defined as a security problem or made into one.

according to different status positions under residence law has a multi-layered effect on the processes of partial inclusion and exclusion that affect the rights of migrants. Therefore social work with migrants and refugees faces discriminatory and racialising regulations based on their respective residence status. At the same time, the absence of rights for certain migrant groups, such as the undocumented, is normalised through processes of "filtering and selecting" (Mezzadra/Neilson 2013, cited in Schütze 2021: 398).

De/serving humanitarianism: The security and border paradigm of migration control is accompanied by a specific form of humanitarian regulation of immigration and asylum (Fassin 2011: 213, cited in Monforte 2020: 49). EU institutions and member states, as well as NGOs and international aid organisations, replace the discourse on (universal) rights of migrants and asylum seekers with a moral discourse of forms of protection based on the discretionary powers of humanitarianism, understood as the protection of human beings from existential threats. The main criterion for assessing who can enter EU territory is vulnerability and the extent of suffering experienced. From this perspective, border policies act as a sorting filter that serves to distinguish people who deserve compassion from others who are deemed undesirable. These border-drawing processes reinforce intersectional exclusionary dynamics based on hierarchies of *race*, *class* and *gender*, which are largely inherited from the colonial history of European states (Monforte 2020: 48; Bhimji 2020: 26).

This postcolonial present also includes camps, which sociologist Bauman (2008: 44ff.) described as a consequence of unequal globalisation. In origin, camps were used during colonial rule to control the population (Briskman 2020).

2.3 Camp as a form of existence

Camps shape the existence of a growing number of migrants and refugees around the globe (Agier 2011). As an integral part of the international refugee and migration regime, camps are not a new challenge for international social work worldwide. Many names and forms of camps can be found, such as camps for refugees and displaced persons, 'anchor centres', migrant camps, waiting zones for people without residence status, transit camps, deportation centres, initial reception centres, ghettos and jungles (Agier 2019: 128). Camps, for all their diversity, have three characteristics: exterritoriality, the regime of exception, exclusion. As "spatially delimited special zones" (ibid.), for Agier they are "non-places" that are usually not marked on any map. The camps are administered according to their own laws, and the freedom of movement of the "residents" is arbitrarily restricted. The permanent social exclusion in this form of accommodation highlights the fact that refugees and migrants are considered a superfluous, undesirable population group that needs to be controlled (Baumann 2007: 81f.).

Beyond such commonalities, the contextual differences of camps in countries of the Global North compared to the Global South must be taken into account. The creation of, and search for, agency on the part of refugees must also be considered, even if this is undoubtedly largely limited by existing structures of violence (cf. Delvin et al. 2021). The majority of refugees do not come to Europe but remain in neighbouring countries or end up (temporarily) in one of the many camps and emergency shelters along the flight routes. Camps in countries of the Global South have been described as "vulnerable places of uncertainty" (Rehklau/Lutz 2018: 249). They are designed as "places of refuge" that are supposed to protect against need and fear, but they cause new suffering and fear. They are supposed to guarantee security and 'save spaces', but they are set up as provisional and often permanent emergency shelters. At best, they offer residents minimal care, but they deny them the right to work and participate in society, thus ending in a life of indefinite waiting. Being in camps means that refugees "are not recognised, are isolated, are barracked, are disciplined, are ignored, are stigmatised, are administered and continue to be persecuted" (Rehklau/Lutz 2018: 249, translation by the A. S.).

Camps in the many *border spaces* around the world serve to (im)mobilise population groups. In her study on German refugee activism, Bhimji interprets the institutional and everyday racism in camps as a colonial legacy and postcolonial present (Bhimji 2020: 26). The power and control mechanisms of the camp are perpetuated in the restrictive asylum legislation, which establishes exclusions along *race*, *class* and *gender* lines. The everyday life of many asylum seekers is characterised by "*Living with Deportability and Detainability*" (Bhimji 2020: 27), a perseverance in life perspectives that are marked by deportation and detention due to illegal residence and criminalisation. Worldwide, this experience is shared by a growing "*global deportspora*" (Nyers 2019: 4), a global "underclass" for whom deportation has become the "*way of life*". In response to the 2014–2016 refugee protection crisis, a study by the *Global Detention Project* examines the criminalisation of migrants and refugees through detention in European countries. A dramatic intensification of practices can be seen in the frequency, reasons, duration and treatment of children and families (Majacher et al. 2020). In resistance to criminalisation and exclusion, protests are mobilised by refugees who are insufficiently supported by social work, where it does not know or use its professional ethics and human rights orientation – as Burzlaff/Eifler (2018: 346) have shown using the example of the Berlin refugee protests in 2015.

3. Refugee activism, solidarity and social work

3.1 Protest movements, civil society in solidarity and human rights

"*We are here, because you were there.*" – With this slogan, Ambalavander Sivanandan, activist and director of the Institute of Race Relations in London, summarised the relationship between European colonialism and migration from former colonies to Europe in the 1980s. Since the mid-1990s, refugee activists in Germany have resorted to the modified slogan: "We are here because you destroyed our countries" (Bendix 2018: 247). In this way, they point to global interconnections and postcolonial, contemporary structures of exploitation and do not want to think of a right to stay which is limited to national borders. In Germany, refugees have become visible as politically active subjects rather than objects of politics, especially in protests since 2012 (Bendix 2018: 247). Social work can learn from the fire of social movements when it makes the demands and voices of refugees and migrants heard. However, social work does not sufficiently give voice to the demands and voices of refugees and migrants (Burtzlaff/Eifler 2018).

The Europeanisation of migration and asylum policies in the 1990s led to the development of activist alliances of migrants and refugees across borders. Social movements of migrants and undocumented persons have developed transnational collective actions, such as the *"European march of the sans-papiers and migrants"* (2014) from Brussels to Strasbourg, the *"European day of struggle for regularisation and for the closure of all detention centres for foreigners"* (2004) or *"A Day without Us"* (2011) with demonstrations and strikes across Europe (Monforte 2020: 51). When migrants express their protest in public, they articulate demands for inclusion and belonging, which in the context of *critical citizenship studies* has been interpreted as a resistant enactment of their citizenship rights: "to 'enact' citizenship and their right to have rights" (Isin/Nielsen 2008, cited in Monforte 2020: 53). These protests by migrants and in particular undocumented migrants challenge the exclusionary and divisive logic of (European) border demarcation (Monforte 2020: 51). The demands of migrants and networks of supporters undermine European border policies with universalist demands such as *"citizenship for all"*, *"no border"*, *"no one is illegal"* or the slogan *"We are all foreigners"*. A radical, universal and post-national "citizenship" is claimed, which has also been described as a post-colonial one (Stierl 2018). It aims to overcome exclusion and demands equal rights for all. At the same time, social movement research highlights that especially migrants with precarious residence status, often without work or housing, as well as those without documents are deprived of material and symbolic resources. If they participate in public protests, they furthermore risk arrest and deportation. In the last decade, this danger has been exacerbated by right-wing parties and anti-migration social movements with their media campaigns and social media attacks in many countries in Europe and worldwide (Steinhilper 2021).

Four essential human rights demands are repeated in the German refugee movement: abolish camps, stop deportations, abolish the residence obligation and recognise the right of refugees to work and education (Bendix 2018: 249). They also demand simplified family reunification, the access to certified interpreters and free legal counselling (Burzlaff/Eifler 2018: 347). Refugees also articulate structural causes of flight that are often overlooked in social work. Networks such as *The VOICE* or the *Caravan for the Rights of Refugees and Migrants* compare the asylum system in Germany with colonial rule (Bendix 2018: 253). Refugee activists, such as those in the network *Afrique-Europe-Interact*, campaign for the right to self-determined development, the right to stay and the right to global freedom of movement and settlement, and they criticise structural causes of flight such as land theft, land grabbing, the destruction of farmers' livelihoods and unfair world trade policies (Kilian/Bendix 2021).

During the refugee movement in 2015/16, refugee activists and their solidarity activities for newly arrived refugees took a back seat. What became visible in the media was the welcome culture, which was described as "white" and "helping" (Bhimji 2020: 9; Bendix 2018: 256) and criticised for the often paternalistic attitude of volunteers and social workers (Schmelz 2018). The sociologist of migration Pries interprets the organising of refugees and their supporters as a common, empowering social and political movement. In forced migration he recognises an "emergent, transnational, civil-social movement comparable to the national workers' movements of the 19th century, which aimed to solve the social question in the struggle between capital and labour" (Pries 2016: 23, translation A. S.). Policies of migration control and deterrence, especially the 'EU-Turkey Deal' of March 2016, largely stopped such a movement at the EU's external borders. It brought with it even more dangerous migration routes and the holding out of people in camps along and beyond the EU borders.

As European countries failed to guarantee social rights for refugees *from above*, solidarity grew *from below*. Existing gaps in social assistance systems and support structures could be partially closed in this way. *Three strands* of solidarity movements have emerged that are able of expanding the scope of action of state-funded social work.

Solidarity movements at a glance

Firstly, the broad welcome movement since 2015 was interpreted as a *European-wide citizens' movement* that aims to promote the reception, arrival and inclusion of refugees in cooperation with local actors (Feinschmidt et al. 2019). For Germany alone, migration researcher Werner Schiffauer estimated that there were 15,000 refugee projects (2016) in which more than five million people were involved – often side by side – with social workers. These initiatives showed everyday solidarity and willingness to help and provided support to improve access to information, accommodation, education and health care, work and community life (Scherr/Scherschel 2019).

Secondly, in many European cities the concept of *solidarity cities/sanctuary cities* is gaining importance for social work (Schmelz 2019; cf. Schmitt's contribution in this volume). Municipalities and cities are a microcosm of social demarcation between desired and undesired immigration (Schmelz 2019). In 2017, *Solidarity City* was founded as an activist network of refugee councils, migrant organisations, left-wing movements, urban policy NGOs, church groups, social workers and academics working internationally with sea rescue initiatives in thinking together EU border policies and social rights in the city. The direct reception of refugees and deportation bans are linked to the democratic shaping of urban social spaces (Schmelz 2019; Kron 2020: 45).

Thirdly, new forms of solidarity with migrants are emerging along the external borders. Since 2014, non-governmental organisations have succeeded in saving tens of thousands of refugees from drowning with their boats. A broad protest movement was built in Europe against the criminalisation of this private sea rescue, fighting to ensure that sea rescue is not a crime (Stierl 2020: 47). *Alarm Phone* runs an impressive project of political solidarity. Activists from Europe and Africa are on standby around the clock for emergency calls from refugees to prevent state actors such as the coast guard from failing to provide assistance in distress at sea. This intervention represents a radical form of solidarity that transcends national borders and humanitarian motivations for aid (Stierl 2019: 105).

3.2 Social Workers without borders and professional ethics

Social workers can not only broaden their perspectives of action through alliances with solidarity movements but also become actors in these movements themselves. One example of social worker activism is *Social Workers Without Borders* (SWWB). *SWWB international* was founded within the framework of the *International Federation of Social Workers* (IFSW) in Australia (2014). In the UK, an independent national organisation was founded in the context of social work in the "Jungle"[32] in Calais (2016).[33] In an anthology, the founders of SWWB (UK) summarise their political, critical-reflective positioning in a programmatic and practice-oriented way on the basis of case studies (Wroe et al. 2019). The case studies cover a broad spectrum of action, ranging from support for unaccompanied minors and single-parent families to work with victims of torture and detention pending deportation.

SWWB opposes the "*deserving-undeserving nexus*" in social work with refugees, migrants and asylum seekers, which links state aid to "vulnerability" assessed by humanitarian standards and draws boundaries between refugees who deserve protection and other migrants who do not. The organisation advocates for a social work that is based on the principles of solidarity, protection and being an ally. Based on the International Standard on Ethics (IASSW 2018), the initiators of SWWB (UK) see the social work profession as having a responsibility to promote social justice and equality, to fight for anti-discrimination and to use and defend its professional integrity in practice (Wroe et al. 2019: 19). In the context of flight and migration the critical question is raised how the 'promotion of human rights', 'respect for diversity' and 'access to equal resources' can be reconciled with social work's involvement in welfare state restrictions that serve as instruments of migration control. Defending the rights of migrants thus becomes a yardstick for preserving the autonomy and integrity of the social work profession: "Defending the rights of asylum seekers, refugees and migrants, then, is just as much about defending the autonomy of our profession to deliver services to all who need it, as it is about opposing immigration control" (Wroe et al. 2019: 21).

The initiators of SWWB (UK) also relate this 'concept of border work', which is based on professional ethics, to national and welfare state border demarcations as a whole. In view of neoliberal policies, these cannot be limited to migrant groups and potentially affect all addressees: "[S]ocial work without borders means not only working across national borders, or those imposed by immigration control, but also transcending those borders imposed by liberalist ideologies and market-led approaches" (Wroe et al.: 2019: 276). SWWB thus assumes that social work as a profession is embedded in the migration and border regime and is involved

---

32 Term for a 'spontaneous' refugee camp in the north of France of people seeking protection to cross the English Channel.
33 In other countries, such as Italy, the association of Assistenti Sociali Senza Frontiere already has a much longer tradition.

in the creation and maintenance of borders within society through various regulations. At the intersection of migration control and social policy, social work can become a crucial actor that confirms and reproduces borders, but it can also shift or subvert them through critical reflection and action (Schütze 2021: 401).

Social work with migrants and refugees and their families as border management at the micro and meso levels needs to be complemented by political demands at the macro level. Ferguson et al. (2018: 104–110) draw on the international ethical standards and a five-point plan for refugee protection (2016) of the international social work associations and draft a list of demands for the policy and practice of social work as a global profession in order to fundamentally transform inhumane structures internationally:

- Safe migration routes: right to fair access to asylum procedures and support along flight and migration routes; dignified reception conditions for all.
- Internment and criminalisation: refugees, asylum seekers and migrants have committed no crime and cannot be "illegal"; deportation centres contradict fundamental human rights and must be closed.
- Support for unaccompanied refugee minors: right to education; protection and access to all welfare services.
- Right to family reunification: a fundamental human right which governments must fulfil.
- Right to work: recognising the skills of refugees and their human dignity.
- Self-organisation and self-help: social workers must recognise the agency of refugees and develop programmes with them (co-design and co-produce).)
- No collusion with discriminatory laws: no cooperation with institutions that undermine social, political and civil rights.

In order to meet such demands, social work cannot accept a framework of action anywhere around the globe that contradicts legal guidelines (Briskman/Ife 2018). First and foremost, social work professionals and agencies are called upon to influence policy and legislation in order to translate human rights standards into applicable law and to enable solidarity-based support for refugees and, if necessary, to use forms of civil disobedience (cf. Scherr 2018: 49; Prasad 2018, 2021). Furthermore, a fundamental role of political social work is to engage and act as an ally with refugee self-organisations to open their voices to political advocacy and establish self-help structures. The political mandate of social work with refugees can begin and become effective in practice through networking at different levels, for example in the context of cooperation with refugee councils and NGOs, which depend on the participation, cooperation and reports of social workers to be able to use evidence from practice for their demands. Another example is the participation in campaigning or strategic litigation through cooperation with NGOs such as Pro Asyl, Amnesty International or the Federal Association for

Unaccompanied Minors. In strategic individual cases, signature collections can be launched to appeal to a petition committee (cf. Schmelz 2021).

Social work can use human rights as its professional ethical compass and, within the framework of the triple mandate, has the opportunity to contribute to structural change in the area of tension between individual help, social control and the self-definition as a human rights profession (Staub-Bernasconi 2019: 83ff.). The triple mandate enables social workers to reject illegitimate and discriminatory mandates and to formulate their own mandates (Prasad 2021: 227). For example, human rights can support social work as analytical tools in the following respects:

- "to evaluate the living situation of a vulnerable group;
- as orientation in mandate conflicts;
- as a 'corrective' on ethical issues,
- as a decision-making tool to classify an order as legitimate (even if not legal);
- in dealing with dilemmas;
- to strengthen one's own argument" (Prasad 2021: 225, translation A. S.).

By reviewing inadequate living conditions in refugee accommodation and/or camps on the basis of human rights standards applicable to all, social workers can name and scandalise them as human rights violations and lack of participation. On this basis, social workers are able to advocate, for example, for minimum standards, grievance mechanisms and concepts for protection against violence based on international human rights standards. A review of the living conditions of racialised people, based on the core provisions of the Convention against Racism, shows that significant experiences such as *racial profiling* or discrimination on the housing and labour markets are not regarded as human rights violations. A human rights violation is seen as an act for which the state is responsible (Prasad 2021). According to Prasad, human-rights-based social work implies that social workers must deviate from their nationally established rules. Human rights are also helpful in dealing with tasks assigned to social workers by employers that contradict the human rights mandate of social work. This is the case when social workers in a refugee shelter inform authorities on the temporary absence of an asylum seeker and, as a result of that, social benefits are reduced (Prasad 2018). Finally, in cooperation with welfare or advocacy organisations social workers can invoke complaints procedures of the UN human rights system (including shadow reports, individual complaints, special rapporteurs, universal periodic review). However, this approach requires competences regarding the complaints procedures and methodological action through campaigning, public relations and lobbying as well as strategic litigation, which need to be further developed in social work curricula (Prasad 2014).

4 "Breaking borders": Women in resistance against gender-based violence and living in camps

All over the world, women are raising their voices in the public against injustices, suffered in contexts of forced migration, human trafficking and trauma. They demand protection of women's and human rights and in particular against gender-based violence (cf. also the contribution by Lohrenscheit in this volume). Nevertheless, sexual assaults, sexism and racism remain largely invisible as a daily structural experience; they are normalised and rarely prosecuted. The case studies of *Nadja Murad* and *Women in Exile* (WiE) show how courageously women break the silence. Nadja Murad has become a global symbol for gender-based violent crimes against Yazidi women. She received the Nobel Peace Prize in 2018 together with the Congolese doctor Denis Mugewe.

Nadja Murad – Winner of the Nobel Peace Prize (2018)

Nadja Murad came to Germany from Iraq in 2015 as part of a so-called *resettlement programme* for refugees run by the government of Baden-Württemberg. She was one of 1,100 Yazidi women who had suffered utmost abuse and violence by the Islamic State of Iraq and the Levant (ISIL). The Yazidi women were admitted to Germany for psychotherapeutic treatment under a UN special initiative (see Zeidan 2018). In 2017, Murad published a biography (Murad 2017), and as tireless campaigner she addresses the public by pointing to gender-based violence as war crime.

The Yazidi human rights activist Murad was born in Koch, Iraq, in 1993. The Yazidis are largely based in Iraq and had long been the target of persecution and discrimination before. When ISIL occupied Murad's village in August 2014, all the Yazidis were rounded up and the women were separated from the men. The men were killed – among them six of Murad's brothers. Older women, including Murad's mother, were also killed. The remaining women, including Nadja Murad, were taken to Mosul, Iraq, and sold into "sex slavery". In total, about 5,200 women were enslaved that year and 5,000 men were murdered. After several attempts to escape, Nadja Murad made her way to the Kurdish-controlled areas of Iraq and finally to Germany via the Resettlement Initiative.

In December 2015, the UN Security Council invited Nadja Murad to speak about human trafficking. She accused the ongoing suffering of the Yazidi community, ISIL's reign of terror and sexual violence as a weapon of war. In 2016, the United Nations appointed Murad as an ambassador for the 'Dignity of Survivors of Human Trafficking'. In cooperation with international organisations, she combines human rights and women's rights work with peacebuilding in her Yazidi region of origin, *Sinjar* in Iraq. The work of the foundation set up by Murad applies a community-based approach. This work is based on the principle that reconstruction measures are developed locally and survivors are empowered to take an active role in the peace process (cf. https://www.nadiasinitiative.org/ (retrieved at 28.02.2024).

As an activist self-organisation, WiE is committed to combating racism, camp accommodation and its psychosocial consequences, as well as it is engaged with regard to the traumas suffered by women and children. WiE organises self-help in its health projects and also advocates for an unconditional right to health with a political list of demands. WiE focusses on inclusive health care for refugee women, which recognises and addresses their special needs and requirements.

WiE fights for a "world without borders", highlighting two demands: on the one hand, WiE calls for overcoming the consequences of colonisation and ending exploitation and plundering of resources; on the other hand, they advocate for "the right to come, the right to go, and the right to STAY!" (WiE 2022) As an initiative of refugee women in Brandenburg, WiE sees itself as a feminist, political and social solidarity group, as a place of learning and living that describes where the personal becomes political and self-empowerment can be experienced. WiE fights fundamentally to abolish the "camp system" because as women they live there without privacy and are exposed to the dangers of sexual and physical violence with their children. The campaign "No camps for women* and children! Abolish all camps!" was run by WiE for several years as a bus tour through various camps throughout Germany (WiE 2022).

Women in Exile as a Poetry Self-Portrait (from: WiE 2020: 21, translation A. S.)

"WiE is a group
a political group
a social group
a group of friends, sisters, mothers and
children,
but not just a group,
it is a family.

A space to learn
about myself, about ourselves, about the
world with its big and small politics about
power relations and about life.

WiE is a space of sharing,
of giving and taking, of coming and going.
It means arriving,
a connection to home,
a mirror of society.

WiE is a collection of stories of
violence, injury, discrimination
– but also one of strength, love, hope and faith.
A space to be myself, to show up
and learn to be more than what I have
been told (and believe) I am.

Women in Exile is
a collective of unheard voices
of immense resistance, knowledge and power.

A movement for human rights
for dignity
for justice
for freedom
and for humanity.
For life.
Life itself.

> Women in Exile is community,
> it means fighting TOGETHER,
> going to the camps and to the streets,
> being loud and shouting out,
> to eat and celebrate together,
> to laugh and cry and be together.
>
> It means fighting and disagreeing,
> cheating, forgiving and being forgiven,
> solidarity and sisterhood.

WiE expanded to *Women in Exile & Friends* in 2011 through the participation of solidarity activists without a refugee history. Since then, women with and without a refugee history have been working together for political change strategies (WiE 2020: 21).

Now it is up to you to discuss how a human-rights-oriented, decolonial and racism-critical social work can be implemented in refugee shelters (Prasad 2018) and how these approaches defend the rights of refugee women and all migrants.

Reflective questions

- For what reasons is it necessary in social work to look critically at statistics and key terms in the context of flight and migration? Explain and discuss using the terms mentioned in the text.
- What is meant by internalisation and externalisation of boundaries? Which challenges do you see for social work with refugees and migrants?
- List the slogans and demands of the activist voices mentioned in the text. What feelings and questions do they trigger?
- What concepts can social work use to deal with the exclusion of people seeking refuge? Discuss your own experiences in social work with refugees and migrants.
- What possibilities do you see for cooperation between activist refugee women and social work, and how should this be structured?

Introductory literature

Boccagni, Paolo/Righard, Erica (2020): Social work with Refugees and Displaced Populations in Europe: (Dis-)continuities, Dilemmas, Developments. In: European Journal of Social Work 23, vol. 3, 375–383.

Schmelz, Andrea (2021): Social Work as a Human Rights Profession in the Context of Refuge and Migration: Global Perspectives. In: Roßkopf, Ralf/Heilmann, Katharina (eds.): International Social Work and Forced Migration Opladen: Budrich, 204–215.

Wroe, Lauren/Larkin, Rachel/Maglajic, Ana Reima (2019) (eds.): Social Work with Refugees, Asylum Seekers and Migrants. Theory and Skills of Practice. London/Philadelphia: Jessica Kingsley Publishers.

Further Reading

Autorinnenkollektiv Meuterei (2022): Grenzenlose Gewalt. Der unerklärte Krieg der EU gegen Flüchtende. Berlin: Assozation A.

Agier, Michel (2019): Lagerwelten. In: Mahlke, Stephan: Lagerwelten. Atlas der Globalisierung. Berlin: Le Monde diplomatique, 128–129.
Agier, Michael (2011): Managing the Undesirables: Refugee Camps and Humanitarian Government. Cambridge: Polity Press 2011.
Balibar, Étienne (2002): Politics and the Other Scene. London/New York: Verso.
Bauman, Zygmunt (2016): Die Angst vor den anderen. Ein Essay über Angst und Panikmache. Frankfurt: Suhrkamp.
Bauman, Zygmunt (2007): Flüchtige Zeiten. Leben in der Ungewissheit. Hamburg: Hamburg Edition.Bendix, Daniel (2018): Migration und soziale Ungleichheit – Perspektiven aus dem Geflüchtetenaktivismus in der BRD. In: Prasad, Nivedita (ed.): Soziale Arbeit mit Geflüchteten. Rassismuskritisch, professionell, menschenrechtsorientiert. Opladen: Budrich, 247–259.
Bhimji, Fazila (2020): Border Regimes, Racialisation Processes and Resistance in Germany. An Ethnographic Study of Protest and Solidarity. Cham: Palgrave Macmillan.
Boccagni, Paolo/Righard, Erica (2020): Social work with Refugees and Displaced Populations in Europe: (Dis-)continuities, Dilemmas, Developments. In: European Journal of Social Work 23, vol. 3, 375–383.
Bojadzijev, Manuala/Liebelt, Claudia (2014): Cosmopolitics, oder: Migration als soziale Bewegung: Von Bürgerschaft und Kosmopolitismus im globalen Arbeitsmarkt. In: Nieswand, Björn/Drotbohm, Heike (eds.): Kultur, Gesellschaft, Migration. Die reflexive Wende in der Migrationsforschung. Wiesbaden: Springer VS, 325–346.
Briskman, Linda (2020). Social work co-option and colonial borders. In: Kleibl, T. et al. (eds.), The Routledge Handbook of Postcolonial Social Work. London: Routledge, 51–60.
Briskman, Linda (2019). Challenging harmful political contexts through activism. In: Webb, Sephen A. (eds.), The Routledge Handbook of Critical Social Work. London: Routledge, 549–560.
Briskman, Linda/Ife, Jim (2018): Extending beyond the legal: social work and human rights. In: Rice, Simon/Day, Andrew/Briskman, Linda (eds.): Social Work in the Shadow of the Law. Alexandra: The Federation Press (5th edition).
Burtzlaff, Miriam/Eifler, Noemi (2018): Kritisch intervenieren!? Über Selbstverständnisse, Kritik und Politik Sozialer Arbeit – oder aber: Was ist der „weiße Kittel" Sozialer Arbeit?. In: Prasad, Nivedita (ed.): Soziale Arbeit mit Geflüchteten. Rassismuskritisch, professionell, menschenrechtsorientiert. Opladen & Toronto, 345–365.
Delvin, Julia/Evers, Tanja/Goebel, Simon (eds.) (2021): Praktiken der Immobilisierung. Lager, Sammelunterkünfte und Ankerzentren im Kontext von Asylregimen. Bielefeld: transcript.
Fassin, Didier (2011): Humanitarian Reason. A Moral History of the Present. Berkeley, CA: University of California Press.
Ferguson, Iain/Ioakimidis, Vasilios/Lavalette, Michael (2018): Social Work in a Global Context. Bristol: Policy Press 2018.
Feinschmidt, Margit/Pries, Ludger/Cantat, Celine (eds.) (2019): Refugee Protection and Civil Society in Europe. Cham: Palgrave Macmillan.
Gal, John/Köngeter, Stefan/Vicary, Sarah (eds.) (2020): The Settlement House Movement Revisited: A Transnational History. Bristol: Polity Press.
Hill, Marc/Schmitt, Caroline (eds.) (2021): Solidarität in Bewegung. Neue Felder für die Soziale Arbeit. Baltmannsweiler: Schneider Verlag.
Isin, Egin/Nielsen Greg (eds.) (2008): Acts of Citizenship. London: Zed Books.
Kasparek, Bernd/Schmidt-Sembdner (2020): Grenzen: Streit hinter den Mauern der Festung Europa. In: Wels et. al (eds.), 44–45.
Kilian, Juri/Bendix, Daniel (2021): Refugee Resistance against Deportation in Germany, Post-Deportation, and Social Work. In: Österreichisches Jahrbuch für Soziale Arbeit 2020, Vol. 2, 51–73.

Kron, Stefanie (2020): Solidarität der Städte. In: Wels et. al (eds.), 44–45.
Lambert, Laura (2020): Die tödlichste Grenze der Welt. In: Wels et. al (Hrsg.), 32–33.
Lavalette, Michael (2019): Popular Social Work. In: Webb, Stephen A. (ed.): The Routledge Handbook of Critical Social Work. Abingdon/New York: Routledge, 536–548.
Lutz, Ronald (2017): Der Flüchtling woanders. Verletzliche Orte des Ungewissen: ein Leben in Lagern. In: Chaderi, Cinur/ Eppenstein, Thomas (eds.): Flüchtlinge. Multiperspektivische Zugänge. Wiesbaden: Springer, 367–380.
Majcher, Izabella/Flynn, Michael/Grange, Mariette (eds.) (2021): Immigration Detention in the European Union. Cham: Springer.
Mecheril, Paul/Castro Varela, Maria do Mar/Dirim, Inci/Kalpaka, Annita/Melter, Claus: Migrationspädagogik. Beltz: Weinheim 2010.
Mezzadra, Sandro/Neilson, Brett (2013): Border as a Method or the Multiplication of Labor. Durham: NC: Duke University Press.
Mohr, Karin (2005): Stratifizierte Rechte und soziale Exklusion von Migranten im Wohlfahrtsstaat. In: Zeitschrift für Soziologie 34, 383–398.
Monforte, Pierre (2020): From „Fortress Europe" to „Refugee Welcome": Social movements and the political imaginary on European borders. In: Fominaya, Flesher Christina/Feenstra Ramòn A. (2020) (eds.): Routledge Handbook of Contemporary European Social Movements: Protest in Turbulent Times. Abington/New York: Routledge, 59–70.
Morris, Lydia (2002): Managing Migration. Civic Stratification and Migrants' Rights. London: Routledge.
Murad, Nadja mit Krajeski Jenna (2017): Ich bin Eure Stimme. München: Knaur Verlag.
Prasad, Nivedita (2014): Teaching the Use of Complaint Mechanisms of UN Treaty Bodies as a Tool of International Social Work Practice. In: Libal, Kathyrn/Berthold Megan S./Thomas, Rebecca/Healy, Lynn (eds.): Advancing Human Rights in Social Work Education. Alexandria: Council of Social Work Education, 143–164.
Prasad, Nivedita (2018): Statt einer Einführung: Menschenrechtsbasierte, professionelle und rassismuskritische Soziale Arbeit mit Geflüchteten. In: Prasad, Nivedita (ed.): Soziale Arbeit mit Geflüchteten. Rassismuskritisch, professionell, menschenrechtsorientiert. Opladen & Toronto: Budrich, 9–32.
Prasad, Nivedita (2021): Rassismus, Migration und Flucht als Themen im Kontext menschenrechtsbasierter Sozialer Arbeit, in: ogsa AG Migrationsgesellschaft (eds.): Soziale Arbeit in der Migrationsgesellschaft, Weinheim: Beltz Juventa 2021, 220–233.
Pries, Ludger (2016): Migration und Ankommen. Die Chancen der Flüchtlingsbewegung. Frankfurt/Main: Campus.
Nyers, Peter (2019): Irregular Citizenship, Immigration, and Deportation. Abingdon/New York: Routledge.
Rehklau, Christine/Lutz, Ronald (2018): Migration und Flucht. In: Handbuch Internationale Soziale Arbeit. Dimensionen – Konflikte – Positionen, Weinheim: Beltz Juventa 2018, 240–257.
Samaddar, Ranabier (2020): The Postcolonial Age of Migration. Abingdon/New York: Routledge 2020.
Scherr, Albert/Scherschel, Karin (2019): Wer ist ein Flüchtling? Grundlagen einer Soziologie der Zwangsmigration. Göttingen: Vandenhoeck & Ruprecht.
Schirilla, Nausikaa (2016): Migration und Flucht. Orientierungswissen für die Soziale Arbeit. Stuttgart: Kohlhammer.
Schmelz, Andrea (2021): Social Work as a Human Rights Profession in the Context of Refuge and Migration: Global Perspectives, in: Roßkopf, Ralf/Heilmann, Katharina (eds.): International Social Work and Forced Migration. Opladen: Budrich, 204–215.
Schmelz, Andrea (2019): „Recht auf Rechte" in Kommunen Europas praktizieren? Lokale Politikstrategien in Deutschland und Italien. In: Arslan, Emre/Bozay, Kemal (eds.): Flüchtlingsbewegungen und symbolische Ordnung – interdisziplinäre Zugänge, Verlag VS Springer, 189–206.

Schmelz, Andrea (2018): (Un-)welcoming refugee politics in Germany: Challenges for social work professionals and volunteers, In: Schmelz, Andrea/Lohrenscheit, Claudia (eds.): Together for justice and peace: International Social Work Education, Gender and the Global Goals for Sustainable Development. Oldenburg: Paulo Freire Verlag, 139–162.

Schwenken, Helen (2018): Globale Migration zur Einführung. Hamburg: Junius 2018.

Schütze, Theresa (2021): Grenzarbeiten – Anschlüsse kritischer Grenzregimetheorie für die Soziale Arbeit. In: ogsa, AG Migrationsgesellschaft (eds.): Soziale Arbeit in der Postmigrationsgesellschaft. Kritische Perspektiven und Praxisbeispiel, Weinheim: Beltz Juventa, 394–405.

Steinhilper, Elias (2021): Migrant Protest. Interactive Dynamics in Precarious Mobilizations, Amsterdam: University Press.

Staub-Bernasconi (2019): Menschenwürde – Menschenrechte – Soziale Arbeit. Die Menschenrechte vom Kopf auf die Füße stellen. Opladen: Budrich.

Stierl, Maurice (2020): Zivilgesellschaft: Neue Generationen der Solidarität. In: Wels et. al (eds.), 46–47.

UNHCR (2020): Global Trends 2020. Geneva: UNHCR.

Van Hear, Nicholas (1998): New Diasporas. London: Routledge.

Wels, Florian et al. (eds.) (2020): Atlas der Migration. Berlin: Rosa-Luxemburg-Stiftung.

Women in Exile (WiE) (2020): Gesundheitsversorgung für alle ohne Diskriminierung. Potsdam: Eigenverlag.

Women in Exile (WiE) (2022): Breaking Borders to Build Bridges. Berlin: edition assemblage.

Wroe, Lauren/Larkin, Rachel/Maglajic, Ana Reima (2019): Social Work with Refugees and Asylum Seekers and Migrants. In: dies. (eds.): Social Work with Refugees, Asylum Seekers and Migrants. Theory and Skills of Practice. London/Philadelphia: Jessica Kingsley Publishers, 17–26.

Wroe, Lauren/Larkin, Rachel/Maglajic, Ana Reima (2019): Concluding Thoughts. In: ibd. (eds.): Social work with Refugees, Asylum Seekers and Migrants. Theory and Skills of Practice. London/Philadelphia: Jessica Kingsley Publishers, 267–278.

Zeidan, Adam (2018): Nadja Murad. Iraqi human rights activist. In: https://www.britannica.com/biography/Nadia-Murad (retrieved at 28.02.2024).

II.5 Solidarity Cities.
Urban Citizenship and Artivism as a Practice of Inclusive Solidarity

Caroline Schmitt

> 15th April – World Art Day
>
> 20th June – World Refugee Day
>
> 31st October – World Day of Cities
>
> 20th December – International Human Solidarity Day

Summary

The chapter[34] provides insight into solidarity-based urban movements that advocate for a city for all people regardless of diversity dimensions such as residency status, nationality and origin. Solidarity city movements, known as sanctuary cities, have existed in the United States since the 1980s and have also spread to Canada. Since the 'long summer of migration', they have become known in Europe under the term solidarity cities. After an introduction to the history and objectives of sanctuary and solidarity cities, the chapter focuses on the concept and practice of municipal city cards as an expression of urban solidarity. Using the case study of the Züri City Card, the chapter discusses the possibilities and challenges of urban citizenship before delving into an artistic approach. Through the example of "Weekends for Moria Kärnten/Koroška", the chapter demonstrates how solidarity alliances, through artistic actions, generate awareness of societal issues and create a public presence in the city (artivism). Finally, the significance of solidarity city movements for International Social Work is discussed and connected to the approaches of Popular Social Work and municipal pedagogy.

1. Social problems and urban solidarity movements

The number of people fleeing, according to the UN Refugee Agency, has more than doubled from 41 million in 2010 to over 100 million by 2022 (UNHCR 2022a). In its annual report for 2021, the UNHCR (2022b) reveals that, by the end of 2021, 83% of displaced individuals found refuge in low or middle-income countries, with 72% of them located in neighbouring countries. Only a small proportion managed to reach Europe. Many people do not survive the journey. For instance, the route across the Mediterranean is considered the deadliest migration path globally (Hentges 2021). According to statistics between 2014 and 2021, at least 22,200 people have drowned in the Mediterranean (Statista 2021). Those who manage to reach Europe despite all the dangers have experienced stages of progression such as being immobilised in camps or prisons. Reports frequently highlight illegal push-backs, indicating a violent rejection of people

---

[34] The chapter contains trains of thought and passages from my contribution Schmitt (2023) and develops them further.

at the borders of their transit or destination countries (Isakjee et al. 2020). In European transit and destination countries, those who have successfully reached a European country, despite the perilous journey, typically live initially in separate accommodations or camps. Since the 1980s, large refugee accommodations and camps in Global North countries have evolved into an increasingly normalised form of housing (Dünnwald 2018; Kreichauf 2016). Studies emphasise the institutionally induced potentials of conflict and violence inherent in the forced cohabitation of many people in close quarters as well as the significant psychosocial burdens associated with such forms of accommodation for those residing there (Kleist et al. 2022). The waiting period until the outcome of the asylum process is characterised by uncertainty about the future and fears. Participation in societal life, such as access to the job market, education, culture, leisure and healthcare, is restricted (Christ et al. 2017). Often, these accommodations and camps are located far from city centres, thus contributing to the spatial isolation of individuals. Additionally, sans-papiers, i.e. individuals without valid residence papers, are excluded from societal life; they remain hidden although they engage in socially relevant activities in the care sector, hospitality or crafts (Knoll et al. 2012). The exclusion of people without secure residency status and individuals living in the shadows from centres and social security systems contradicts civil society attempts to create safe places for all (Scherr 2022: 427). Such attempts are primarily found in cities.

1.1 Cities on the move

Cities are considered places where people live together in all their diversity and where "confrontation with diversity is part of everyday life" (Yıldız 2013: 19). The urban environment is characterised by a "coexistence of strangers among strangers, which moves people and shapes spaces" (Hill 2018: 97). In comparison to nation-states, cities have more accessible leeway for shaping their environments and have increasingly distanced themselves from national and European migration policies in recent years. Educator Cudak and sociologist Bukow (2016) refer to urban societies as spaces of possibility and primarily examine the potentials of inner-city neighbourhoods. These "not only provide meeting points for people in search of a new life perspective but also have long facilitated the stabilisation and everyday integration of mobility and diversity" (ibid.: 5). However, cities and neighbourhoods should not be romanticised. They are not only expressions of cosmopolitan developments, as right-wing extremist and racist movements can also appropriate urban spaces; likewise, restrictive urban policies can manifest exclusion (Doomernik/Ardon 2018: 93). Nevertheless, looking at the local level often reveals that cities do not simply accept these developments (Hill/Schmitt 2021a: 37). According to Mayer (2014), urban spaces play a noteworthy role in social movements. Activities range from flash mobs to the occupation of parks or the transformation of roads into green spaces. A "radical-democratic insistence" (ibid.: 38) is evident not only in immediate urban environments but also in "post-, ex- and sub-urban spaces" (ibid.: 39), which connect with urban areas and break down the dichotomy of city and countryside.

1.2 "A city for all"

An example of creating cosmopolitan spaces is the urban movements of sanctuary cities and solidarity cities. As social movements, they aim to bring about "cultural, social and political changes to existing societal conditions" (Lahusen 2013: 717). They function as a "network of organisations, groups and individuals [...] that seeks to promote societal change through protest actions" (ibid.). Their underlying idea is based on the concept of urban citizenship, understood as the social, political, cultural and economic participation of individuals in societal life (Marshall 1950) without the requirement of holding the citizenship of a specific country. The ability to participate should be open to anyone present, with immigration status playing no role in this regard (Wenke/Kron 2019: 9–10). The concept of urban citizenship challenges an understanding of participation that primarily grants full access to socially relevant goods to citizens of a specific country. In our nation-state-structured world, opportunities for participation depend not exclusively but centrally on the citizenship acquired by an individual through the principles of birthplace (jus soli), descent (jus sanguinis) or a combination of these citizenship principles (Ataç/Rosenberger 2013: 48). In contrast, approaches to urban citizenship place the location of residence as a relevant factor in participation (jus domicili) at their core and advocate for a right to the city for all people (Doomernik/Ardon 2018: 93). These approaches have been actively discussed in the U.S. and Canada since the 1980s and have also entered scholarly and urban political debates in Europe (Füchslbauer 2022).

Calls for a city for all can be traced back, among others, to the French sociologist Henri Lefebvre (1996), who criticised an urban landscape oriented towards consumption and capitalism and envisioned the urban as a need-oriented space for encounters. Recent approaches emphasise the processual nature of citizenship, moving the concept away from "static and state-centric interpretations" (Hess/Lebuhn 2014: 13) and focusing on "urban appropriation practices 'from below'" (ibid.). This highlights urban design practices and struggles of social movements related to issues of migration and displacement as well as to problems such as the displacement of low-income and low-wealth population groups from city centres, racial practices like racial profiling and the denied and fought-for accessibilities of the city for people with disabilities.

> **Urban citizenship** refers to social search movements as well as concrete practices that aim to decouple the right to participation from the 'belonging' to a particular nation state assigned by citizenship. Instead it seeks to anchor participation rights locally – at the place of residence or the focal point of individuals' lives (Schilliger 2018). The debate on urban citizenship has been actively pursued since the 1980s in the United States and Canada and has been translated into concrete strategies by sanctuary cities. In the meantime, these approaches are also gaining relevance in Europe and are intended, among other things, to give illegalised, but also otherwise marginalised groups of people access to services and goods in a city. Urban citizenship movements thus position themselves as a subversive response to an increasingly restrictive national and supranational (migration) policy.

1.3 Sanctuary cities in the U.S. and Canada

The earliest initiatives of sanctuary cities date back at least to the 1980s in the U.S. state of Arizona (Füchslbauer 2022: 87–88). The background was the influx of refugees fleeing war and torture from Central American countries such as Guatemala and El Salvador, coupled with a simultaneously restrictive asylum practice during the presidency of then-U.S. President Ronald Reagan (1981–1989). Despite their experiences of violence, refugees were rarely granted asylum or received minimal protection, compelling them to undertake dangerous border crossings in the Sonoran Desert. In response to these dire situations, it was not governmental bodies but rather religious organisations and individuals from the United States and Mexico that attempted to organise safer escape routes for these people. Moreover, facing an unrealistic expectation of federal support, they pressured city governments to take action, leading to an increasing number of cities declaring themselves "refugee sanctuary zones" (ibid.: 88). In 1985, for instance, San Francisco passed a City of Refuge resolution. The ordinance adopted in 1989 prohibits "urban authorities and police officers from cooperating with federal authorities in the identification, pursuit, detention, and deportation of migrants without legal status" (Wenke/Kron 2019: 5). In 2013, the Canadian city of Toronto similarly enacted an ordinance with a comparable focus (Bauder 2019: 41). Both in the U.S. and in Canada, more than 500 cities have now declared themselves as sanctuary cities (a list for the USA can be found here: https://cis.org/Map-Sanctuary-Cities-Counties-and-States; Kron/Maffeis 2021: 169). Sanctuary cities "share the common belief that all city residents, regardless of their immigration status, should be treated as equal citizens" (Schmelz 2019: 191). They refer not only to "the city in a narrow geographical, sociological and political dimension but also to municipalities and communities, thus including rural areas" (ibid.: 192). These cities and communities employ various strategies, such as city IDs, allowing all residents to identify themselves to local authorities, regardless of whether they have proof of residency or a state driver's license (Bauder 2016: 176). The "Don't Ask, Don't Tell" (DADT) policy implies that, for instance, the police and other authorities do not inquire about immigration status, and residents can file a police report, enrol their children in school or rent an apartment based on the city ID.

A prominent example is the New York City Identification Card (IDNYC), introduced in 2015 in New York City under then-Mayor Bill de Blasio in response to long-standing demands from social movements for a city ID. The IDNYC has since served as a recognised identification document in schools, administrations and some private businesses like banks in New York City. It is issued by the city government, requiring proof of residence in the city. Homeless individuals can note the address of a support organisation. No information about immigration status needs to be provided for issuance. In 2016, the card was evaluated, with approximately 10% of New York City residents, around 900,000 people, using the IDNYC at that time. For 25%, the card served as their only identification document. 70% of respondents expressed support for the idea. Students, among others, use the ID to gain free or discounted access to cultural institutions and events. City sociologist Lebuhn (2016) concludes that, while the card opens up important potentials for participation, its limitation lies in not enabling the use of social welfare benefits. This highlights the ambivalence of sanctuary city concepts: aiming to support refugees, undocumented individuals, low-income individuals and those without secure immigration status, they nevertheless remain limited and should not falsely convey a sense of security, as they cannot override higher-level legislation and do not guarantee protection, for example from deportation (Scherr/Hofmann 2018).

2 Solidarity cities in Europe – practices and interventions

The concepts from the U.S. and Canada have garnered interest and support in Europe as well, especially with the increasing numbers of forced migrants, contributing to the emergence and growth of solidarity cities – the common term used in Europe. These concepts from overseas can, on the one hand, be characterised as traveling concepts. On the other hand, they never entail a one-to-one transfer from one space to another. Instead, it is essential to reflect on the international journey of these ideas and practices, always considering their translation into local, regional and national contexts.

With a focus on the European continent, networks like the *Solidarity Cities* (https://solidaritycities.eu/) have formed since 2015. In this network, mayors unite in their desire for cosmopolitan approaches to dealing with forced migration, advocating for support and urban spaces from the EU. Participating cities include Amsterdam, Barcelona, Berlin, Bremen, Gaziantep, Leeds, Lucerne, Ljubljana and Vienna. This should be distinguished from the network *Solidarity City: eine Stadt für alle* (https://solidarity-city.eu/de/), primarily involving activists from Germany and Switzerland. In their flyer, participants demand the right to basic services for all people, access to city infrastructures, education and further training, medical advice and care, culture, political participation and the right to stay (Solidarity City 2017).

The international movement *Seebrücke* (https://seebruecke.org/) also places municipalities and cities at the centre, urging them to declare themselves a "Safe Haven", advocating for the decriminalisation of sea rescue and calling on cities to accommodate more people with refugee experiences than the legally mandated number.

An overview of solidarity initiatives in Europe can be found on the platform "Moving Cities" (https://moving-cities.eu/de), launched in October 2021, supported by the Heinrich Böll Foundation and continuously expanding. As of the summer of 2022, the platform lists over 700 cities and 14 networks across Europe. Their strategies include attempts to establish a municipal city ID, roundtable discussions, cooperative employment projects, inclusive housing forms and independent asylum counselling centres.

Subsequently, two solidarity city activities from Switzerland and Austria will be presented, drawn from the majority of activities. These case studies originate from the research project "Weltoffene Solidarität in der Stadt" (Cosmopolitan Solidarity in the City), conducted by the author since April 2021 at the University of

Klagenfurt, funded by a "Globalbudget" (one-line budgeting). The project takes forms of solidarity engagement in the Alpine-Adriatic region and the D-A-CH region as its starting point and examines who the actors of these solidarities are, the understanding of solidarity cities they unfold and the practices they use to bring this into the public sphere.

> The concept of **solidarity** has become widespread with the 'long summer of migration', the COVID-19 pandemic and Russia's war of aggression against Ukraine, which began in February 2022. Laitinen (2013) differentiates between four different contexts of appropriation of this concept, which has historically been used in very different ways: First, the term is understood as the glue that holds society and communities together (*social solidarity*). Secondly, the concept is interwoven with the ideal of *fraternité* (brotherhood* and sisterhood*) and is negotiated as a political state to strive for and as a welfare state principle (*civic solidarity*). Thirdly, solidarity is an attitude and demand in civil society struggles for more justice and against oppression (*political solidarity*). The fourth context of appropriation refers to solidarity as an universalist, ethical principle and moral response to human existence (*human, moral and global solidarity*). Solidarity movements in cities adhere to a comprehensive understanding of solidarity, emphasising mutual connection and the assumption of responsibility by vastly different individuals. They advocate for unconditional and globally conceived solidarity (Susemichel/Kastner 2021; Broden/Mecheril 2014), along with a redistribution of societal goods accessible to all people (Lessenich 2020). Such as understanding of solidarity does not view solidarity as something exclusive, as a connection only among ostensibly similar individuals who share a common origin, religion or similar socialising contexts. Instead, it is about inclusive solidarity under conditions of diversity; in its cosmopolitan thought, it should not exclude anyone. At the same time we observe that the idea of solidarity is also appropriated by far-right, racist, anti-feminist, anti-queer and homophobic groups, constructing an exclusive 'we' group and, consequently, an exclusive solidarity confined to the members of this 'we' group – for example, based on gender, nationality or skin colour (Haase 2020). Such appropriations and distortions of the concept of solidarity are at odds with an understanding oriented towards social justice and inclusion. This is different with groups that use the concept of solidarity to draw attention to their own experiences of discrimination – for example, as a woman*, a refugee*, a BIPoC* (Black, Indigenous, People of Colour) or a homeless person*. These individuals use group construction to address social inequalities and demand solidarity with their concerns as well as equal rights and participation for all. If they achieve their goals, their solidarity activities may subside. As shown here, solidarity is a yardstick for societal relations that have become imbalanced and for social inequalities that are perceived and deemed unacceptable (Hill/Schmitt 2021b). Solidarity, along with freedom and equality, is one of the fundamental principles of human rights. In the "Global Social Work Statement of Ethical Principles" by the International Federation of Social Workers (2018), solidarity is enshrined as a central social work principle: "Social workers actively work in communities and with their colleagues, within and outside of the profession, to build networks of solidarity to work toward transformational change and inclusive and responsible societies" (ibid.: n.p.).

2.1 The "Züri City Card" – a city card for all residents of Zurich

The city of Zurich is one of the first cities in Europe to decide on the introduction of a city card following the example of the United States and Canada. Holders of the "Züri City Card" should be able to gain access to cultural offerings and be granted access to municipal services and healthcare. The idea of such a card received approval in the Zurich City Council in October 2018, followed by several years of debate. In May 2022, a referendum took place in which the majority of Zurich residents supported the card, initiating the implementation process. In recent years, the city of Zurich has become a solidarity laboratory, especially for those cities that aim to follow this example and translate self-declarations as a solidarity city into concrete strategies. The following passages are based on a guided interview conducted in October 2021 (Przyborski/Wohlrab-Sahr 2010: 138–145) with Bea Schwager[35], a protagonist of the debate. They provide insight into the idea of the city ID card and the current status of its implementation.

"Focus on the city"

Bea Schwager is the head of the "Sans-Papiers Anlaufstelle Zürich" (SPAZ, https://sans-papiers-zuerich.ch/) and the president and board member of the "Züri City Card Association" (https://www.zuericitycard.ch/). The SPAZ association was founded in April 2005 by trade unions, migrant organisations and individuals. The background to this was a "paradigm shift in the trade unions" (lines[36] 121–122), which began to recognise Sans-Papiers as workers. Together with legal experts and "leftist lawyers" (line 133), they formed a movement and finally an umbrella organisation, leading to the establishment of SPAZ. Bea Schwager had been involved in activism for years at this point. She is a trained interpreter and a bookseller and has studied and worked in the field of development cooperation. She joined SPAZ full-time and established the counselling centre (lines 32–34). SPAZ's responsibilities include advisory services, support for Sans-Papiers in enrolling their children in school, accessing healthcare, political lobbying (lines 154–161), "awareness-raising work" (line 188), "communication" (line 189) and "public relations" (line 189). The goal is to shape a solidary framework for "Swiss-wide politics" (line 194) and "a collective regularisation of Sans-Papiers" (line 190). With their demand for regularisation, the team faced resistance from the "National Council and Council of States, which is responsible for such issues, as well as the Cantonal Council" (lines 194–196), encountering a firm opposition. Since SPAZ made no progress at the national and cantonal levels, the team decided to "focus on the city" (line 201). At the time of the interview, the city of Zurich was "left-green governed, and the parliament was left-green dominated" (lines 201–202). The exploration of urban possibilities led to the "demand for the introduction of a city card" (line 203). The Züri City Card Association was established to support this initiative in addition to SPAZ.

---

35 The author would like to thank Bea Schwager for the enriching interview and the insights into the commitment of SPAZ and the Züri City Card Association.
36 Refers to the corresponding lines in the transcript of the interview.

(Trans-)Urban Networks

Bea Schwager had heard through her various engagements that the city of New York defines itself as a sanctuary city and has introduced a city card (lines 216–218). She invited individuals from New York City and Toronto to Zurich through several events: "They told us how it works in Toronto regarding this Don't Ask, Don't Tell directive from the authorities" (lines 421–423). She is also connected with initiatives from other "cities in Switzerland" and cities in other countries, such as activists in Frankfurt am Main (lines 433–440). The transurban exchange highlights how tightly interwoven urban citizenship activities are beyond individual locations. Starting points elsewhere serve as flagship projects and inspiration, leading to knowledge exchange across various cities and countries.

Concerning Zurich, the activists aim to provide Sans-Papiers with access to "municipal and private services" (lines 447–448) through a municipal city card and ensure "residence security" (line 449) by having the police "accept the card" (line 450). This would enable Sans-Papiers to file criminal reports and witness statements, allowing them to "live without constant fear" (line 450). The existence of the card would help Sans-Papiers to "know they are a recognised part of the city, and if people exploit Sans-Papiers ... the better the legal protection, the more Sans-Papiers can defend themselves" (lines 488–492).

Political negotiations

In order for the city card to function, it is essential that both the city and cantonal police genuinely recognise the Züri City Card as a valid identification document and refrain from conducting their own checks on residency status. However, there are concerns among certain members of the municipal and city councils about the potential reaction from the canton:

> "This has a long history in Zurich [...] because [...] the canton keeps interfering in municipal matters [...], which was then [...] suddenly a great fear on the part of the city council that, if the city police were now to recognise this [...] city ID card on the city territory, the cantonal police could come and say, now we are going to start controlling again in the city of Zurich because the city police are no longer doing their job properly" (lines 233–241).

While the idea of the Züri City Card is generally supported by the city council and civil society, and while Bea Schwager has successfully raised awareness for the cause among city council members ("we then sought conversations with various other city council members, and initially [...] everyone found the idea very good", lines 219–226), the idea faces "scepticism" in parts of the population and politics (lines 231). Bea Schwager explains how a petition came about and legal opinions were sought:

> "In the city council, this petition was approved with a large majority. Thus, the city council, i.e., the executive, was given the mandate to develop a proposal for implementation within two years [...] and [...] then the

city council commissioned one and later another legal opinion from the University of Zurich. [...] both of these opinions turned out entirely in our favour, essentially stating that issuing an official city card does not violate overarching laws. The city has the leeway to issue such a card, and it would indeed provide a good opportunity to address the lack of access to justice that Sans-Papiers face" (lines 257–269).

In September 2021, the city council finally approved a framework credit of 3.2 million Swiss francs for the preparation of the Züri City Card; however, a civic committee called for a referendum against it. The Züri City Card has become a legal and public negotiation project (Morawek 2019). Consequently, on 15th May 2022, a popular vote was held on the Züri City Card. The people of Zurich voted in favour of introducing the city card, with a yes vote share of 51.69%. In the coming months and years, it will be revealed how the implementation will be approached. However, the case study already illustrates the potential scope that cities have for creating solidary cities. At the same time it becomes apparent that supportive networks are necessary for success – besides political authorities and institutions. In Zurich it was ultimately the citizens of various constituencies who decided on the project's implementation.

Meanwhile, Bea Schwager summarises what she and all other stakeholders are aiming for, namely the creation of an "inclusive city where everyone who lives here has equal rights, and no one is discriminated against" (lines 561–562).

2.2 "Weekends for Moria Carinthia/Koroška". Artivism in the Alps-Adriatic region

While the previous chapter focused on the idea and practice of municipal ID cards, the following elaborations shift to an artistic approach to urban citizenship. In Kewes' interpretation (2016), urban citizenship encompasses not only institutionalised forms of solidarity but also serves as an umbrella term for creative practices that, through artistic means, unlock, renegotiate and expand opportunities for participation for all people in a city (ibid.: 145–146). A well-known example of visualising and addressing societal issues through art is the graffiti of the British street artist Banksy (see: http://banksy.co.uk/). Banksy places his works in places all over the world, drawing attention to the need for sea rescue and humane asylum and migration policies, among other things.

Figure 1: Graffiti by Banksy "Child with telescope and vulture", Calais beach (Photography: Caroline Schmitt, 2020)

Interlocking art and protest

Artful protest practices challenging the migration policies of individual nation-states and the EU while presenting them with solidarity narratives can also be heard at one's doorstep. An example of this is seen in protest practices during the "Weekends for Moria Kärnten/Koroška" in Austria, regularly visible in the city of Klagenfurt am Wörthersee. During the "Weekends for Moria Kärnten/Koroška", people camp in tents on central squares in the city to criticise Austrian and European asylum policies and the living conditions in refugee camps worldwide. The goal is to imagine and implement new possibilities for coexistence. This is a translocal movement initiated in December 2020 in response to the catastrophic conditions in the Moria camp on the Greek island of Lesbos, starting in the city of Innsbruck and now taking place in a similar form in other EU countries and additional Austrian cities such as Vienna, Graz, Linz, and Villach. In Klagenfurt, the weekends are organised by the association "Kärnten andas" and a core group of dedicated individuals, including students, artists, people with refugee experiences and social workers.

Figure 2: Weekends for Moria, tents and banners, Klagenfurt (Photography: Caroline Schmitt, 2021)

The organisers[37] maintain contacts in various refugee camps, among others in Greece and Bosnia and Herzegovina, in order to support local organisations and initiatives and to transfer donations. Their demands are: "Evacuate all camps! Take people in! Stop deportations!" A characteristic feature of the "Weekends for Moria Kärnten/Koroška" is the use of artistic means and solidarity practices. Events have taken place where slam poets presented specially written slam texts, filling the urban space with solidarity narratives. A band named "Solband", led by singer Baback Soleymani, who fled from Iran to Austria, regularly performs at many of these events. Additionally, a rapper delivered solidarity rap songs, raising awareness not only among the core group of activists but also reaching a broader audience (Schmitt 2022). The artistic performances reflect a negotiation of dominant orders of belonging in the city and countryside. They provide space for new narratives and urban identities that aspire to be inclusive, considering all people in the city.

The interlocking of artistic protest with socio-critical concerns is negotiated in art and science under the term artivism. Artivism means "activism through and by

---

37 The author sincerely thanks all those involved in the "Weekends for Moria Carinthia/Koroška" (especially Bettina Pirker and Martin Diendorfer from "Kärnten andas", Baback Soleymani and his "Solband", the multimedia artist Barbara Ambrusch-Rapp and Mighty M. aka Himmeldach as well as all other committed people) for opening their door to this research and for supporting it.

art" (Suchet/Mekdjian 2016: 2) and is a characteristic of recent social movements in particular (Schmitz 2015: 10), which sharpen public perception of social problems, "de-automate" (Koch 2021: 249) and ultimately "stimulate the collective sense of possibility" (ibid.) through their colourful, cheerful, imaginative and aesthetically conscious protest.

> ***Artivism*** is a neologism composed of the words 'art' and 'activism' (Salzbrunn 2019). The term refers to the combination of protest and artistic practices with the political goal of initiating social change (Mekdjian 2018: 39). Artivism is not a movement in its own right but a multifaceted practice that destabilises common hierarchies, thereby mobilising and adding a joyful component to protest. This form of protest art can be situational and temporary or longer-term. It is made visible in publicly accessible places and ranges from graffiti art, flash mobs and theatre to raps and slam texts. Artivism is sometimes used to demand inclusive forms of citizenship and to shake up social orders (Zebracki 2020: 149). Entrenched dichotomies such as 'migrant' and 'non-migrant' or 'other' and 'normal' are questioned and transformed (Mekdjian 2018: 47–48). The beginnings of artivism date back to the late 19th century and the early 20th century (cf. in detail on the history of artivism Brigouleix 2019).
> Artistic projects and forms of work that initiate community development – understood as interventions in urban or rural communities – are also part of social work studies at many universities in Germany and abroad. They are usually not discussed as 'artivism' but rather categorised under the term 'cultural education'.

Protest under the wire tent

In the course of the research project "Cosmopolitan Solidarity in the City", the practices of the "Weekends for Moria" were ethnographically studied, and conversations were conducted with artists, including multimedia artist Barbara Ambrusch-Rapp (https://barbara-rapp.com). She unfolds her performance art under a wire tent, into which she quietly weaves messages at the edge of the events. In the interview the artist describes her art as a way to address societal problems and raise awareness of injustice in society: "As an artist, I naturally have the opportunity to make all these issues visible. In other words, not to make (them) disappear, as many want" (lines 258–263). Her performances are a 'need' for her in the face of the isolation of people on the run. The young woman wants to create "awareness [...]: Yeah, hey, you know? There is much, much more happening in the background" (lines 532–534).

Figure 3: Weekends for Moria, "(No)Hope", Artivism in front of the city theatre in Klagenfurt (Photography: Caroline Schmitt, 2021)

She explains the performance as follows:

> "I tried to make people [CS: meaning people on the run] visible as individuals in the middle of the main square in a way that was as unobtrusive as possible. I put up a wire tent […] dressed in white […] sat on the ground […] for one and a half to two hours. Off stage in silence. Because the suffering of these people also happens offstage […] [I] tied the writing in. […] a white Hope horizontally […]. And a turquoise No vertically in the O […]. I did this performance several times. On several weekends for Moria. And depending on the mood, which was political at the time, I sometimes tied a little more to the white Hope. And sometimes more to the turquoise No. […] turquoise stood […] for the [CS: Austrian] federal government […] for the party. Because the No from that side was also particularly vehement" (lines 17–32).

Silence and visibility at second glance are means that the artist uses to address the suffering of forced migrants *"with dignity"* (lines 128–144) and to confront the viewers with society's looking away or only conditionally looking at the living conditions of people on the run. The white clothing symbolises *"the hope that maybe things will somehow continue in a positive way"* (lines 128–140). Turquoise stands for the Austrian People's Party (ÖVP), which primarily represents a rejectionist migration policy. The dynamic performance illustrates how, from the artist's point of view, party political decisions have a direct impact on the life situation and future prospects of forced migrants. Sitting under the wire tent, she symbolises the imprisonment of forced migrants in a life-threatening situation and at the same time the possibility of looking through the wire and hoping for a better life.

Empathy spaces

The protest art is accompanied by emotionality in the audience. Towards the end of the events, conversations with the audience and the solution of the performance take place (lines 39–59). One thought of the artist is to be 'rescued' from the wire tent, especially by that point. Throughout the entire event, a wire cutter is placed next to the tent for this purpose. When the tent is opened, the artist is moved by all the concern directed towards her and, at the same time, is exposed—just like the 'rescuing person'—to the observing gazes of the audience.

> "That was always such a beautiful act. [...] the caution, the cutting open [...]. 'Yes, be careful when you get out. Don't hurt yourself and all that.' That, that touched me very much. [...]. That was definitely visible as an art performance. [...] [But] as soon as someone comes and cuts me out. He or she is suddenly the focus of everyone's attention [...] [I] discussed this with the organiser Bettina Pirker beforehand: 'Yes, what do I do when I go out?' [...] Should I thank her now for saving me? No [...] it is [...] a human act to help someone in need. And then I just disappeared quietly in the background. [...] [P]eople looked around for a long time to see where I was going and what I was doing now. [...] Well, what about the people who are fleeing? Who are now being rescued? They will probably be the focus of a lot of attention. What are they doing now? [...] Will they behave properly?" (lines. 77–122).

The artist, through her performance, creates a space of attention for the living situation of displaced people. She connects the city's public with the lived realities of displaced individuals. The wire cutter symbolises the responsibility to take action against the 'imprisonment' in the wire tent. The performance critically engages with societal discourses, such as the debate that displaced people are responsible for themselves if they embark on a dangerous escape route, owe gratitude to the 'receiving' society or should remain inconspicuous. The artist confronts the audience with these debates, creating a space where care for each other and mutual responsibility become the focus. From a social work perspective, this space can be seen as a space of empathy, expanding and changing perspectives on the experiences of displacement – with the aim of creating a new togetherness in global and urban society.

To what extent activities like these contribute to a sustainable engagement of the public with questions of forced migration remains a question to be further investigated.

3 Conclusion and outlook. Popular Social Work and solidarity-based professionalism

The article has provided an insight into solidarity-based urban movements, using examples from sanctuary and solidarity cities. It explores the associated debates on urban citizenship and concrete practices such as city IDs and artivism. The "new new social movements" highlighted in this article (see Straub's contribution in this volume) are significantly driven by activists and institutionalised forms of solidarity, manifested in organisations like SPAZ and the Züri City Card Association.

In activist circles, individual social workers actively participate, supporting the endeavour to create solidary urban spaces. They gather in urban areas and envision inclusive coexistence that breaks down divisions between 'locals' and 'foreigners', 'refugees' and 'settled residents', between an 'us' and 'them'. These visions emphasise commonalities, mutual responsibility and awareness (Kubaczek/Mokre 2021). The solidary practices and concepts go beyond dominant integration appeals that require refugees to fit into a challenging-to-describe, pluralised 'residential society'. Instead, the focus shifts to urban spaces, local political strategies and the ways all members of society deal with refugee-related issues in terms of their transformative potential to create solidarity and inclusion on the ground – a mission to which social work is also dedicated.

Inclusion here means reimagining and modelling urban, rural and regional coexistences with the aim of not excluding anyone. This understanding is based on inclusive solidarity (Schwenken/Schwiertz 2021) and encompasses a resolute stance against marginalisation and discrimination in a transnationalised and plural society. As an urban bottom-up strategy it is a response to societal tendencies of exclusion and division and stems from the idea of a socially just world for all (Schmitt 2021: 406). Inclusive solidarity is characterised precisely by the fact that human connections and a commitment to one another do not stop at origin or nationality; instead, people with different biographies and life experiences stand up for each other.

Sometimes loud and sometimes quiet, sometimes through artistic means, sometimes through urban policies, social movements take shape against the backdrop of such commitment and can culminate in institutionalised forms of solidarity – such as a city ID. Participation in these forms of engagement is not conceptualised through citizenship understandings but rather as participation for all those present in specific locations and cities.

For social work, these practices are highly relevant and can be connected with community-oriented approaches such as community work or discussions on cultural education. A look into the history of social work reveals that the development of social work is closely linked to emancipatory social movements (see the contributions by Straub in this volume). These movements often share common concerns with social work and advocate in various ways for the reduction of social inequalities and the establishment of social justice (Maurer 2019). At the same time, social movements such as the labour movement and new women's movements (see the contribution by Lohrenscheit in this volume) have, in many cases, been critics of social work perceived as too state-compliant and uncritical (Wagner 2009).

The major challenges of our time, such as wars and displacement, the climate crisis and poverty (see the contributions by Schmelz in this volume), once again provide a reason for revitalising the connections between social movements and professionals in social work to collectively change course. The World Bank estimates that by the year 2050 there will be more than 200 million people fleeing due to climate-related factors (Statista 2022); wars, poverty, water scarcity, famines, and widening income and wealth disparities are increasing globally. Thus, migration movements will not simply disappear but are an expression of unequal living conditions in our world. A sustainable engagement with these disparate living conditions calls for globally open places, cities and regions, as demanded by the United Nations' Sustainable Development Goals (SDGs): "Make cities and human settlements inclusive, safe, resilient and sustainable" (https://sdgs.un.org/goals/goal11).

Solidarity city movements embrace this demand and can be crucial partners for internationally reflected social work without co-opting civil society engagement. Kunstreich (2017) suggests the concept of solidarity professionalism for this purpose. This refers to a professionalism that reflects societal and political issues in their significance for all people and is particularly in solidarity with marginalised individuals or groups. Social work can thereby "free itself from its structurally conservative embedding in the hegemonic order" (ibid.: 123). At the core of Kunstreich's argumentation is the "social code 'with'" (ibid.: 124), understood as a collective societal design by social work professionals together with social movements, initiatives and people particularly affected by the crises of our time. Solidarity then means collective action and the creation of solidary spaces, as presented in this article. Recent works, including Schmidt (2022), revive such an approach and explicitly focus on city and space-related concepts and the idea of municipal pedagogy, aiming to enable "cooperative forms" (ibid.: 197) among various status groups and milieus of civil, economic, administrative and (professional) political actors in a neighbourhood, district, city or region. This would create "collaborative thinking and action factories" (ibid.: 198) that reconnect societal transformation visions and practices to state institutions (ibid.: 202).

Internationally, such intertwining of social movements, local actors and social work is discussed under the term 'Popular Social Work'. Similar to Schmidt's considerations on municipal pedagogy, Popular Social Work acknowledges the interconnections between social movements and social work and sees it as an opportunity to think beyond state-organised social work (Jones/Lavalette 2013). The latter does not become obsolete but benefits from collaboration with dynamic forms of social support 'from below', which, as shown in the examples in this article, are not exclusively provided by trained social workers. A connection of these interventions with "official social work" (Lavalette/Ioakimidis 2017: 122) appears significant, as the latter, due to its state embedding, often intervenes less progressively and demandingly in exclusionary policies, especially in countries of the Global North. Approaches like Popular Social Work, solidarity professionalism and municipal pedagogy offer perspectives for social work to engage even more strongly than before in the struggle for urban citizenship and to form a strong voice and sustainable practices in dealing with exclusion and social inequalities together with social movements.

Now, at the conclusion of this article, you, as students and (future) practitioners or researchers in social work, are now invited to develop your own understanding of social work against the backdrop of the provided ideas. Are you encouraged by the presented solidary practices in this article to walk through your social spaces with open eyes and let your gaze be guided by the question of where practices of a solidary coexistence also show up in your life worlds? Where are solidary cities, places and regions being developed in the sense of urban citizenship? How are the actors doing this? And what points of connection do you see for an internationally and at the same time regionally and locally oriented social work?

> **Reflective questions**
>
> - What societal issues do the solidarity city movements respond to? What understanding of solidarity and inclusion is unfolded in these movements?
> - How does urban citizenship differ from nation-state oriented citizenship concepts?
> - Where do possibilities and limitations in the idea of a city for all manifest?
> - What potentials do you see in the intersection of artivism and social work?
> - What connections do you see between solidarity-based urban movements and internationally oriented social work?

Introductory literature

Bauder, Harald (2016): Sanctuary Cities: Policies and Practices in International Perspective. In: International Migration 55, 2, 174–187.
Bauder, Harald (2019): Migration und Citizenship: Vom Geburtsprivileg zum Domizilprinzip. In: Grünendahl, Sarah J./Kewes, Andreas/Ndahayo, Emmanuel/Mouissi, Jasmin/Nieswandt, Carolin (Hrsg.): Staatsbürgerschaft im Spannungsfeld von Inklusion und Exklusion. Wiesbaden: VS, 31–47.
Broden, Anne/Mecheril, Paul (Hrsg.) (2014): Solidarität in der Migrationsgesellschaft. Bedeutung einer normativen Grundlage. Bielefeld: transcript.
Hill, Marc/Schmitt, Caroline (2021b): Solidarität in Bewegung. Neue Felder für die Soziale Arbeit. In: Hill, M./Schmitt, C. (Hrsg.): Solidarität in Bewegung. Neue Felder für die Soziale Arbeit. Reihe Grundlagen der Sozialen Arbeit. Baltmannsweiler: Schneider Verlag Hohengehren, 11–32.
Kubaczek, Niki/Mokre, Monika (Hrsg.) (2021): Die Stadt als Stätte der Solidarität. Wien u.a.: transversal.
Lahusen, Christian (2013): Soziale Bewegungen. In: Mau, Steffen/Schöneck, Nadine M. (Hrsg.): Handwörterbuch zur Gesellschaft Deutschlands. Wiesbaden: VS, 717–729.
Lebuhn, Henrik (2016): „Ich bin New York". Bilanz des kommunalen Personalausweises in New York City. In: Luxemburg 3, 114–119.
Susemichel, Lea/Kastner, Jens (2021): Unbedingte Solidarität. In: Susemichel, Lea/Kastner, Jens (Hrsg.): Unbedingte Solidarität. Münster: UNRAST, 13–48.
Yildiz, Erol (2013): Die weltoffene Stadt. Wie Migration Globalisierung zum urbanen Alltag macht. Wiesbaden: transcript.

Further reading

Ataç, Ilker/Rosenberger, Sieglinde (2013): Inklusion/Exklusion – ein relationales Konzept der Migrationsforschung. In: Ataç, Ilker/Rosenberger, Sieglinde (Hrsg.): Politik der Inklusion und Exklusion. Göttingen: V&R unipress, 35–52.

Brigouleix, Emilie (2019): A Brief History of Artivism. http://artivism.elaninterculturel.com/wp-content/uploads/2019/06/2-Intro-Emilie.pdf (retrieved at 28.02.2024).

Christ, Simone/Meininghaus, Esther/Röing, Tim (2017): „All Day Waiting". Konflikte in Unterkünften für Geflüchtete in NRW, https://www.ssoar.info/ssoar/handle/document/61651 (retrieved at 28.02.2024).

Cudak, Karin/Bukow, Wolf-D. (2016): Auf dem Weg zur Inclusive City. In: Behrens, Melanie/Bukow,Wolf-Dietrich/Cudak, Karin/Strünck, Christoph (Hrsg.): Inclusive City. Überlegungen zum gegenwärtigen Verhältnis von Mobilität und Diversität in der Stadtgesellschaft. Wiesbaden: VS, 1–20.

Doomernik, Jeroen/Ardon, Djoeke (2018): The City as an Agent of Refugee Integration. In: Urban Planning 3, 4, 91–100.

Dünnwald, Stephan (2018): Die Renaissance der Lager. Die Ankerzentren setzen eine deutsche Tradition der Ausgrenzung fort und rufen deren Ursprünge direkt wieder auf. https://archiv.akweb.de/ak_s/ak640/15.htm (retrieved at 28.02.2024).

Füchslbauer, Tina (2022): Soziale Arbeit in Städten: Für alle! Urbane Schutzzonen für undokumentierte Migrant_innen. In: Österreichisches Jahrbuch für Soziale Arbeit 4, 1, 84–103.

Haase, Katrin (2020): Exkludierende Solidaritäten. Herausforderungen im Kontext der Wohnungslosigkeit. In: Soziale Arbeit 69, 4, 146–152.

Hentges, Gudrun (2021): Kriminalisierung solidarischen Handelns in Europa am Beispiel der Seenotrettung. In: Hill, Marc/Schmitt, Caroline (Hrsg.): Solidarität in Bewegung. Neue Felder für die Soziale Arbeit. Baltmannsweiler: Schneider Verlag Hohengehren, 114–134.

Hess, Sabine/Lebuhn, Henrik (2014): Politiken der Bürgerschaft. Zur Forschungsdebatte um Migration, Stadt und *citizenship*. In: sub/urban. zeitschrift für kritische stadtforschung 2, 3, 11–34.

Hill, Marc (2018): Eine Vision von Vielfalt. Das Stadtleben aus postmigrantischer Perspektive. In: Hill, Marc/Yildiz, Erol (Hrsg.): Postmigrantische Visionen. Erfahrungen – Ideen – Reflexionen. Bielefeld: transcript, 97–120.

Hill, Marc/Schmitt, Caroline (2021a): Solidarity Cities. Auf dem Weg zu einer neuen „Weltsolidargesellschaft"? In: Sozialmagazin. Die Zeitschrift für Soziale Arbeit 46, 7/8, 33–41.

Hofmann, Rebecca/Scherr, Albert (2017): Verwahrung in Aufnahmelagern oder Willkommenskultur? Eine Fallstudie zur Erstaufnahme von Geflüchteten. https://ratfuermigration.files.wordpress.com/2018/08/vorstudie_hofmann_scherr_2017.pdf (retrieved at 28.02.2024).

International Federation of Social Workers (IFSW) (2018): Global Social Work Statement of Ethical Principles. https://www.ifsw.org/global-social-work-statement-of-ethical-principles (retrieved at 28.02.2024).

Isakjee, Arshad/Davies, Thom/Obradović-Wochnik, Jelena/Augustová, Karolína (2020): Liberal Violence and the Racial Borders of the European Union. In: Antipode 52, 6, 1751–1773.

Jones, Chris/Lavalette, Michael (2013): The two souls of social work: exploring the roots of 'popular social work'. In: Critical and Radical Social Work 1, 2, 147–65.

Kewes, Andreas (2016): Urban Citizenship – Oder: Über den Versuch, dem „System" auf Augenhöhe zu begegnen. In: Rother, Stefan (Hrsg.): Migration und Demokratie. Studien zur Migrations- und Integrationspolitik. Wiesbaden: VS, 139–160.

Kleist, Olaf J./Dermitzaki, Dimitra/Oghalai, Bahar/Zajak, Sabrina (Hrsg.) (2022): Gewaltschutz in Geflüchtetenunterkünften. Theorie, Empirie und Praxis. Bielefeld: transcript.

Knoll, Alex/Schilliger, Sarah/Schwager, Bea (2012): Wisch und weg! Sans-Papiers-Hausarbeiterinnen zwischen Prekarität und Selbstbestimmung. Zürich: Seismo.

Koch, Lars (2021): Über artivistische Interventionen. Invektivität, Medien, Moral. In: Kulturwissenschaftliche Zeitschrift 6, 1, 247–266.

Kreichauf, René (2016): Das Flüchtlingslager. Raumtheoretische Zugänge. In: Ludwig, Joachim/von Eschenbach, Malte Ebner/Kondratjuk, Maria (Hrsg.): Sozialräumliche Forschungsperspektiven. Disziplin, Ansätze, Zugänge und Handlungsfelder. Berlin: Barbara Budrich, 207–221.

Kron, Stefanie/Maffeis, Stefania (2021): Die Stadt als sicherer Hafen: Kosmopolitismus und gelebte Solidarität. In: Susemichel, Lea/Kastner, Jens (Hrsg.): Unbedingte Solidarität. Münster: UNRAST, 159–172.

Kunstreich, Timm (2017): Ein Schritt aus der Sackgasse heraus: soziale Arbeit als solidarische Professionalität. In: Schweizerische Zeitschrift für Soziale Arbeit/Revue suisse de travail social 21/22, 117–126.

Laitinen, Arto (2013): Solidarity. In: Kaldis, Byron (Hrsg.): Encyclopedia of Philosophy and the Social Sciences. Thousand Oaks a.o.: Sage Publications, 948–950.

Lavalette, Michael/Ioakimidis, Vasilios (2017): Popular social work in extremis: two case studies on collective welfare responses to social crisis situations. In: Social theory, empirics, policy and practice 13, 2, 117–132.

Lefebvre, Henri (1996): Writings on Cities. Selected, translated and introduced by Eleonore Kofman and Elizabeth Lebas. Oxford/Malden: Blackwell Publishers.

Lessenich, Stephan (2020): Doppelmoral hält besser: Die Politik mit der Solidarität in der Externalisierungsgesellschaft. In: Berliner Journal für Soziologie 30, 113–130.

Marshall, Thomas Humphrey (1950): Citizenship and social class and other essays. Cambridge: Cambridge University Press.

Maurer, Susanne (2019): Soziale Bewegung als strukturierendes Element des Sozialraums. In: Kessl, Fabian/Reutlinger, Christian (Hrsg.): Handbuch Sozialraum, Sozialraumforschung und Sozialraumarbeit, 2. Aufl. Wiesbaden: VS Springer, 359–380.

Mayer, Margit (2014): Soziale Bewegungen in Städten – städtische soziale Bewegungen. In: Gestring, Norbert/Ruhne, Renate/Wehrheim, Jan (Hrsg.): Stadt und soziale Bewegungen. Stadt, Raum und Gesellschaft. Wiesbaden: Springer VS, 25–42.

Mekdjian, Sarah (2018): Urban artivism and migrations. Disrupting spatial and political segregation of migrants in European cities. In: Cities 77, 39–48.

Morawek, Katharina (2019): Städtische Bürgerschaft und der kommunale Personalausweis. In Zürich setzen sich zivilgesellschaftliche Akteure für urban citizenship ein. In: Wenke, Christoph/Kron, Stefanie (Hrgs.): Solidarische Städte in Europa. Urbane Politik zwischen Charity und citizenship. Berlin: Rosa Luxemburg Stiftung, 5–16.

Przyborski, Aglaja/Wohlrab-Sahr, Monika (2010): Qualitative Sozialforschung, 3. Aufl. München: Oldenbourg.

Salzbrunn, Monika (2019): Artivisme, https://revues.ulaval.ca/ojs/index.php/anthropen/article/view/30581 (retrieved at 28.02.2024).

Scherr, Albert (2022): (Un-)sichere Orte. In: Kessl, Fabian/Reutlinger, Christian (Hrsg.): Sozialraum, Sozialraumforschung und Sozialraumarbeit. Wiesbaden: VS, 427–436.

Scherr, Albert/Hofmann, Rebecca (2018): Sanctuary Cities – Zufluchts-Städte. In: Gesemann, Frank/Roth, Roland (Hrsg.): Handbuch Lokale Integrationspolitik. Wiesbaden: VS, 869–882.

Schilliger, Sarah (2018): Urban Citizenship. Teilhabe für alle – da, wo wir leben. In: Aigner, Heidrun/Kumnig, Sarah (Hrsg.): STADT FÜR ALLE! Analysen und Aneignungen. Wien: Mandelbaum, 14–35.

Schmelz, Andrea Frieda (2019): „Recht auf Rechte" für Flüchtlinge in Kommunen Europas praktizieren? In: Arslan, E./Bozay, K. (Hrsg.): Symbolische Ordnung und Flüchtlingsbewegungen in der Einwanderungsgesellschaft. Wiesbaden: VS, 189–206.

Schmidt, Marcel (2022): Das „just-city"-Konzept als normativer Bezugspunkt für die Soziale Arbeit im Kontext raumbezogener sozialer Klimagerechtigkeit? In: Pfaff, Tino/Schramkowski, Barbara/Lutz, Ronald (Hrsg.): Klimakrise, sozialökologischer Kollaps und Klimagerechtigkeit. Spannungsfelder für Soziale Arbeit. Weinheim/Basel: Beltz Juventa, 192–204.

Schmitt, Caroline (2021): Inklusive Solidarität: Ethnografische Erkundungen im urbanen Raum. In: soziales_kapital wissenschaftliches journal österreichischer fachhochschulstudiengänge soziale arbeit 24, 392–410.

Schmitt, Caroline (2022): Jenseits der Geflüchtetenunterkunft. Urban Art am Wörthersee. In: Sozialmagazin. Die Zeitschrift für Soziale Arbeit 47, 1/2, 62–71.

Schmitt, Caroline (2023): Solidarische Beziehungen in der Stadt. Von Stadtausweisen, Artivism und Popular Social Work. In: Sozialmagazin. Die Zeitschrift für Soziale Arbeit 48, 1/2, 72-81.

Schmitz, Lilo (2015): Einleitung. In: Schmitz, Lilo (Hrsg.): Artivismus. Kunst und Aktion im Alltag der Stadt. Bielefeld: transcript, 9–16.

Schwenken, Helen/Schwiertz, Helge (2021): Transversale und inklusive Solidaritäten im Kontext politischer Mobilisierungen für sichere Fluchtwege und gegen Abschiebungen. In: Dinkelaker, Samia/Huke, Nikolai/Tietje, Olaf (Hrsg.): Nach der „Willkommenskultur": Geflüchtete zwischen umkämpfter Teilhabe und zivilgesellschaftlicher Solidarität. Bielefeld: transcript, 165–192.

Solidarity City (2017): Flyer. https://solidarity-city.eu/app/uploads/2017/10/Solidarity_City_Flyer_de.pdf (retrieved at 28.02.2024).

Suchet, Myriam/Mekdjian, Sarah (2016): Artivism as a Form of Urban Translation: An Indisciplinary Hypothesis, https://halshs.archives-ouvertes.fr/halshs-01437039/document (retrieved at 28.02.2024).

Statista (2021): Geschätzte Anzahl der im Mittelmeer ertrunkenen Flüchtlinge in den Jahren von 2014 bis 2021 (Stand 22. Juli). https://de.statista.com/statistik/daten/studie/892249/umfrage/im-mittelmeer-ertrunkenen-fluechtlinge/ (retrieved at 28.02.2024).

Statista (2022): Anzahl der Menschen weltweit, die bis zum Jahr 2050 aufgrund des Klimawandels innerhalb ihres Landes/ ihrer Region zur Flucht gezwungen werden könnten (Prognose; in Millionen), https://de.statista.com/statistik/daten/studie/1263402/umfrage/anzahl-moeglicher-klimafluechtlinge-weltweit-bis-2050-nach-region/ (retrieved at 28.02.2024).

UNHCR (2022a): Global Trends. Website. https://www.unhcr.org/globaltrends/, 28.02.2024.

UNHCR (2022b): Global Trends. Forced Displacement in 2021. Kopenhagen: UNHCR. https://www.unhcr.org/62a9d1494/global-trends-report-2021 (retrieved at 28.02.2024).

Wagner, Leonie (Hrsg.) (2009): Soziale Arbeit und Soziale Bewegungen. Wiesbaden: VS.

Wenke, Christoph/Kron, Stefanie (2019): Solidarische Städte In Europa. Urbane Politik Zwischen Charity Und Citizenship. In: Wenke, Christoph/Kron, Stefanie (Hrsg.): Solidarische Städte in Europa. Urbane Politik zwischen Charity und citizenship. Berlin: Rosa Luxemburg Stiftung, 5–16.

Zebracki, Martin (2020): Public artivism: queering geographies of migration and social inclusivity. In: Citizenship Studies 24, 2, 131–153.

II.6 Environment, Ecology, Climate and Sustainability: Global Movements towards Ecosocial Transformation

Andrea Schmelz

>5th June – World Environment Day
>
>22nd May – International Day for Biological Diversity
>
>13th October – International Day for Disaster Risk Reduction

Summary

The chapter highlights the connections between environmental and climate movements and a "green", ecosocial international social work. It chooses three focal points: First, it shows how environmental and climate justice movements have emerged historically up to the present and have become significant as a frame of reference in social work. Secondly, selected approaches and positions of *Green Social Work*, *Ecosocial Work* and *Ecological/Environmental Social Work* will be discussed. Thirdly, Wangari Matthai (1940–2011) is portrayed as a global pioneer of the environmental movement, who became a role model worldwide as an environmental, women's, human rights and peace activist from Kenya. The grassroots work of the *Green Belt Movement (GBM)*, which she founded, is presented as a practice model for ecosocial community development and women's empowerment in Kenya. This is all about a transformative ecosocial work that advocates for social and ecological justice and positions the profession as an agent of ecosocial transformation and sustainable development.

1. Social movements in the context of environment, climate and sustainability

In European countries, the human-nature relationship has long remained a marginal topic in professional social work discourses. In many parts of the world, however, such as India, Latin America, the USA, Canada and Australia, social workers have been involved in various forms of environmental and climate activism for decades. In the following, we will look at how the environmental and climate movement have developed from an initially loose connection to social work to a mainspring of environmental and climate justice.

1.1 Movement for environmental justice and sustainability

Historically, *environment* and *ecology* have played a role in the profession since its inception. A late explicit reference to these issues in social work in the Global North is partly due to the fact that social workers did not perceive themselves as part of the environmental movement, as it was a movement that excluded low-income classes and *people of colour* (Erickson 2018; Agyeman 2005). Using the USA as an example, Erickson distinguishes *four phases* how a middle-class, white environmental movement has developed to a movement for environmental and climate justice (Erickson 2018: 5ff.).

A *first* phase of the environmental movement extended from the end of the 19th to the middle of the 20th century, when social work has been emerging. For the pioneers of social work, Jane Addams and Mary Richmond, the focus was not directly on the natural environment and relationships between people and the environment but in *neighbourhood work*. For instance, dealing with environmental impact and natural resources played a significant role in the form of sanitation, waste disposal, access to green spaces, city parks and land and improved quality of air and water in general (Erickson 2018: 6; Staub-Bernasconi 1989). The *second* phase of the environmental movement was marked by the book *Silent Spring* (Carson 1962), which generated a growing awareness of the environment and nature conservation in social work as well. This worldwide bestseller documented the destructive impact of pesticides and herbicides on the natural environment. As a result, birds, bees and other insects that are fundamental to the protection of biodiversity, human health and well-being were threatened with extinction (Erickson 2018: 7).

Sustainability, Global Sustainable Development Goals (17 SDGs), Global Agenda for Social Work and Social Development (2010–2020 and 2020–2030)

The concept of sustainability for future generations dates back to the 18th century in Germany in the context of forestry. Reforestation should contribute to the preservation of resources for future generations. Globally, the concern for, and the protection of, natural resources for future generations is part of the indigenous world knowledges.

Today's concept of sustainable development is based on the globally known definition of the term by the Brundtland Commission (*World Commission on Environment and Development* – WCED 1987). This reads as follows: "*Sustainable Development is development that meets the needs of the present without compromising the ability of future generations to meet their own needs.*" The Rio Earth Summit and the Agenda 21 (1992) have contributed to society and the economy pursuing a triple bottom line of sustainability through a variety of activities: social, environmental and economic.

The Brundtland definition (1987) has already thought together social and environmental justice on a global level, which today is set out in the UN agenda of 17 *Sustainable Development Goals* (SDGs) (*Transforming Our World: The 2030 Agenda for Sustainable Development*). The SDGs are specified by 169 sub-goals. The most important overall goal is to fight poverty worldwide (*SDG 1: End poverty for all*). The second goal aims at ending hunger and achieving food security and quality (*SDG 2: End hunger, achieve food security and improved nutrition and promote sustainable agriculture*). Other goals focus on environmental and ecological issues and sustainability (*SDG 11: Sustainable cities and communities; SDG 13: Climate action*). The most frequent criticism and evident contradiction refers to the adherence to economic growth (*SDG 8: Promote sustained, inclusive and sustainable economic growth, full and productive employment and decent work for all*). The 17 global SDGs coincide with social work's areas of responsibility, which include health, poverty and hunger, social inequality, shaping cities and communities, ecological justice and peace. The SDGs therefore also build the action framework of the *Global Agenda of Social Work and Social Development* (2010–2020 and 2020–2030) of the

three world associations of social work. In a separate priority area, the *Global Agenda* commits to the promotion of *sustainable communities*.
In three workbooks, social work teachers and trainers around the world developed teaching and learning materials on "green"/ecosocial social work (Powers/Rinkel 2017-2019). The third workbook highlights a social work practice example for each of the 17 SDGs, e.g. clean energy production in the USA (SDG 7), sustainable consumption and production in South Africa (SDG 12) or sustainable forest management in communities in India (SDG 15). For the editors, the post-growth perspective is necessary to realise the SDGs (cf. Rinkel/Powers 2019; Stamm 2021: 63f.).

It was not before the *third* phase, the late 1970s, that social work began to address environmental racism under the impact of the civil rights movement. In a predominantly black neighbourhood in Warren County (North Carolina, USA), protests arose when toxic waste was to be stored in the immediate vicinity. The study *Toxic Wastes and Race* (1987) (cf. Bullard et al.: 2007; Bullard 2005) showed the far more frequent storage of toxic waste in BIPoC-neighbourhoods (Black people, Indigenous people and people of colour) compared to white ones. Robert Bullard, sociologist and activist (Texas Southern University), conceptualises environmental racism as "any policy, practice or guideline that (intentionally or unintentionally) discriminates against individuals, groups, or communities on the basis of 'race' or 'major colour'" (Bullard 1994: 1037, cited in Imeh/Hey 2021: 4). Environmental racism was a form of structural racism, of which BIPoC are affected to a greater extent, regardless of whether they live in the Global North or the Global South.

The movement for environmental justice reached beyond this racist discrimination in the US and brought in decolonial perspectives from the Global South, which demanded recognition and redress for colonial injustices against people, land grabbing and resource theft. In 1991, the *First National People of Colour Environmental Leadership Summit* convened as an international congress in Washington, D.C., which brought BIPoC-perspectives on environmental justice from the Global South and the Global North. The delegates adopted 17 fundamental principles of environmental justice which were expanded to "*10 Principles for Just Climate Change Policies*" (2002) by the *Indigenous Environmental Network* (EIN – USA) (Tokar 2019: 16). Among other things, reparations are demanded for 500 years of colonisation and oppression with their far-reaching exploitation of natural resources and human labour. Many civil society organisations such as the *World Rainforest Movement*, *Friends of the Earth International* or the *Third World Network* have also pointed to the struggles of indigenous and local peasant populations in the Global South. Profit-oriented economic and trade policies have been held responsible for the exploitation of natural resources and human labour (Tokar 2019: 17). The Brundtland Report (1987) and the Rio Earth Summit (1992) marked the beginning of the sustainability movement. It became involved in global-local and transnational actions for fair trade, alternative economies and peace, but often it neglected local environmental injustices against BIPoC. In the sustainability movement, too, the committed people mostly came from the *white* middle class (Erickson 2018: 12).

In today's fourth *phase*, social and ecological environmental and climate damage is being considered more closely on a local and global level, based on the categories of *race*, *class* and *gender*. In Europe, the dominant narrative of a *white* environmental, climate and sustainability movement is pushing the voices of indigenous resistance movements and black representatives of the current climate protests into the background. In international professional discourses, these outlined historical contexts have accelerated the development of concepts such as *Ecological/Ecospiritual*, *Environmental* or *Green Social Work*.

> **Environmental justice, ecological justice and climate justice**
>
> Environmental injustice is defined as "inequitable exposure of communities of colour, and communities of poverty, to environmental risks due primarily to their lack of recognition and political power" (Agyeman et al. 2016: 322, cited in Erickson 2018: 9). *Environmental Justice* assumes that all people have the same right to be protected from environmental harm. It asks in particular for benefits and disadvantages from the perspective of humans and not of nature or the (in)animate environment in general. *Ecological justice*, on the other hand, is interested in the preservation of the natural environment and assigns an independent value and subjectivity to nature and planet Earth. Most authors, however, do not make a clear conceptual distinction between environmental justice and ecological justice (e.g. Peeters 2016, 2022; Erickson 2018; Dominelli 2012). With vigour the *Deep Ecology* approach addresses ecological justice (e.g. Besthorn 2012).
>
> In the context of climate change and, among others, the reports of the Intergovernmental Panel on Climate Change, the concept of *climate (in)justice* became widespread: Climate change already affects the people the hardest who contribute the least to the climate crisis. These are mainly population groups in the Global South who live in marginalised and vulnerable situations. These are people who live in countries with low carbon emissions but who suffer in great measure from the ecological-social consequences of the climate crisis, the causes of which are predominantly the responsibility of the Global North.

1.2 Global movement for climate justice and new climate protests

Climate justice has developed since the 2010s into a conceptual term that encompasses various complementary movements worldwide. In the Global South, the demand for climate justice unites a variety of indigenous and other land rights movements that have been advocating for their rights for many decades (e.g. Noble 2018). These include rainforest dwellers who oppose new mega-dams and palm oil plantations, African and Latin American communities who oppose land grabbing for industrial agriculture and the production of agrofuels, Pacific islanders who fear the loss of their homeland because of rising sea levels, and small farmers who fight for food security and basic land rights.

The climate movement presents itself as a loosely connected, yet very active, overarching structure. It is supported, shaped and used by a wide range of civil society actors active in climate policy (Garrelts/Dietz 2014: 7). A distinction must be made between a radical and a moderate direction (cf. Tokar 2019: 17):

- The radical direction demands climate justice from a power-critical position due to a far-reaching crisis of the prevailing political and economic system. This includes organisations such as the *Climate Justice Now!* coalition with more than 400 organisations or the *La Via Campesina* network with almost 200 organisations from more than 80 countries. In both networks, mainly indigenous and smallholder voices are represented.
- The moderate direction is based on the paradigm of ecological modernisation. According to this, environmental and climate problems can be solved politically, economically and technologically within existing institutional structures and power relations. Solutions are seen in line with the idea of "green" economic growth and technological innovation. Environmental organisations such as *Friends of the Earth* or the campaign organisation *350.org* are assigned to this direction.

In global climate protests, new actors emerged at the end of 2018 – most notably *Fridays for Future* (FFF) and *Extinction Rebellion* (XR). Both FFF and XR responded to the global ecological crisis with new, worldwide mobilisation power. Albeit they have been building on decades of protests by climate and environmental movements, they show new characteristics (Moor et al. 2021: 623f.). Firstly, the campaigns have mobilised a historically large number of students, including a disproportionate number of female participants and newcomers to the climate justice movement. Secondly, they mainly use forms of civil disobedience, even though the protest methods are not fundamentally new. Thirdly, both groups mainly target local or national governments, whereas previous climate protests were directed at transnational institutions and fossil fuel corporations. For the future of the movement it is contested whether the prognostic claim "listen to science" will be sufficient for the long-term mobilisation or whether a radicalisation of forms of action will occur (Moor et al. 2021: 625f.). A more radical protest movement we encounter in the action of the *Last Generation* (LG). In Germany, this movement emerged from a hunger strike by climate activists. In 2021, LG was formed as an alliance of climate and environmental activists who intensified non-violent forms of protest against government inaction on climate policy in Germany and many other countries. With more radical forms of civil disobedience, the activists want to bring about an immediate reversal in climate policies in order to avert climate collapse.[38] The forms of action range from blockades of road, air and railway traffic to iconoclasm in museums.

Fridays for Future (FFF) and Extinction Rebellion (XR)

On Friday, 20th August 2018, Greta Thunberg, then 15 years old, skipped school to initially protest alone in front of the Swedish Parliament. On 9th September 2018, she initiated the hashtag *#Fridays for Future* (FFF), whereupon the protests quickly spread (Moor et al. 2021: 620). FFF is on the one hand about the already visible effects of the climate crisis, primarily in countries of the Global South, and on the other hand about justice between generations regarding the climate and living conditions of subsequent generations. Against

---

38 https://www.letztegeneration.de/ (retrieved at 28.02.2024).

the background of the Covid-19 pandemic and the outbreak of war in Ukraine, many FFF activists link their ecological climate protest with social support in neighbourhoods and refugee aid. The profile of FFF has become visible as largely *white*, middle- to upper-class oriented and predominantly female (Posemk 2021: 188). Racist exclusionary practices were evident in media coverage, among other things: while the media celebrated Greta Thunberg as a climate heroine at the World Economic Forum in Davos (2019), FFF activist Vanessa Nakate from Uganda was cut out in the press photo. In September 2023, the 13th global climate strike took place in more than 150 countries around the world but lost mobilisation power due to multiple other disasters such as war, hate, populism and poverty around the globe.

In October 2018, the *Extinction Rebellion* (XR) movement emerged in the UK, a more radical movement in its forms of action, which was represented in 75 countries (2020). XR describes itself as a decentralised and international network. It applies non-violent, creative and high-profile methods to fight CO_2 reduction and the protection of biodiversity. XR focuses on three core objectives: *Tell the truth; act now; beyond politics*, and acts on the basis of civil disobedience. Compared to FFF, XR's forms of action are more radical and use, for example, street blockades, hunger strikes or planting trees in front of parliament and company buildings. While FFF is considered a "grassroots movement", XR is criticised for emotionalising and instrumentalising young people for its "end times" or "end of the world" scenarios and even for antisemitic statements.[39]

From the perspective of social work, the twofold question arises as to what impulses for social workers can be deduced from the activities of the movements and what contribution social workers can make to social movements (Stamm 2021: 137). According to Stamm, social movements such as FFF and XR could be a source of inspiration and a critical companion for critical-ecological social work. In Germany in the 1970s, the concerns and demands of the environmental movement were already significant in social work practice as alternative projects and self-help, without ecological practice formats acquiring a recognised status in Germany's social work. The climate crisis and Covid-19 open up new opportunity structures for practice forms of socio-ecological justice (cf. e.g. Schmelz 2021, 2022). In social work, children and young people are among the largest target groups; therefore social workers are called upon to position themselves on the demands of the FFF movement. Strikes as a central method of FFF refer to schools, where many social workers in Germany work (cf. Stamm 2021: 140). At the same time, FFF's radius of action extends far beyond the school. For children and adolescents, FFF opens up an informal educational and learning space (Costa/Wittmann 2021), where children and adolescents from school types besides the secondary school level participate less.

Common issues of *Fridays for Future* and social work are intergenerational justice, human rights and participation (Moor et al. 2021: 620f.; Stamm 2021: 140). These are particularly action-oriented for the rights of children and young people with regard to ecological and climate-friendly participation and chances for the

---

[39] Cf. debate on Extinction Rebellion: TAZ, 7.10.2019, https://taz.de/Debatte-um-Extinction-Rebellion/!5632122/ (retrieved at 28.02.2024).

future (cf. Schramkowski 2022: 120ff.). This also includes the possibility that specific child and youth welfare organisations are newly founded or expanded and, for example, anchor an ecological orientation in their mission statement. Furthermore, social work can advocate for the participation of marginalised groups, especially because social movements such as FFF and XR are criticised for being less inclusive but *white*, middle-class and Eurocentric. Social work could mobilise youth participation in the climate movement beyond the urban middle-classes through inclusive social work practice projects (cf. Stamm 2021: 140). Today, when organisations like *Black Earth* think of environmental and climate damage together with coloniality, (environmental) racism and other dimensions (and conditions) of oppression, they build on the starting point of the movement for environmental justice and the protests of the past generations (Imeh/Hey 2021: 15). Similar to the *First National People of Colour Environmental Leadership Summit* (1991), *Black Earth* locates the climate crisis in the historical context of slavery and colonialism.

2. Green(ing) social work: approaches, concepts and positions on environment and ecology

Since the 1960s and 1970s, environmental and climate movements have given social workers an impetus to understand nature destruction and environmental injustice as a professional mandate and to incorporate them into practice, theory, research and education of social work. The strategy of *Greening Social Work* has been called for in order to systematically integrate ecosocial transformation in social work approaches and practices, in particular into social work curricula (e.g. Jones 2018; Schmelz 2022). Due to the global climate movement, since the 2010s social work has also increasingly focused on climate impacts for disadvantaged communities in the Global South (e.g. Mason/Rigg 2018). Firstly, selected proposals for the systematisation of relevant approaches are described below, without providing a complete overview here. Secondly, the *green social work* and ecological perspectives will be focussed on.

2.1 Overview on international approaches

Green Social Work, Environmental Social Work and *Ecosocial Work* have emerged as most significant approaches. The common intersection of these approaches is summarised as the ecosocial paradigm (Rambaree et al. 2019: 205) of social work: "*Ecosocial work is social work, with all its depth and breadth, but it approaches the analysis of social problems, issues and concerns with ecosocial paradigm or lens, rather than an anthropocentric lens*" (Matthies/Närhi 2016, cited in Rambaree et al. 2019: 206). According to this definition, ecosocial work is not to be understood as a special field, but all social work should also be ecosocial and transformative. *Ecosocial Work* combines an ecocentric perspective with indigenous knowledge and spirituality, takes up *Deep Ecology* perspectives, is critical of capitalism and advocates for degrowth perspectives. The only overview in German (Stamm 2021) prefers the concept of *eco-critical social work* and refers to Nähri/Matthies, the pioneers of this approach in Europe (Nähri/Matthies

2016). The two pioneers list the following systematisation of approaches (Närhi/Matthies 2016: 29–32; Dörfler 2021):

- Ecological Social Approach in Social Work (Jef Peeters, Belgium; Margret Alston/Jennifer McKinnon, Australia)
- Deep Ecological Social Work (Fred Besthorn, USA)
- Eco-Spiritual Social Work (Mel Gray, Australia; John Coates, Canada)
- Green Social Work (Lena Dominelli, Great Britain)
- Social-Ecological Social Work (Jef Peeters, Belgium)
- Environmental Social Work (Mel Gray/John Coates/Tiani Hetherington, Australia)

With regard to the current state of the international debate (2021), Stamm highlights three main areas: ecological-critical social work, the concept of *Green Social Work* and Australian approaches such as the *Transformative Eco-Social Model* (Boetto 2019; Stamm 2021: 53). These exemplary attempts of systematisation do not represent approaches or positions that can be clearly distinguished from one another, nor are they to be regarded as completed in their development.

2.2 Green(ing) Social Work

Green Social Work (GSW) has been conceptualised in a leading role by Lena Dominelli, drawing on indigenous knowledge as well as partly on other existing approaches. As an academic environmental and climate activist, she founded the *Climate Justice Program* (IFSW) in 2009. GSW is also understood as a catch-all term for an eclectic mix of ideas and practices that refers to a wide range of approaches in contexts of ecology, environment, sustainability and the global climate (Ferguson et al. 2018: 111). On the one hand, GSW is considered a radical approach because it brings together the theory and practice of environmental activism and justice and calls for ecosocial transformation of unfair systemic conditions (Ife 2016). On the other hand, the concept is also criticised for conceptual vagueness and not clearly named points of connection to ecology and the environment (Stamm 2021: 46). At the same time, it is conceded that GSW has inspired international professional discourses and is establishing itself as a practice of *ecosocial work* (Stamm 2021: 53). GSW defines itself as a paradigmatic practice model which should not be understood as a theory.

GSW aims to develop a "new paradigm" (Dominelli 2018: 10) for critical social work theorists and practitioners, which seeks to assert *environmental justice* as an integral part of social justice in theory and practice and focuses on *community action*. The interventions of GSW serve both for the protection of the environment and improved human well-being. Dominelli relates GSW to the social dimensions of disasters, whether they are man-made or nature-induced. The former range from climate change to poverty, the latter include natural incidents such as earthquakes or volcanic eruptions that can become disasters in the face of vulnerabilities as well as human (in)action (Dominelli 2019: 234). Dominelli defines:

"Green social work is a holistic approach to practice involving environmental degradation in all its forms and focuses on the impact of social structures and human intentionality in the exploitation of the earth's resources, social and physical. It emphasizes interdependencies between people, plants, animals and planet earth as the site in which life occurs, ... it centres social justice within a duty to care for and about all living things, animate and inanimate" (Dominelli 2019: 233).

GSW is seen as a transdisciplinary, holistic approach (Dominelli 2018: 9), which calls for preventive action by the profession beyond the reactive strategies of social work. Dominelli points out two fundamental perspectives here. Firstly, in response to environmental crises and natural disasters social work should not limit itself to offering social assistance and humanitarian aid to the affected local population. According to Dominelli, GSW reshapes social work action because it is based on a co-production of knowledge and action in transdisciplinary settings, multi-professional teams and empowerment – before the (natural) disaster, during the disaster and in the reconstruction (Dominelli 2018: 13f.). Secondly, GSW pursues preventive action strategies. Significant here are the consequences for human environmental and public welfare due to environmentally harmful, capitalist modes of consumption and production that damage the limited available resources of planet "Earth". With regard to these two perspectives, Dominelli identifies multiple tasks for GSW to address the social vulnerability of people affected by climate change and environmental crises: advocacy, mobilisation, co-production of community-level solutions, dialogue facilitation and curriculum development (Dominelli 2018: 16). GSW is therefore particularly aiming at the adaptation or reorientation of social work curricula (Schmelz 2022). Furthermore, GSW involves a variety of partly new roles for social workers, who can be facilitators, coordinators, community mobilisers, mediators, counsellors, trainers and educators, psychosocial therapists and translators of scientific knowledge (Dominelli 2012: 199).

GSW originated in the context of disaster relief and research, but it has been expanded via the "Routledge Handbook of Green Social Work", among others, by further approaches from a "green" social work practice (Dominelli 2018, 2019; Schmelz 2021: 225f.). Dominelli (2012: 174f.) is particularly committed to ensuring that the "estimated 370 million [indigenous] people on planet Earth" can preserve their livelihoods despite pressures on their land rights. According to Dominelli (2012: 183), many indigenous groups experience colonisation, marginalisation, destruction of their cultures and languages, loss of land and other resources. Many of these ongoing struggles of indigenous people place a great strain on the protection of their livelihoods and natural environment, for example in the Amazon rainforest, the Pacific Islands, Canada, Alaska and Northern and Central Australia. Furthermore, Lena Dominelli presents a wide range of examples of green social work around the globe. They range from improving urban housing (ibid.: 40f.) to psychosocial support and counselling for those affected by toxic waste (ibid.: 72f.), to renewable energy and income generation interventions in communities at risk of poverty (ibid.: 76) and mediation in communities to resolve water conflicts (ibid.: 161f.). The "Routledge Handbook of Green Social Work" furthermore develops practical examples of green social work in different contexts: e.g. in areas of "green" agriculture (Dominelli et al. 2018: 159ff.), psychosocial support in the context of disaster-induced migration (ibid.: 307ff.) or community-based interventions for specific target groups such as children or people with disabilities (ibid.: 407ff.). The discussion of a "green" curriculum development and the presentation of relevant case studies from Australia, New Zealand and the USA (ibid.: 511ff.) plays an important role. In summary, *greening social work* is to be understood as an open programme of a political, transformative social work. It can also be understood as a professional-political positioning and a call to the discipline to deepen ecological perspectives in the theory and practice of social work. This perspective calls for a critical alliance with ecologically oriented approaches, a few of which are briefly outlined below (cf. e.g. Schmelz 2022).

2.3 Ecology and ecofeminism as a challenge

Ecological as well as ecocentric perspectives are proposed with different emphases. Jef Peeters, for example, emphatically shows in his approaches that in view of the impending ecological collapse a social and economic transition is indispensable. A radical change must start at different levels: ecological, technological, economic, social, political and institutional. It relates to energy production, consumption, the monetary system, the mobility of people, food production and distribution, and the organisation of the labour market and care (Peeters 2016: 178f.). Gray and Coates (2019: 175f.) also call for a transformed economic system beyond greed for profit and growth, as well as the rejection of the opposition (dualism) of humans and nature. For both authors, humans are to be understood as dependent on, and part of, nature. It must be recognised that we humans are in relationship with other humans, animals and plants as well as the animate and inanimate environment. Such a perspective strengthens the understanding that individual lifestyles and prevailing patterns of behaviour in society affect people all over the world as well as other species and the planet's ecosystem. Changing behaviour at the individual level can also be fostered by a spiritual connection to nature, which is expressed in indigenous perspectives such as Buen Vivir[40] (cf. Dörfler 2021: 25).

In Western thought, the *Deep Ecology* movement of the 1990s took up indigenous worldviews and linked them to a plea for radical ecological justice that puts nature, not people, at the centre. Deep Ecology, following the Norwegian philosopher Arne Naess (1912–2009), advocates an ecocentric human-nature relationship (Besthorn 2012: 253). It is closely related to *Eco-Spirituality* (e.g. Coates 2003; 2013), which thinks together ecology and spirituality, i.e. an emotional-empathic human-nature relationship, and assumes that the well-being of humans and

---

[40] The South American concept means "good life" and stands for the harmony of the nature-human relationship, the reduction of social inequality, a solidarity-based economy and way of life, and a democratic design of society and community. The concept criticises Western development thinking and neoliberal economic thinking.

the planet cannot be separated. While indigenous knowledge is highly valued, capitalist growth thinking and Western consumerism are rejected (Coates 2013: 74–77). An uncritical reference to indigenous knowledge in countries of the Global North implies the danger of cultural appropriation and Eurocentrism (Schmelz 2022: 31). Stamm explicitly warns against romanticising and idealising misinterpretations (Stamm 2021: 36f.): "Not in every case does a Western view of nature conservation and animal protection coincide with the needs and attitudes of all 'indigenous' people" (cf. Tester 2013: 112, quoted from Stamm 2021: 37). In an extreme case, the Deep Ecology approach is even associated with a biologism and racism-approach, whereby humans are assumed to be "pests" for the planet (Opielka 2017; Tester 2015, cited after Stamm 2021: 36). The potential danger of ecology being appropriated by right-wing extremist groups does exist. However, critical ecological perspectives today primarily stand for a "solidary togetherness" of humans and nature, without which humans cannot exist. If the ecosystem reaches its critical tipping points, the existential basis of human life are threatened to be irrevocably lost.

Ecofeminist perspectives also take a critical perspective on the interaction of ecological crises, the oppression of women and the gendered division of labour in patriarchal capitalism (Noble 2018: 238; Noble 2021: 95; Mies/Shiva 1995/2016). A prominent pioneer of ecofeminism is *Vandana Shiva* (Shiva 1989; Mies/Shiva 1995/2016), whose writings highlight the congruence between the exploitation and destruction of nature and the oppression and discrimination against women. She makes this point about the situation of women in the Global South, especially smallholder farmers, and opposes the dominant capitalist, patriarchal mode of economy. Both as a practice approach in social work and in climate policy, ecofeminism amplifies women's voices and advocates for an intersectional approach to experiences of exploitation and discrimination. The aim is to change power relations and empower women to become part of a community-driven movement for ecological justice (Alston et al. 2019: 181f.). Ecofeminism was accused of essentialism because it attributed to women a higher connection to nature compared to men and declared this to be a female essence. Later on, ecofeminism has evolved through intersectional perspectives into *queer ecology*, which questions heteronormative attributions (e.g. Gaard 2017).

The ecosocial approach of the *Green Belt Movement (GBM)* analysed below is an influential example of ecosocial *community development* and women's empowerment, which was developed in Kenya with a global impact. The work of Wangari Mathaai (1940–2011), the founder of GBM, is attributed to ecofeminism, although she did not explicitly define herself an ecofeminist, and she is not a social worker. The GSW-approach of the *Green Belt Movement* shows with vigour how social work in countries of the Global North can learn from the Global South.

3. Wangari Maathai and Green Belt Movement (GBM)

Today, Maathai is regarded a "global icon" (Kanago 2020: 12) of the environmental and climate movement. Within the framework of the GBM, Maathai linked local and global engagement. She saw care for the Earth as a global responsibility that required the attention and participation of all the Earth's inhabitants. She perceived the planet as a "diseased entity" and designed a simple but effective way to restore its health: planting trees (Kanago 2020: 81). Helmut Spitzer emphasises the special significance of Matthai's and GBM's work for a "social work that is power-critical, politically engaged and transformative" (Spitzer 2022: 338, translation A. S.), while facing an ecological-social collapse (Spitzer 2022). In the following, the opportunities of GBM and the action of Wangari Maathai for ecosocial transformation are highlighted. The literature on the *Green Belt Movement* emphasises the exemplary character of the movement. There is a lack of published evaluations or analyses for an empirical-critical assessment of the short-, medium- and long-term effects of the Green Belt Movement.

3.1 Life and work of Maathai: environmental injustice and colonialism

Maathai was a pioneer in many ways. She was born on 1st April 1940 in Ihithe, a small village in the central highlands of Kenya, which was still under British colonial rule until 1963 (Spitzer 2022: 339; Maathai 2008; documentary film "Taking Root"). She grew up with great affinity to nature and within a polygamous family system. Maathai was the first woman in her family to graduate with a degree in biology. In Kenya, she became the first woman to hold doctoral and professorial degrees in the 1970s.

Through the internationally well-known grassroots movement GBM, Maathai became famous beyond the borders of Kenya. GBM is an environmental movement that combined local community development with tree planting and economic activities by women. The movement advocated for the vision of a reforested Kenya, where the destructive power of colonialism is countered by a practice of *healing* people and nature. In the course of violent colonisation and missionisation, the Kenyan people's relationship to nature was largely reduced to economic exploitation. Ecological exploitation and destruction continued after decolonisation through the influence of corrupt power elites (Spitzer 2022: 341).

Tree planting campaigns were already the core idea of the predecessor organisation *Save the Land Harambee* (Harambee: Swahili for "pulling together"), founded by Maathai. *Harambee* symbolised community work and was a motto for a social realignment. Maathai was also called Mother of Trees (Swahili: *Mama miti*). She used methods of civil disobedience to resist the Kenyan authoritarian regime of Daniel arap Moi and was imprisoned several times (Namulandah 2014: 15f., 87f.). Within the framework of the GBM, she has fought since 1989, for example, for the preservation of the Uhuru Leisure Park in Nairobi (Kenya) with a size of 13 ha, where a skyscraper with 60 floors was to be built. She also engaged in non-violent resistance with the opposition group *Release Political Prisoners* to free prisoners (Spitzer 2022: 342). While the GBM was focused on the socio-ecological problems of the rural population, Maathai's struggle for Uhuru Park in Nairobi was related to freeing urban poor from their overcrowded, unhealthy slum dwellings (Kanago 2020: 81).

Wangari Maathai has received many international awards for her activism, including the *Right Livelihood Award* (1984, Alternative Nobel Prize), the Jane Addams International Women's Leadership Award (1989) and the Nobel Peace Prize (2004) in recognition of her commitment to peace, democracy and sustainable development. From 2003 to 2005, Maathai was able to promote her vision of environmental and climate justice as Deputy Minister for Environment and Natural Resources. On 25th September 2011, Maathai died of cancer. At the time of her death, the GBM had spread to numerous countries with the participation of more than one million women who had planted more than 50 million trees (Kanago 2020: 12).

For Maathai, planting trees meant planting hope and peace. In GBM, environmental and climate protection united with women's rights, human rights and democracy work on the basis of activism, political education and environmental education. A politically engaged, "green" and ecosocial work emanates from the green belt movement.

3.2 Learning from the Green Belt Movement – an integrated approach to ecological-social community development

GBM shows many starting points for transformative social work (Spitzer 2022: 342). Hereby, social work itself is seen as an actor of socio-political processes on micro, meso and macro levels. As a biologist, Maathai thought of the natural ecosystem in its interaction with the human living world in scientific analysis. She highlighted that the impact of the climate crisis and accelerated environmental degradation will increase the exclusion of vulnerable and marginalised populations, in particular women (Spitzer 2022: 344). In the following, we will explore learning potentials of the ecosocial approach in GBM and how these impact on politically engaged social work in the Global North:

Firstly, the value orientation of GBM is linked to ecospiritual/ecological concepts of social work (Maathai 2010). These emphasise, among other things, an emotional relationship and respectful interaction with nature. These include:

- Love of nature expressed in lifestyle and commitment to environmental protection;
- Respect and gratitude for natural resources linked to the three Rs: *reduce, reuse* and *recycle*;
- Self-empowerment and personality development;
- Willingness to serve the community and to volunteer (cf. Graneß et al. 2019: 293).

Today we also encounter the sustainable use of natural resources and the principles of *reduce – reuse – recycle* in the post-growth movement, which advocates sustainable, solidarity-based and ecological-social management and living (Schmelz 2022: 30). Its forms of practice are, e.g., repair cafes, swap meets and social farming, which are increasingly finding their way into social work.

Self-help, voluntary commitment and self-empowerment are also emancipatory basic principles of social work (cf. e.g. Schmelz 2022: 30).

Secondly, GBM applies an integrated multi-dimensional approach to an ecosocial transformation that addresses the interactions of environmental, social and political problems (Maathai 2003). In this holistic approach, environmental protection, poverty alleviation, community healing and individual agency and self-empowerment) work together. Through activism, the movement contributes to repairing the human-nature relationship and overcoming political violence. Collective and individual healing processes start locally to solve practical issues aiming at community building and collective change. The community recovered as soon as the ecosystem has been regenerated. Maathai summarised as follows:

> "Recognizing that sustainable development, democracy and peace are indivisible is an idea whose time has come ... Today we are faced with a challenge that calls for a shift in our thinking, so that humanity stops threatening its life-support system. We are called to assist the Earth to heal her wounds and in the process heal our own – indeed to embrace the whole of creation in all its diversity, beauty and wonder" (Maathai 2004, para 7, 22).

Thirdly, the GBM includes a programme of self-help following Harambee, which means "Let's all pull together" in Swahili. The prerequisite here is that people take problems into their own hands and work for solutions. Harambee is the motto of a self-help movement that is still very important today and goes back to Kenya's first president, *Jomo Kenyatta* (Kanago 2020: 81–84). The GBM targets rural communities and made it its mission to empower the people in order to transform their land and their lives. An important goal was also to encourage impoverished rural people to move beyond environmental conservation to economic independence and sustainability – and this was meant to a revolutionary development from below.

Fourthly, GBM focuses on the empowerment of women in rural communities. It is about solving practical issues in rural communities for which women traditionally are assigned responsibility. The basic idea is first of all reforestation, so that firewood resources are created and fertile soils are preserved. In addition, income-generating measures for women become effective through newly established tree nurseries and training measures (Kanago 2020: 86). In this way, women can become economically independent, empowered and aware of their rights and can resist gender-based oppression. In doing so, the green belt movement relies on the interaction and potential for change of both genders through environmental education (Graneß et al. 2019: 298).

Maathai summarised the GBM's transformative, environmental education work as *The Wrong Bus* syndrome (cited in Spitzer 2022: 347; Maathai 2010: 167ff.). She bases this on the most frequently used means of transport on the African continent and asks the critical question of what to do when persons realise that they are on the "wrong bus". The advice here is not fatalistic waiting but to "stop the bus" and develop an alternative route. According to Spitzer, this is where one of the core tasks of social work comes in. It consists of supporting and enabling people to perceive and name "what is actually wrong" (Spitzer 2022: 347). Maathai countered scepticism towards GBM's environmental work with the story of the little hummingbird: "What do you think you can do? You are too small to light the fire. Your wings are too small and your back is so small that you can only bring a small drop of water at a time: But when (the other little animals) wanted to discourage it again and again, it turned to them without wasting time and said to them: 'I am doing my best.' And that is what we should all do. We should always feel like a hummingbird" (Kanago 2020: 14). So change starts from what each one of us can do.

The methods of action of the GBM can be seen as an exemplary orientation framework for "green" social work and ecosocial transformation, which has intersections with intervention formats in social work worldwide and implicitly influenced practice projects all over the world. Maathai and GBM are able to unfold transformative learning potentials for social work as a decolonial, gender-sensitive and ecosocial practice of community development. In Europe, for example, forms of solidarity economy and agriculture, as well as the concerns and action formats of the aforementioned post-growth movement, are connectable to the GMB (e.g. Elsen 2020; Burkert et al. 2017; Liftin 2014). In the agricultural cooperative system in Italy, the concept of ecosocial agriculture has been established, whose five action approaches show significant interfaces with GBM: (1) support for disadvantaged people; (2) strengthening of the community; (3) environmental education and education for sustainable development; (4) environmentally friendly, organic-ecological farming; (5) nature and resource conservation measures (Bernhard et al. 2020: 15f., quoted from Stamm 2021: 137).

In summary, "green" social work and ecosocial transformation are essential future tasks in international social work that are in progress. "*Co-Building a New Eco-social World: Leave no one behind*" is the motto of a global eco-social campaign of the *International Federation of Social Work* (IFSW) (2022). The aim is to bring together individuals, communities and people's experiences to work with inter- and transnational organisations to advocate for a new, socially and ecologically just world in the face of the climate crisis and Covid-19. In the spirit of the motto of the Global UN Sustainable Development Goals Agenda, this is about thinking and acting in an ecologically and socially inclusive way and leaving no one behind. The campaign takes up in particular the Latin American *Buen Vivir*, the African *Ubuntu*[41] and human rights principles: "Buen Vivir, love and care of people and the planet, responsibilities and rights; Respect, dignity, harmony and justice; Diversity, belonging, reciprocity and equity; Ubuntu, togetherness and community."[42] The Green Social Work agenda (Dominelli 2012) provides for social workers at local, national and international levels to address environmental and social injustices in a practical way.

---

41   Ubuntu is a South African philosophy of humanity that means "I am because we are". It emphasises the solidary relationships of people with each other and with the planet.
42   https://www.newecosocialworld.com/ (retrieved at 28.02.2024).

> **Reflective questions**
>
> - How would you personally describe your relationship with nature or the environment? What role do environmental degradation and climate change play in your everyday life?
> - Explain the main phases of the environmental and climate movement in terms of their respective significance for social work.
> - How did the concept of environmental racism emerge? Why did it become significant for social work?
> - How can the special role of the *Fridays for Future* movement for social work be described?
> - What are the core elements of *Green Social Work*? Where can you find approaches to ecosocial social work in your local community?
> - How do you assess the impact of the *Green Belt Movement* from the perspective of international social work?

Introductory literature

Dominelli, Lena (2012): Green Social Work. From Environmental Crisis to Environmental Justice. Cambridge, UK: Polity Press.

Dominelli, Lena et al. (2018) (eds.): The Routledge Handbook of Green Social Work. London: Routledge.

Erickson, Christina L. (2018): Environmental Justice as Social Work Practice. New York: Oxford University Press.

Matthies, Aila-Leena/Närhi, Kati (eds.) (2017): The Ecosocial Transition of Societies. The Contribution of Social Work and Social Policy. London: Routledge.

McKinnon, Jennifer/Alston, Margret (eds.) (2016): Ecological Social Work: Towards Sustainability. London/New York: Palgrave.

Nesmith, Ande A. et al. (2021): The Intersection of Environmental Justice, Climate Change, Community, and the Ecology of Life. New York: Springer.

Further reading

Alston, Margret/Hazeleger, Tricia/Hargreaves, Desley (2019): Social Work and Disasters. A Handbook for Practice. London/New York: Routledge.

Agyeman, Julian (2005): Sustainable Communities and the Challenge of Environmental Justice. New York: University Press.

Bernhard, Armin/Elsen, Susanne/Nicli, Sara (2020): Einleitung: Öko-soziale Landwirtschaft – Ein Ansatz gesellschaftlicher Transformation und nachhaltiger Entwicklung. In: Elsen, Susanne/Angeli, Sergio/Bernhard, Arnim/Nicli, Sara: Perspektiven der sozialen Landwirtschaft unter besonderer Berücksichtigung der Entwicklungen in Italien. Bozen: bu, press, 1–19.

Besthorn, Fred H. (2013): Radical Equalitarian Ecological Justice. In: Gray, Mel/Coates, John/Heatherington, Tiani (eds.): Environmental Social Work. London/New York: Routledge, 31–45.

Besthorn, Fred H. (2012): Deep Ecology's Contributions to Social Work: A ten-year retrospective. In: International Journal of Social Welfare 21, no. 3, 248–259.

Boetto, Heather (2019): Advancing Transformative Eco-social Change: Shifting from Modernist to Holistic Foundations. In: Australian Social Work 72, no. 2, 139–151.

Bullard, Robert D. et al. (2007): Toxic Wastes and Race at Twenty 1987-2007: Grassroots Struggles to Dismantle Environmental Racism in the United States. Cleveland: The United Church of Christ.

Bullard, Robert D. (2005): The Quest of Environmental Justice. San Francisco, CA: Sierra Club Books.
Burkart, Corinna/Schmelzer, Matthias/Treu Nina (eds.) (2017): Degrowth in Motion(s). 32 alternative paths to social-ecological transformation. Munich: ökonom.
Carson, Rachel (1962): Silent Spring. Boston: Houghton Mifflin.
Coates, John (2003): Ecology and Social Work: Toward a New Paradigm. Halifax: Fernwood Publishing.
Coates, John (2013): Ecospiritual Approaches: A Path to Decolonizing Social Work. In: Gray, Mel/Coates, John/Bird, Yellow Michail /Hetherington, Tiani: Decolonizing Social Work. London: Routledge, 63–85.
Coates, John/Gray, Mel (2019): How green is social work? Towards an ecocentric turn in social work. In: Payne, Malcolm/Reith-Hall, Emma (eds.): The Routledge Handbook of Social Work and Social Theory. London: Routledge, 171–180.
Costa, Jana/Wittmann, Elena (2021): Fridays for Future als Lern- und Erfahrungsraum: Befunde zu Beteiligungsformaten, den Motiven und der Selbstwirksamkeitserwartung von Engagierten. . In: Journal of International Educational Research and Development Education 44, no. 3, 10–15.
Dominelli, Lena (2018): Green Social Work in Theory and Practice: a New Environmental Paradigm for the Profession. In: Dominelli, Lena et al. (eds.): The Routledge Handbook of Green Social Work, London: Routledge, 9–19.
Dominelli, Lena (2019): Green Social Work, Political Ecology and Environmental Justice. In: Webb, Stephen A. (ed.): The Routledge Handbook of Critical Social Work, London New York: Routledge, 233–243.
Dörfler, Lisa (2021): Ansätze ökokritischer Sozialer Arbeit in internationalen Theoriediskussionen . In: FORUM sozial, Vol. 2, 24–28.
Elsen, Susanne (2019): Eco-social transformation and community-based economy. Abingdon: Routledge.
Ferguson Iain/Ioakimidis, Vasilios/Lavalette, Michael (2018): Global Social Work in a Political Context. Bristol. New York/London: Lexington Books.
Gaard, Greta (2017): Critical Ecofeminism. Landham: Rowan & Littlefield.
Garrelts, Heiko/Dietz, Matthias (2014): Introduction: Contours of the Transnational climate movement. In: Dietz, Matthias/Garrelts, Heiko (eds.): Routledge Handbook of the climate change movement. Abingdon/New York 2014, 1–17.
Graneß, Anke/Kopf, Martina/Kraus, Andrea M. (2019): Feministische Theorie aus Afrika, Asien und Lateinamerika. Stuttgart: utb.
Gray, Mel/Coates, John/Hetherington, Tiani (2012) (eds.): Environmental social work. London: Routledge.
Haunss, Sebastian/Sommer, Moritz/Fritz, Lisa (2020): Fridays for Future. Konturen einer neuen Protestbewegung. In: Haunss, Sebastian/Sommer, Moritz (eds.): Fridays for Future - Die Jugend gegen den Klimawandel, pp. 7-14. Bielefeld: Transcript. https://doi.org/10.14361/9783839453476-001 (retrieved at 28.02.2024).
Ife, Jim (2016): Community Development in an Uncertain World: vision, analysis, practice. Port Melbourne: Cambridge University Press.
Ituen, Imeh/Tatu Hey, Lisa (2021): Der Elefant im Raum – Umweltrassismus in Deutschland. Berlin: Heinrich Böll Foundation November 2021. (https://www.boell.de/de/2021/11/26/der-elefant-im-raum-umweltrassismus-deutschland (retrieved at 28.02.2024).
Jones, Peter (2018): Greening Social Work Education: transforming the Curriculum in Pursuit of Eco-social Justice. In: Dominelli, Lena et al. (eds.): The Routledge Handbook of Green Social Work. London and New York: Routledge, 558–568.
Kanago, Tabitha (2020): Wangari Maathai, Athens: Ohio University Press.
Litfin, Karen (2014). Ecovillages: Lessons for Sustainable Community. United Kingdom: Polity Press.

Maathai, Wangari (2003). The Green Belt Movement: Sharing the Approach and the Experience. New York, NY: Lantern Books.
Maathai, Wangari (2004): Nobel Lecture. https://www.youtube.com/watch?v=dZap_QlwlKw (retrieved at 28.02.2024).
Maathai, Wangari (2008): Africa, my life. Memoirs of an indomitable woman. Cologne: DuMont.
Maathai, Wangari (2009): The Challenge for Africa. New York: Pantheon.
Maathai, Wangari (2010): Replenishing the Earth: Spiritual Values of Healing Ourselves and the World. New York: Doubleday Image.
Mason, Lisa Reyes/Rigg, Jonathan (2019): People and Climate Change: Vulnerability, Adaptation, and Social Justice. New York: Oxford University Press.
Merton, Lisa/Dater, Alan (2008): Taking Root. The Vision of Wangari Maathai. Documentary. Marlboro Productions/Soundchef Studies.
Mies, Maria/Vandana, Shiva (1995/2016): Ecofeminism. The liberation of women, nature and oppressed peoples. A new world is born. 2nd, revised edition. Neu-Ulm: AG SPAK.
Namulundah, Florence (2014): Wangari Maathai. Visionary, Environmental Leader, Political Activist. New York: Latern Books.
Ngunjiri, Faith Wambura (2014): "I Will Be a Hummingbird": Lessons in Radical Transformative Leadership from Professor Wangari Maathai. In: Jallow, Baba G. (ed.): Leadership in Postcolonial Africa. An Introduction. New York: Palgrave Macmillan, 123–141.
Matthies, Aila-Leena/Närhi, Kati (eds.). (2017): The Ecosocial transition of Societies. The Contribution of Social Work and Social Policy. London: Routledge.
McKinnon, Jennifer/ Alston Margret (eds.) (2016): Ecological Social Work: Towards Sustainability. London/New York: Palgrave.
Moor, de Jost/De Vydt, Michiel/Uba, Katrin/Walström (2021): New Kids on the Block: staking stock to the recent cycle of climate activism. In: Social Movement Studies 2021, vol. 20, no. 5, 619–625.
Närhi, Kati/Matthies, Aila-Leena (2016): Conceptual and Historical Analysis of Ecological Social Work. In: McKinnon, Jennifer/Alston Margret (eds.): Ecological Social Work: Towards sustainability. Hampshire, UK, 21–38.
Nesmith, Ande A. et al. (2021): The Intersection of Environmental Justice, Climate Change, Community, and the Ecology of Life. New York: Springer.
Noble, Carolyn (2018): Green social work requires a Green politics. In: Dominelli, Lena et al. (eds.): The Routledge Handbook of Green Social Work, London and New York, 569–572.
Noble, Carolyn (2021): Ecofeminism to Feminist Materialism: Implications for Anthropocene Feminist Social Work. In: Bozalek, Vievienne/Pease, Bob (eds.): Post-Anthropocentric Social Work. Abingdon/ New York: Routledge, 95–107.
Peeters, Jef (2016): A Safe and Just Space for humanity: The Need for a New Concept of Well-being. In: McKinnon Jane/Alston, Margret (eds.): The Ecological Social Work. London/New York: Palgrave Macmillan, 177–196.
Peeters, Jef (2022): Sustainability and new Economic Approaches. An exploration for social work research. SPSW Working Paper No.CeSo/SpSW/2022-01. Leuven: Centre for Sociological Research, KU Leuven.
Posmek, Jana (2021): Fridays for Future – Empirische Einblicke in ein Feld gemeinschaftlichen Aufbegehrens „ökologischer" Subjekte. In: Hill, Marc/Schmitt, Caroline (eds.): Solidarität in Bewegung. Neue Felder für die Soziale Arbeit. Hohengehren: Schneider Verlag, 179–196.
Powers, Meredith C. F./Rambaree, Komalsingh/Peeters, Jef (2019): Degrowth for Transformational Alternatives as Radical Social Work Practice. In: Critical and Radical Social Work, vol. 7, no. 3, 417–433. doi.org/10.1332/204986019X15688881497178 (retrieved at 28.02.2024).

Rinkel, Michaela/Powers, Meredith C. F. (eds.). (2019): Social work Promoting Community and Environmental Sustainability. A workbook for global social workers and educators (Vol. 1-3). Geneva: International Federation of Social Work (IFSW).

Rucht, Dieter/Ronk, Dieter (2020): Mobilisierungsprozesse von Fridays for Future. Ein Blick hinter die Kulissen. In: Haunss, Sebastian/Sommer, Moritz (eds.): Fridays for Future - Youth against climate change (pp. 95-114). Bielefeld: Transcript. https://doi.org/10.14361/9783839453476-004 (retrieved at 28.02.2024).

Schmelz, Andrea (2022): Greening Social Work im Antrhopozän. In: Pfaff, Tino/Schramkowski, Barbara/Lutz, Ronald (eds.): Klimakrise, sozialökologischer Kollaps und Klimagerechtigkeit. Weinheim: Beltz Verlag, 22–36.

Schmelz, Andrea (2021): Green Social Work für eine post-pandemische Welt. Klimakrise, Covie-19 und das Anthropozän. In: Lutz, Ronald/Steinhaußen, Jan/Kniffki, Johannes (eds.): Corona, Gesellschaft und Soziale Arbeit. Neue Perspektiven und Pfade. Weinheim: Beltz Juventa, 220–233.

Sinha, Sunny (2013): Maathai, Wangari. In: Encyclopedia of Social Work. doi: 10.1093/acrefore/9780199975839.013.1123 (retrieved at 28.02.2024).

Schramkowski, Barbara (2022): Ökologische Gewalt als Kindeswohlgefährdung? In: Pfaff, Tino/Schramkowski, Barbara/Lutz, Ronald (2022) (eds.): Klimakrise, sozialökologischer Kollaps und Klimagerechtigkeit. Weinheim: Beltz Juventa, 120–132.

Shiva, Vandana (1989): The Gender of Life: Women, Ecology and the Third World. Berlin: Rotbuch.

Spitzer, Helmut (2022): Wangari Maathai. Das Vermächtnis einer afrikanischen Friedensnobelpreisträgerin für eine transformative Soziale Arbeit. In: Pfaff, Tino/Schramkowski, Barbara/Lutz, Ronald (eds.): Klimakrise, sozialökologischer Kollaps und Klimagerechtigkeit. Weinheim: Beltz Verlag, 338–350.

Stamm, Ingo (2021): Ökologisch-kritische Soziale Arbeit. Geschichte, aktuelle Positionen und Handlungsfelder. Opladen: Budrich.

Tokar, Brian (2019): On the Evolution and Continuing Development of the Climate Justice Movement. In: Routledge Handbook of Climate Justice. Abingdon/New York: Routledge, 13–26.

United Church for Christ Commission for Racial Justice (1987): Toxic Wastes and Race in the United States: A National Report on the Racial and Socio-Economic Characteristics of Communities with Hazardous Waste Sites. New York.

II.7 Indigenous Movements in International Social Work

Monika Pfaller-Rott & Ute Straub

9th August – Day of the World's Indigenous Populations[43]

> **Summary**
>
> Indigenous approaches are an element of "social work of the South". Local and indigenous support systems and traditions have long been disregarded or suppressed in the course of colonisation and professional imperialism (Midgley 2010). Social work has contributed significantly to the loss of cultural roots and thus to the destruction of an identity-forming framework that is indispensable for personality development. In recent years, "forgotten knowledge", also "tacit" or "implicit knowledge" (Polyani 1985), has experienced a renaissance due to the louder and more self-confident voices from the Global South (liberation movements, movements for the rights of indigenous peoples), which also includes the demand to include indigenous approaches as equal in the canon of social work approaches. These approaches gave and still give impulses for the further development and decolonisation of social work. Indigenous approaches play an important role in the context of ecosocial work or green social work. This is the starting point for many indigenous movements that are directed against the destruction of their ancestral settlements, their traditional ways of life and against the exploitation of nature, as can be found in the approaches of Deep Ecology or Eco-Spirituality (cf. the contribution by Schmelz in this volume).
> For a better understanding of the historical and current situations of indigenous peoples, it is essential to consider their rights. However, their implementation too often fails due to state ignorance or profit interests. The demands of indigenous peoples are exemplified by two social movements in Mexico and Guatemala. The Buen Vivir (Good Life) movement is strongly linked to the philosophy of indigenous peoples, a movement focusing on a harmonious relationship between the individual, society and the environment, contrary to a Western capitalist view. Rigoberta Menchú Tum, a Quiché Maya from Guatemala, is portrayed as an important representative and initiator of indigenous movements.

1. Indigenous knowledge and international social work[44]

In 2014, the International Association of Schools of Social Work (IASSW), the International Federation of Social Workers (IFSW) and the International Council on Social Welfare (ICSW) adopted a revised version of the Global Definition of the Social Work Profession, which identifies indigenous knowledge as an essential

---

43 By resolution 49/214 of 23rd December 1994, the United Nations General Assembly decided that the International Day of the World's Indigenous Peoples should be observed on 9th August each year. In 1982, the inaugural meeting of the UN Working Group on Indigenous Populations was held on that date.
44 The first section is partly based on an article for the socialnet encyclopaedia: Straub, Ute (2020): Indigene Ansätze in der Sozialen Arbeit. socialnet Lexikon. Bonn: socialnet, https://www.socialnet.de/lexikon/Indigene-Ansaetze-in-der-Sozialen-Arbeit (retrieved at 28.02.2024).

component of professional knowledge (Straub 2015): "Underpinned by theories of social work, social sciences, humanities and indigenous knowledge, social work engages people and structures to address life challenges and enhance wellbeing" (IFSW 2015). A text addition explains the background:

> "The present definitional determination affirms that not only Western scientific theories and Western practice experience form the basis of social work, but that this basis is also influenced by indigenous knowledge in particular. To value Western theories and knowledge generated in the cultural West alone as valuable knowledge and indigenous knowledge as inferior to it is part of the colonial legacy. This process should be stopped. And by recognising that indigenous peoples in every region, country and area have their own values, their own way of understanding and their own way of sharing their knowledge, the historical Western colonialism and Western hegemony in the field of science shall be overcome by listening to and learning from indigenous peoples around the world. Knowledge in the field of social work is co-created and influenced by indigenous peoples. They should be adequately applied not only in the local environment but also at the international level" (https://www.ifsw.org/what-is-social-work/global-definition-of-social-work/ (retrieved at 28.02.2024)).

There is a good reason for talking about indigenous knowledge, because it is controversial whether one can speak of an "indigenous social work". Social work as a profession is an "invention" of the Global North and established itself in Europe and the United States as a specific response to industrialisation and mass poverty of the late 19th century. In contrast, it was successively imposed on the countries of the South in the form of so-called development aid and international exchange programmes (cf. Healy 2008: 136), while traditional local and indigenous aid systems were disregarded or suppressed (Noyoo 2018). However, renowned authors who are recognised in the debate on indigenous approaches propagate indigenous social work, e.g. in the title of the standard work "Indigenous Social Work around the World" (Gray et al. 2010).

We adopt the terms "indigenous approaches" and "traditional knowledge" in this paper and address the issue of "indigenous science".

1.1. Indigenous peoples – definition

> "When people talk about 'peoples' today, they almost always refer to 'nations' in the sense of the populations of modern nation states. However, in this way, on the one hand, an inexistent socio-cultural homogeneity was ascribed to the latter, while, on the other hand, the existence of most peoples' living today was negated, especially of those whose ancestors lived in the Asian, African and Oceanic colonies, but also in the countries of Latin America, which became politically independent already at the beginning of the 19th century. These peoples found themselves, in the then generally accepted scheme of development, opposed to the North Atlantic and the 'civilised', who had migrated from the North Atlantic countries,

as 'savages', 'barbarians' or 'primitives' who were to be somehow and as far as possible 'developed' culturally, linguistically, religiously, legally and politically" (Krotz 2011: 445).

This attitude has not changed across the board, but through the activism of indigenous movements in particular a social awareness has emerged of the value that can be attributed to indigenous knowledge for the future of humanity as a whole, both in the context of ecological issues and for community-oriented approaches (cf. Straub 2020a). It can no longer be denied that the "development model" of the Global North, which has so far been regarded as universally valid, is increasingly endangering people and nature. How can we rethink a "civilisation" that, on the one hand, achieves a better balance of the different orders for humanity (economic, cultural and spiritual) but, on the other hand, considers nature as an equal entity beyond anthropocentric ways of thinking? Indigenous approaches can point the way here.

But first, back to the definition: How are indigenous peoples (currently) defined? The UN proposes the following characteristics (https://www.un.org/esa/socdev/unpfii/documents/5session_factsheet1.pdf (retrieved at 28.02.2024)):

- Self-identification as indigenous peoples at the individual level and being accepted by the community as their member
- Historical continuity with pre-colonial and/or pre-settler societies
- Strong link to territories and surrounding natural resources
- Distinct social, economic or political systems
- Distinct language, culture and beliefs
- Forming non-dominant groups of society
- Resolved to maintain and reproduce their ancestral environments and systems as distinctive peoples and communities (As a rule, they belong to a non-dominant group and differ in language, cultural and religious/spiritual views.)[45]

Some authors (especially in sub-Saharan African countries) argue that "indigenous" refers to the traditional local approaches of the formerly colonised population. Here it is also applied to non-indigenous culture. The following are mentioned in particular: Ubuntu/Hunhu as a current of African humanism that focuses on the well-being and harmony of the community (Ditlhake 2020; Mayaka/Truell 2021). What remains unclear in this definition is the demarcation from indigenous peoples according to the UN definition (see above), who are also oppressed and/or marginalised by the majority population in the countries of the Global South (for example Himba in Namibia, Sandawe in central Tanzania) and are existentially threatened by land grabbing or the designation ofnature reserves in their habitat (e.g. the Maasai in Kenya and Tanzania). In this definition, "local", "traditional" and ""indigenous" knowledge are used synonymously.

---

45 A basic text on this can be found at www.ifsw.org/indigenous-peoples1/ (retrieved at 28.02.2024).

In our paper, the above definition is used when referring to "indigenous peoples and tribes" or "indigenous knowledge".

1.2. Indigenous cosmovision

Despite the different living conditions and spaces of indigenous peoples, which need to be carefully analysed, there are many commonalities in indigenous worldviews (cf. Straub 2020a). Indigenous knowledge is based on the following worldview premises:

- *Relational worldview* or *cosmovision* refers to a worldview in which people think and perceive themselves in terms of relationships. Hart (2010) describes this perspective on the world as a "mental lens". It helps on a cognitive, affective and intuitive level to understand the individually "inscribed" social and spiritual map (cf. Hart 2010: 2). The foundations for knowledge/insights and knowing are holistic, cyclical and dependent on relationships in the community, with ancestors and with nature. Thus, not the universe but a multiverse in the form of diverse parallel worlds is the subject of this worldview (cf. Cajete 2020: 2), which leaves room for the non-obvious and non-apprehensible.

- *Ecospirituality* is expanded spirituality and a "perspective that finally offers a place for indigenous approaches" (Coates et al. 2006). It is thus a central paradigm for indigenous movements and has a political dimension (cf. Straub 2020b). The background to this is a worldview that is not based on dichotomies but on eco-spiritual contexts and emphasises the interdependence of people, communities and the natural environment. It measures a good life and well-being by the extent to which it succeeds in creating harmony and liberating ecological thinking from the narrow anthropocentric view (cf. ibid.: 18-21). This kind of questioning of the special status of the human species is a fairly recent philosophical issue in the (Christian) Global North, triggered by the loss of biodiversity and the realisation of dependence on non-human living beings. This broader conception of quality of life thus also reflects post-materialist values.

- *We-thinking* describes connectedness with others and at the same time demands respect for otherness. Otherness is not a threat but a constituent part of life (in the community). We-thinking is seen as part of the implementation of human dignity (cf. Cobbah 1987, quoted from Hapanyengwi-Chemhuru/Makuvaza 2014: 8).

- *Blood-memory* (Baskin 2010) as intergenerational experiential knowledge refers to the interconnectedness of all perspectives of life and survival that are essential for present and future generations, incorporating ancestral lore and the belief that people are part of the "web of life" and that their destiny is linked to that of their ancestors. Fundamental to this is the relationship between people and the spiritual world (cf. Simpson 2000, quoted in Hart 2010: 3).

- *Healing* is not understood in a purely medical sense but is about restoring the balance between people, the social and ecological environment, the mental/spiritual dimension and cosmic processes. It helps the individual and the group to orient themselves in the sense of community healing. One approach that reflects this principle is restorative justice. It is based on the philosophy that justice must help to *restore* the community that has been torn apart or damaged by an offence. It stands in contrast to punishment and retribution; instead, it is designed for reparation, reconciliation and healing (cf. Ross 2014). Healing processes are accompanied by ceremonies, often by communal dances.

One question asked in indigenous communities for self-assurance is: "What kind of ancestor do you want to be?" This question illustrates the cyclical way of thinking in indigenous knowledge: The answer includes the present as well as the future and is at the same time the view into the (anticipated) past. It includes the reference to the ancestors and the responsibility for future generations, which finds its expression in present behaviour. It calls for the use of indigenous wisdom and ancestral knowledge that contribute to the survival and well-being of the human community and the salvation of the Earth's life support systems (cf. Cajete 2020: 10). This basis of indigenous approaches is transferred into concrete "pre-professional" support services, i.e. into social commitment contexts through kinship or ethnic ties. The associated traditional customs or ritual acts are often entrusted to specially empowered persons such as elders, wise women or healers who have no conventional training in social work. When these activities are integrated into social work practice, we speak of indigenisation, i.e. the linking of northern social work and traditional indigenous approaches. This is where professionalism and scientifically based practice, as understood in the tradition of European knowledge systems, come in, which is why the term and process of indigenisation are critically examined (see section 1.4).

As a consequence of the above, in this paper we do not speak of indigenous social work but of indigenous approaches in social work.

Indigenous Knowledge Systems (IKS) are an important resource. These tried and tested traditional ways of thinking and acting, transmitted over many generations, make sense in current practice, as they have always addressed today's urgent problems of food supply, human and animal health, education, the environment and the management of natural resources (United Nations 2014: esp. points 12, 22, 26).

Many of these approaches have been adopted in one form or another in indigenised social work in the Global North as well (cf. Straub 2012: 53–59).

1.3 Indigenisation and decolonisation

Introduced into the professional discussion as early as 1972 by Shawky, "indigenisation of social work" describes how approaches imported from the North can be adapted to local conditions (cf. Gray et al. 2010: 15–18). Why did the term only find its way into international social work many years later? Why is indigenisation also viewed critically?

On the first question: Apart from a pronounced Eurocentrism (including the Anglo-American perspective) and a hegemonic claim that saw "real" social work only in that professionalised form that developed in the context of industrialisation and the social question, there may be the following reasons for the neglect:

For a long time, indigenous knowledge about support systems was only passed on orally and therefore (so far) not sufficiently described (cf. Noyoo 2007). Local and indigenous approaches to support have been and still are mainly carried out in practice, often far away from academic discussions in rural communities living away from the centres, from where there were and still are hardly any viable paths into the professional discussion.

Internationalisation and the drive to respect the discipline of social work on a global level presupposes formal professionalisation and standardisation of training/studies and practice, which limited the perception of the diversity of support approaches, especially for collectively organised and assembly-oriented support. Thus, the call for evidence-based practice became louder and louder, and the perception and appreciation of proven "pre-professional" approaches, local/indigenous knowledge and spirituality found little space.

On the second question: After a controversial debate about a one-sided or mutual influence of northern and southern approaches, there is now agreement that indigenisation refers to a bottom-up process that is dynamic, reciprocal and integrative. It is designed to revitalise and develop local/indigenous approaches, but also to modify northern approaches (Barise 2005; Osei-Hwedie/Rankopo 2010; Gray/Coates 2010). Some authors criticise "indigenised social work" as an outdated concept and would like to see it replaced by "cultural relevance". The actual concern, the implementation of a politically understood culturally relevant social work, is withheld (cf. Gray/Coates 2010). The concept of indigenisation is a disparagement and does not take into account the different local and cultural conditions in the very diverse indigenous communities. Furthermore, there is a danger of exploiting indigenous values such as spirituality or community orientation by reinterpreting them in favour of approaches that are still dominated by the North (cultural appropriation).

A fundamental modification of the profession requires a second critical perspective: the decolonisation of social work. The "global power matrix" set up by colonialism (and educational imperialism), the dominance of a European-influenced way of thinking and its epistemic supremacy are critically analysed. "It is not about finding culturally sensitive forms of knowledge or celebrating culturally 'others' as bearers of alternative concepts. Nor is it about learning from 'others', but it's about opening up new spaces beyond dominant knowledge structures from the perspective of those excluded by them and thus decentring dominant discourses" (Schirilla 2018: 116). What is called for is the "provincialisation" of Northern concepts in practice and research, i.e. a view that sees the Anglo-European version of social work as one of several possible ones that is no longer at the centre but – together with others – on the periphery. The admission of several universalisms is also propagated, namely a turning away from the claim to be able to subsume the diversity of reality under a single universally valid principle or set of rules (Tamburro 2013).

1.4. Indigenous science

Formal (academic) training and evidence-based practice are opposed to experiential knowledge and intergenerational remembering. Professional (predominantly individual) help starts from other premises than we-thinking and conferencing. Measurability and standards are difficult to reconcile with spirituality, cosmovision and the rejection of dichotomous perspectives. The academic community from the North, especially in German-speaking countries, reacted to the new definition with a mixture of perplexity and dismay. Perplexity because the topic had hardly found its way into the professional discussion in Europe. Is it because they feared falling back into pre-professional conditions, thus endangering the hard-won recognition as a scientific discipline?

Meanwhile, a broader debate is developing around the question of whether one can speak of an indigenous science. Cajete (2020), as an advocate of indigenous science, presents a working definition and identifies as its object the "stock of traditional environmental and cultural knowledge unique to a group of people and serving to sustain them over generations in a particular bioregion. Indigenous science [...] can also be called 'traditional ecological knowledge' (TEK) [...]" (Cajete 2020: 2, translation by author). Indigenous science he classifies as a "multi-contextual" system, a "high-context" body of knowledge built up over generations. In contrast, he describes Western science as a "low-context" view that does not expand contexts but reduces them to a minimum with a focus on material objectivity, either-or logic and reproducibility (cf. Cajete 2020: 2).

Whichever way this debate goes: If social work in study, practice and research is to be culturally appropriate at the global level[46], i.e. of benefit to the local population and indigenous minorities, it must reconceptualise itself. The "International Indigenous Voices in Social Work" conferences, which have taken place annually since 2013 with indigenous and non-indigenous participants from all over the world, make a contribution to this. In 2022, the programmatic motto was: "Indigenous Social Workers: Reclaim, Rename, Reframe".

2. Rights of indigenous peoples

According to the United Nations, an estimated 5,000 different indigenous peoples live in more than 90 states, to which up to 450 million people belong (cf. UN 2021)[47]. These make up around 6 per cent of the world's population, but 19 per cent of the people living in poverty (cf. BMZ 2021). Exploitation, displacement and land grabbing by profit-oriented companies, often in cooperation with the respective political elites, who seek to maximise profits by plundering natural commons (e.g., monocultures, mining, wind power, hydropower projects)[48], and

---

46 Culture is understood as non-static, transcultural and cross-cultural.
47 UN (2021): We, the Indigenous Peoples in the United Nations, https://zeitschrift-vereinte-nationen.de/suc he/zvn/heft/vereinte-nationen-heft-42021 (retrieved at 28.02.2024).
48 See further: Collectives in Action (ed.) (2019): The world is us. Buen Vivir and the defence of habitats in Mesoamerica. Collectives in Action. Münster: UNRAST.

experiences as labour slaves were (and are) the order of the day for indigenous peoples.

The occupation of Wounded Knee in 1973 in South Dakota was the catalyst for the founding of the International Indian Treaty Council (IITC). As a political organisation of the American Indian Movement, representatives of the IITC travelled to the headquarters of the UN Human Rights Commission in Geneva in 1974 and demanded to be admitted to the community of nations in order to be able to represent themselves, as they saw no sign that the USA or Canada would stand up for their rights. The IITC was the first indigenous organisation to be granted consultative status by the UN Economic and Social Council (ECOSOC) in 1977.

At the international level, the ILO (International Labour Organisation) enacted Convention 169 on Indigenous Peoples ("Convention concerning Indigenous and Tribal Peoples in Independent Countries") in 1989. This is the only binding instrument under international law on the rights of indigenous peoples[49]. This convention lays down the collective rights of indigenous peoples in territorial and cultural matters and those of self-identification. It is based on the recognition of the aspirations of indigenous and tribal peoples to exercise control over their own institutions, ways of life and ideas of development. Thus, anti-discrimination measures should be supported nationally and the situation of poverty and marginalisation of indigenous peoples should be reduced. In the process, indigenous peoples were granted the right to dispose of their natural resources in their territories (cf. Schilling-Vacaflor 2010: 32–33).

In this article, we focus on Latin America because this is where a particularly large number of indigenous peoples and tribes live and where indigenous movements have long been very present on the political stage. Here, various indigenous organisations and groups from all over Abya Yala[50] came together for the first time in 1990 for a meeting in the Ecuadorian capital Quito to pave the way towards a plurinational America (cf. Rinke et al. 2009: 346). In the "Declaración de Quito y Resolución del Encuentro Continental de Pueblos Indígenas" (1990)[51] various demands were made, e.g. for spirituality and a relationship with nature and for the defence of indigenous culture, education and religion as a mark of identity. Another demand relates to the defence and preservation of natural resources as well as self-organisation in their use. There is also a demand for recognition of the right to life, to land and to practice culture. Some of these aspects are reflected in the UN Declaration almost 20 years later.

---

[49] The Office of the United Nations High Commissioner for Human Rights (OHCHR) also cites five other international conventions as the foundation of indigenous peoples' rights: the Universal Declaration of Human Rights (1948), the International Convention on the Elimination of All Forms of Racial Discrimination (ICERD) (1965), the Civil (1966) and Social (1966) Covenants and the Convention on the Elimination of All Forms of Discrimination against Women (CEDAW) (1979).
[50] Abya Yala: pre-colonial name for the American continent before the arrival of Christopher Columbus and the Europeans. The term is also used in indigenous organisations as an opposite term for "America".
[51] See: Declaración de Quito y Resolución del Encuentro Continental de Pueblos Indígenas. Quito, 17–21 de julio de 1990, Quito: CONAIE 1990, pp. 1–5.

In 2007, the "Declaration on the Rights of Indigenous Peoples" was adopted in a UN General Assembly (cf. UN 2007). Significantly, the four countries that were particularly abusive to their indigenous peoples initially voted against it; Australia voted in favour in 2009, the US and New Zealand in 2010 and Canada in 2016.

The Convention guarantees indigenous peoples legally binding protection as well as entitlement to a variety of fundamental rights. The most important are: full guarantee of human rights and fundamental freedoms (Art. 2, 3), right to shape their own future (Art. 6, 7), right to cultural identity and to community structures and traditions (Art. 4), right to land and resources (Art. 13–19), right to employment and decent working conditions (Art. 20), right to education and access to means of communication (Art. 21), right to participate in the making of decisions affecting these peoples (Art. 6), equality before the administration and the judiciary (Art. 2, 8, 9). Especially with regard to the right to self-determination and the right to land, natural resources and political autonomy, the UN "Declaration on the Rights of Indigenous Peoples" goes beyond Convention 169 of the ILO (cf. Schilling-Vacaflor 2010: 35, quoted from Anaya 1996: 53). Indigenous peoples are to be consulted[52] as soon as plans concerning them are developed for legislative decisions, resource exploitation measures or road construction. However, everyday life shows that this and other rights are violated time and again. Areas under tribal administration continue to be threatened by the extractive industries – in addition to deforestation of vast areas and oil and gas pipelines, recently also by the interests of the "green" energy industry in search of raw materials for the "climate-friendly" high-performance batteries of the future.

The implementation of these proclamations is therefore far from guaranteed. For this reason, numerous indigenous movements have formed[53].

3. Indigenous movements in Latin America/Abya Yala

Depending on specific interests and different interpretations of cultural or ethnic relations, the goals of political actions in Latin America range from changing the national discourse to revolutionary strategies (cf. Altmann 2013: 47–48). In this complex field, the focus in the following section is on the exemplary presentation of the situations of indigenous people and their movements in Guatemala and Mexico around the 500-year "celebration"[54] and the discussion around Buen Vivir, which is relevant for Latin America. Finally, the relevance of global cooperation is presented, both from indigenous peoples for the exchange and

---

52 "UN Declarations are generally not legally binding; however, they represent the dynamic development of international legal norms and reflect the commitment of states to move in certain directions, abiding by certain principles [...]. It is in that sense that the Declaration has a binding effect for the promotion, respect and fulfilment of the rights of indigenous peoples worldwide. The Declaration is a significant tool towards eliminating human rights violations against the over 370 million indigenous people worldwide and assisting them and States in combating discrimination and marginalization" (UN 2007: FAQ).
53 On the development of the indigenous struggle for recognition at the UN, see: https://dgvn.de/meldung/indigene-bei-den-un-noch-lange-nicht-am-ziel (retrieved at 28.02.2024).
54 Indigenous peoples proposed in 1987 at the *American Non-Governmental Conference* at UN headquarters in Geneva that 1992 be declared the UN's "Year of Mourning" for the beginning of colonialism, African slavery and the genocide of the Indigenous Peoples of the Americas. As a result, they fought for a Decade for the World's Indigenous Peoples, which officially began in 1993 (Dunbar-Ortiz 2019: 33-34).

implementation of their concerns and from social work, in order to make clear the importance of indigenous knowledge for the profession and discipline.

3.1. Indigenous movements and the 500th anniversary of the "discovery" of America 1992

Since the conquest and the founding of nation states, there have been numerous struggles for resistance and emancipation by indigenous peoples. These movements are linked to demands for autonomy. Around the anniversary celebration of the "discovery" of America in 1992, the resistance of indigenous movements increased, as in their eyes this is not an occasion for celebration but marks the beginning of a sorrowful history of genocide and years of oppression. In some countries, the day is now celebrated under different auspices: in Venezuela as "Indigenous Resistance Day", in Argentina as "Respect for Cultural Diversity Day", in Bolivia as "Decolonisation Day" and in Ecuador as "Interculturality Day". The following two examples illustrate the situation of indigenous peoples and explain the demands of indigenous movements (see section 2).

In Chiapas, Mexico, an armed uprising of indigenous people began on 1st January 1994. In homage to the hero of the Mexican Revolution Emiliano Zapata, this movement calls itself Ejército Zapatista de Liberación Nacional, EZLN (Zapatista Army of National Liberation). This grouping aims to draw attention to the underprivileged situation and ongoing exclusion of Mexico's indigenous population, drawing in particular on new technologies and global networking (cf. Rinke et al 2009: 352). Above all, the first "Declaración de la Selva Lacandona" (Declaration from the Lacandon Jungle), which is understood as a declaration of war against the state, illustrates their situation: the indigenous people see their current living situation and identity as shaped by 500 years of struggle, first against enslavement, then in the War of Independence against Spain in the 19th century, then in resistance against the US expansionism, against a 30-year dictatorship and always (still and again) against land grabbing and resource exploitation, exclusion and poverty[55]. They also complain that their liberation work is unjustifiably associated with drug trafficking, drug guerrillas, banditry, etc. Their movement adheres to constitutional law and stands under the banner of justice and equality.

Not only in Mexico but also in Guatemala indigenous people such as Mayan leader Rigoberta Menchú, whose portrait can be found below, are fighting for justice and against racism, discrimination, oppression and exploitation. "The scorched earth policy, that is, the destruction of entire villages in Guatemala was pursued by the army with the intention of eliminating the witnesses to its crimes [...]" (Menchú 1999: 269). Scorched earth policy meant the total annihilation, the extermination of the indigenous people with all their ideals (e.g., their close relationship to nature, to Mother Earth, the close connection to ancestors and

---

55 Comandancia General del EZLN: Declaración de la Selva Lacandona (1993). http://palabra.ezln.org.mx/comunicados/1994/1993.htm (retrieved at 28.02.2024).

responsibility for descendants[56]) by the army in Guatemala. To save their lives and to protect themselves from torture, indigenous people fled to the mountains and lived there for almost 15 years.

As a result of the 500th anniversary of colonisation in 1992, a positive development is that the common criticism of this neo-colonial event increased cohesion among indigenous peoples. On the negative side, they feel exploited by countless environmental activists and intellectual groups who have appropriated their ideas and positions and taken over the authorship of them.

> "Never was it said: 'That's what Chief Descage said' or: 'That's what a Mayan chief said, that's what a Chortí[57] or a Chamula[58] or a midwife said'. It was never admitted that these ideas had roots thousands of years old, and so the indigenous person seemed to have no world of thought of his own" (Menchú 1999: 299).

An important step towards further uniting the indigenous peoples was the World Conference of Peoples on Climate Change and the Rights of Mother Nature (with its "Declaración de la Conferencia Mundial de los Pueblos sobre el Cambio Climático y los Derechos de la Madre Tierra" 2020) held under the auspices of the Bolivian government in April 2010.

> "More than 5,000 representatives of NGOs and social movements from 174 countries and 25,000 Bolivian activists discussed alternatives to the capitalist development model [...]. In their farewell declaration, they called for a new political, economic and social system based on the following principles: 'harmony between and with all; complementarity, solidarity and equality; collective, social and economic development and equality; collective well-being and satisfaction of basic needs in harmony with Mother Earth; respect for the rights of Mother Earth and human rights; recognition of human beings on the basis of their essence and not on the basis of their possessions; elimination of all forms of colonialism, imperialism and interventionism; and peace between peoples and with Mother Nature [...]'" (Lopez Ayala: 2017)

Portrait Rigoberta Menchú

The human rights activist Rigoberta Menchú Tum, a Quiché Maya, daughter of a Christian catechist and a midwife trained in Mayan medicine, is born on 9th January 1959 in Chimel, Guatemala. Civil war breaks out in 1960. Indigenous communities are under general suspicion of supporting the rebels and are systematically displaced, abducted or murdered. By the time peace is

---

56 E.g. Laura Vicuña Perera Manso, who campaigns for the preservation of the Amazon and the rights of indigenous peoples, says: "We are invited and asked to take care of ourselves, because we ourselves are nature, we are earth, we are air and we are forests."
57 Chorti is an indigenous people and is found in the countries of Guatemala, Honduras and El Salvador.
58 Chamula is a place in Mexico with a very high proportion of indigenous people who are descendants of the Maya.

concluded in 1996, 200,000 Guatemalans, mostly Maya, die, 450 Maya villages are destroyed and one million people are displaced.

Rigoberta Menchú attends a Catholic boarding school and comes into contact with the ideas of liberation theology and the women's movement. During the Guatemalan civil war, her family is close to the guerrilla movement, which opposes the military dictatorship supported by the USA and campaigns for the land claims of the small farmers (campesinos). Most of the family members are killed because of their political commitment. Between 1982 and 1984, at the height of the 36-year civil war in Guatemala, tens of thousands, mostly Maya, flee to Mexico, including Rigoberta Menchú – she is 21 years old at the time. She was only able to return to Guatemala 13 years later (cf. Beltrán 1999: 11).

In 1979, Rigoberta Menchú, like her father and brothers, joined the Comité de Unidad Campesina (Committee for Rural Workers' Union, CUC) and served as a delegate to the UN. Later, as a leading member of the indigenous movement, she represented its interests in the United Nations Working Group on Indigenous Populations, UNWGI (cf. Miná 1999: 14; Menchú 1999: 218ff.). At the age of 23 she is already a founding member of the organisation for the documentation and denunciation of human rights violations. She also becomes a member of the radical "Popular Front 31 January" with the aim of teaching the indigenous peoples and campesinos oppressed by the military dictatorship how to establish resistance by organising themselves (cf. Zimmermann 2001: 122–123). Another important activity from 1882 – from exile – is her involvement in the Representación Unitaria de la Oposición Guatemala (ruog), an association of opposition groups in which she campaigns at national level for fair land distribution, better living conditions and fair wages (Comité de Unidad Campesina 1996: 40). She acts as a representative of indigenous rights at the international level and appears as a speaker and activist at forums all over the world. She becomes the leader of indigenous and women's organisations and a symbolic figure, especially for the indigenous people (cf. Zimmermann 2001: 114).

She achieved worldwide fame through her autobiographies "Yo, Rigoberta Menchú" (1983), "Rigoberta Menchú – Granddaughter of the Maya" (1999) and "Rigoberta Menchú: Life in Guatemala" (Burgos 1984 – now in its 12th edition). Even if she did not experience everything herself exactly as it is reproduced in the (dictated) autobiography, as can be shown, it is worth noting her comment: "I'd like to stress that it's not only my life, it's also the testimony of my people" (Menchú 1983: 3). She knows how to use the marketing of her story to attract even more attention to the concerns of the indigenous people and to achieve international condemnation of the Guatemalan military dictatorship (cf. Zimmermann 2001: 113).

In 1992, Rigoberta Menchú was awarded the Nobel Peace Prize for her fight for the prosecution of crimes against the indigenous population in Guatemala. This makes her not only the youngest laureate up to that time but also the first indigenous one. In her speech, she denounces the subjugation of the indigenous people by the Europeans and pays tribute to the millions of victims.

She then returned to Guatemala with other exiles and used the prize money to found the Rigoberta Menchú Tum Foundation (Fundación Rigoberta Menchu Tum – FRMT), whose aim is to support Mayan communities and genocide survivors in finally demanding justice after decades and to enforce appropriate legal proceedings. It has been successful in many important cases: the trial of former dictator Efraín Ríos Montt (2013), the conviction of the police chief responsible for the massacre of activists at the peaceful demonstration that

> killed her father (2015) and the case of women survivors of sexual slavery at the hands of the military (2016).
> Rigoberta Menchú receives many other awards, the endowments of which she invests in humanitarian projects, e.g. in the nationwide expansion of the pharmacy chain Farmacias Similares, which aims to distribute medicines at low cost (Salud para Todos). As president of this organisation, Menchú has come under fierce attack from big pharmaceutical companies because she wants to shorten the patent life of specific AIDS and cancer drugs in order to increase their availability and affordability.
> In 1996, she was appointed UNESCO Special Ambassador for the Promotion of a Culture of Peace and the Rights of Indigenous People. She runs twice – unsuccessfully – for the office of President of Guatemala but achieves a revival of the discussion about a stronger representation of indigenous peoples in politics.
> Finally, a comment she made at a UN summit in Geneva on the issue of human rights: "We are not butterflies, we are thinking human beings. Why is it not accepted that today's world could learn something from indigenous peoples?" (Minà 1999: 15)
> The importance of Rigoberta Menchú's commitment to the indigenous movements cannot be overestimated. She proves that resistance can lead to making oneself heard internationally. And not only that: she also shows how well-networked activism with the aim of demanding justice can also obtain it.

An indigenous concept that already has influence on Western thinking is Buen Vivir.

3.2 Buen Vivir as an alternative concept to development

Latin America as well as the entire Global South are measured in their "development" against a linear notion of civilisation and progress based on a matrix of global power/superiority of the Global North. In contrast, the Buen Vivir approach presented here shows a concept of development that includes more than material progress, economic growth and one-dimensional assessment. Buen Vivir represents a multiple break with conventional concepts: it breaks with traditional concepts of development, invokes indigenous cosmovisions and traditions, and focuses on the relationship with nature (cf. Fatheuer 2011: 17).

The revival of the concept of Buen Vivir took place in Bolivia and Ecuador, countries where indigenous peoples make up a large part of the population. The indigenous and Andean idea of the good life (Buen Vivir[59] or Sumak Kawsay[60]) is based on a traditional worldview that strives for a harmonious relationship between the individual, society and the environment and is thus a counterproposal to the prevailing capitalist and anthropocentric view of the Global North[61].

---

59 Buen Vivir can be translated as "living well" or "collective well-being".
60 Sumak Kawsay is a multiple economic, political and cultural proposal focused by different social actors with different interests (Altmann 2016: 55).
61 "We are witnesses that the common house lives in agony, with a lack of air to breathe, of pure water to irrigate the land and the forests [...]. We are not receptive to this agony and the silent death of the earth. Many of us, numbed by the separation we make from the earth and from the sons and daughters of the earth, observed, 'whatever the earth does, it will be done to the sons and daughters of the earth'" (Laura Vicuña Perera Manso, 2022, author's translation).

Buen Vivir is clearly distinguished from the idea of the individual good life. It is only conceivable in a social context, mediated by the community in which people live. Walsh (2010: 18) sees it as the result of the social, political and epistemic capacity to act of the indigenous movement, which points to the urgency of a radically different social contract. It is thus a system of knowledge and life whose basis is both the community of people and nature and the spatio-temporal totality of existence.

Buen Vivir was integrated into the constitutions of Ecuador and Bolivia in 2008 and 2009. Both countries see the reconstitution of their constitutions as a final break with colonial history, which is why the presence of the indigenous movement in the constitutional processes was of fundamental importance. In this way, communitarian structures and participatory models of democracy were strengthened (cf. Fatheuer 2011: 14). Another important feature is the self-image as a "plurinational state", an innovation in Latin America, whereby the recognition also explicitly refers to non-indigenous groups such as Afrodescendants or the mestizo population (cf. ibid.: 20).

The preamble of the "Cortesía Constitución de la República del Ecuador" (2008) emphasises the decision to build a new form of coexistence based on Buen Vivir and Sumak Kawsay, to build a new way of living together in harmony with the environment and accepting diversity. Looking at the other focal points (including water and food, nature, education, health, work and social security, housing, culture, social communication, science, ancestral knowledge, biodiversity, ecosystems, alternative energies), the social, economic and epistemic importance to be attached to Buen Vivir becomes clear.

As everywhere, the difference between constitutional reality and the constitutional text is a challenge. Do these two constitutions contain rather good wishes mixed with laws, or is it even mere constitutional poetry or constitutional populism, as critics believe (cf. Fatheuer 2011: 15)? Even if the implementation threatens to fail due to postcolonial obstacles and even if the danger cannot be denied that the concept of Buen Vivir, similar to the African Ubuntu, is depoliticised and can degenerate into an empty phrase: these constitutions contain visions, and they are directed towards the future. Their central feature is that they are transitive constitutions, i.e., they explicitly aim at change and their message is the commitment to the good life as a constitutional goal and the recognition of nature as a legal subject. In any case, the integration of the indigenous worldview into the constitution has united and strengthened the indigenous movement (Altmann 2014: 89–90). Numerous transnational Latin American organisations as well as global cooperations emerged.

3.3. Global cooperation

With the worldwide activities of indigenous movements, their history repeatedly comes into the focus of political publicity at national and international level. Among other things, the unwillingness of Latin American countries to honour their promises of citizenship and equal rights is denounced. As a result, numerous transnational Latin American organisations emerged and joined forces with other international movements such as the World Council of Indigenous Peoples (cf. Hatzky/Potthast 2022:182). Over time, support from the United Nations (UN) intensified. Further global support – such as from the international umbrella organisations of social work IFSW and IASSW (cf. Straub's contribution in this volume) – contributes to understanding and respect for different cultures and to incorporating indigenous knowledge into training, teaching, research and practice, thus giving international social work an important role in decolonising and reconceptualising the profession.

4. Conclusion

Indigenous approaches are an enrichment for social work and can contribute to its further development towards more community-oriented practices. No international congress can be imagined without the topics of ecology and spirituality. As examples show, cooperation between international social work and indigenous movements helps to lend weight to their demands for the assertion of their rights and the protection of their territories and their natural resources and to make them visible and audible. We ourselves have learned and adopted a lot from the indigenous people in this contribution – for which we are grateful.

In the face of global climate change, the indigenous concept of healing and Buen Vivir, i.e. of the balance between people, the social and ecological environment and the spiritual dimension, can no longer be ignored. Laura Vicuña Perera Manso, who campaigns for the preservation of the Amazon and the rights of indigenous peoples, emphasises: "We ourselves are nature, we are earth, we are air and we are forests" (Vicuña Perera Manso 2022).

"Healing through Story, Song and Dance" – this was the title of a lecture at an ICSW congress. This is to be understood as an invitation to listen to each other, to try out different forms of communication and to go and stay in movement(s) together.

Reflective questions

- Which indigenous peoples are you familiar with? Research the question of whether and, if so, how indigenous knowledge plays a role in your everyday live.
- "What kind of ancestor do you want to be" – how would you answer this question for yourself?
- "Provincialisation of northern concepts of social work in practice, teaching and research" – what is your position on this demand? Please justify your position.
- What references do you see between indigenous approaches (e.g. worldview premises, …) and a selected field of work in social work?
- Discuss the term "decolonisation of social work".

Introductory literature

Dunbar-Ortiz, Roxanne (2019): The International Indigenous Peoples´ Movement: A Site of Anti-Racist Struggle against Capitalism. In: Vishwas Satgar: Racism After Apartheid. Challenges for Marxism and Anti-Racism. Published by: Wits University Press.

Fatheuer, Thomas (2011): Buen Vivir. A brief introduction to Latin America's new concepts for the good life and the rights of nature. Volume 17, ed. Heinrich-Böll-Stiftung. https://www.boell.de/sites/default/files/assets/boell.de/images/download_de/Buen_Vivir_engl.pdf (retrieved at 28.02.2024).

Menchú, Rigoberta (2010²): I, Rigoberta Menchú: An Indian Woman in Guatemala: Verso

Straub, Ute (2020a) "A Relational Worldview" – an indigenous perspective and it's impact on (extended) Social Work". In: Straub, Ute/ Rott, Gerhard/ Lutz, Ronald (ed.): Indigenous and Local Knowledge. Volume Nr IX Social Work of the South. Opladen:Paulo Freire-Verlag, 113–129.

Further reading

Altmann, Philipp (2013): Plurinationality and Interculturality in Ecuador: The indigenous movement and the development of political concepts. In: Iberoamericana. Nordic Journal of Latin American and Caribbean Studies. Vol. 43/1-2, 47–66.

Altmann, Philipp (2014): Good Life as a Social Movement Proposal for Natural Resource Use: The Indigenous Movement in Ecuadorin: Consilience, No. 12, pp. 82-94. Published by: Columbia University.

Avenir Social (2019): Die IFSW/IASSW Definition der Sozialen Arbeit von 2014. Bern: AvenirSocial, 26.04.2019. https://avenirsocial.ch/wp-content/uploads/2018/12/definitive-deutschsprachige-Fassung-IFSW-Definition-mit-Kommentar-1.pdf, 28.02.2024.

Barise, Abdullah (2005): Social Work with Muslims: Insights from the Teachings of Islam. In: Critical Social Work, Vol. 6, No 2, https://ojs.uwindsor.ca/index.php/csw/article/download/5660/4627?inline=1 (retrieved at 28.02.2024).

Baskin, Cynthia (2010): Strong Helpers' Teachings: The Value of Indigenous Knowledges in the Helping Professions. Toronto: Canadian Scholars' Press.

Beltrán, Esteban (1999): Einführung. In: Rigoberta Menchú. Enkelin der Maya. Autobiographie. Göttingen: Lamuv Verlag.

Bundesministerium für wirtschaftliche Zusammenarbeit und Entwicklung (BMZ) (2021): Menschenrechte. Rechte indigener Völker. https://www.bmz.de/de/entwicklungspolitik/rechte-indigener-voelker (retrieved at 28.02.2024).

Burgos, Elisabeth (1994): Rigoberta Menchú. Leben in Guatemala. Bornheim-Merten: Lamuv Verlag.

Cajete, Gregory A. (2020): Indigenous Science, Climate Change, and Indigenous Community Building: A Framework of Foundational Perspectives for Indigenous Community Resilience and Revitalization. In: Sustainability 2020, 12, 9569. DOI:10.3390/su12229569.

César Vargas, Samantha (2019): Die Methodik der Enteignung der indigenen Bevölkerung. In: Kollektive in Aktion (eds.) (2019): Die Welt sind wir. Buen Vivir und die Verteidigung von Lebensräumen in Mesoamerika. Kollektive in Aktion. Münster: UNRAST.

Coates, John/Gray, Mel/Hetherington, Tiani (2006): An 'ecospiritual' perspective: Finally, a place for Indigenous approaches. In: British Journal of Social Work, Vol.7, H. 2.

Constitution de la República del Ecuador (2008): www.oas.org/juridico/pdfs/mesicic4_ecu_const.pdf (retrieved at 28.02.2024).

Comitè de Unidad Campesina (1996⁴): Rigoberta Menchù. Klage der Erde. Der Kampf der Campesinos in Guatemala. Göttingen: Lamuv Verlag.

Declaración de la Conferencia Mundial de los Pueblos sobre el Cambio Climático y los Derechos de la Madre Tierra (2020). www.fuhem.es/2010/05/20/declaracion-de-la-conferencia-mundial-de-los-pueblos-sobre-el-cambio-climatico-y-los-derechos-de-la-madre-tierra/ (retrieved at 28.02.2024).

Ditlhake, Kefilwe (2020): Ubunto/Botho culture: An indigenous African value system and community development. In: Straub, Ute /Rott, Gerhard/ Lutz, Ronald (eds.): Indigenous and Local Knowledge in Social Work. Band Nr. 8, Sozialarbeit des Südens. Opladen: Paulo Freire Verlag, 159–176.

Gray, Mel/Yellow Bird, M./Coates, John (2010): Towards an Understanding of Indigenous Social Work. In: dies. (eds.) (2010): Indigenous Social Work around the World. Towards Culturally Relevant Education and Practice. Southhampton: Ashgate, 13–29.

Hapanyengwi-Chemhuru, Oswell/Makuvaza, Ngoni (2014): Hunhu: In Search of an Indigenous Philosophy for the Zimbabwean Education System. In: Journal of Indigenous Social Development, Vol. 3 (1), 11–15.

Hart, Michael A. (2010): Indigenous Worldviews, Knowledge, and Research: The Development of an Indigenous Research Paradigm. In: Journal of Indigenous Voices in Social Work, 1(1), 1–16.

Hatzky, Christine/Potthast Barbara (2022): Lateinamerika seit 1930. Berlin: De Gruyter.

Healy, L. (2008): Introduction: A brief journey through the 80 year history of the International Association of Schools of Social Work. In: social work & society (social work and society), Vol. 6 (1), 1–13.

IFSW (International Federation of Social Workers): Global Definition of Social Work. https://www.ifsw.org/what-is-social-work/global-definition-of-social-work/ (retrieved at 28.02.2024).

International Labour Organization (ILO) (1989): C169 - Indigenous and Tribal Peoples Convention (No. 169). https://www.ilo.org/dyn/normlex/en/f?p=NORMLEXPUB:12100 :0::NO::P12100_ILO_CODE:C169 (retrieved at 28.02.2024).

International Federation of Social Workers (IFSW) (2015): Global Definition of the Social Work Profession. ifsw.org/get-involved/global-definition-of-social-work/ (retrieved at 28.02.2024).

International Federation of Social Workers (IFSW) (2015): World Indigenous Peoples Day message. https://www.ifsw.org/world-indigenous-peoples-day-message/?utm_source=News+signup&utm_campaign=7a89e5faf9-RSS_EMAIL_NEWS&utm_medium=email&utm_term=0_f1659bc18d-7a89e5faf9-81609601 (retrieved at 28.02.2024).

Krotz, Stefan (2011): Die UN-Erklärung über die Menschenrechte der indigenen Völker. In: Stimmen der Zeit, Heft 7/11, 445–459.

López Ayala, Tatiana (2017): Das Buen Vivir als alternatives Entwicklungskonzept? Eine wissenschaftstheoretische Einordnung. In: Wentzlaff-Eggebert/Traine, Martin (eds.): Arbeitspapiere zur Lateinamerikaforschung, Universität zu Köln.

Mayaka, Bernard; Truell, Rory (2021): Ubuntu and its potential impact on the international social work profession. In: SAGE. International Social Work. Vol. 64(5), 649–662.

Midgley, James (2010): Promoting Reciprocal International Social Work Exchanges: Professional Imperialism Revisited. In: Gray, Mel/ Coates, John/ Yellow Bird, Michael (eds.): Indigenous Social Work around the World. Towards Culturally Relevant Education and Practice. Southhampton: Ashgate, 31–45.

Minà, Gianni (1999): Vorwort. In: Rigoberta Menchú. Enkelin der Maya. Autobiographie. Göttingen: Lamuv Verlag.

Noyoo, Ndangwa/Boon, Emanuel (eds.) (2018): Indigenous Social Security Systems in Southern and West Africa. African Sun Media.

Noyoo, Ndangwa (2007): Inequality and Human Development in South Africa: Implications for Social Work. In: Rehklau, Christine/ Lutz, Ronald (eds.): Sozialarbeit des Südens. Bd.2, Schwerpunkt Afrika. Oldenburg, 109–120.

Osei-Hwedie, Kwaku/ Rankopo, Morena (2010): Developing Culturally Relevant Social Work Education in Africa: The Case of Botswana. In: Gray, Mel/ Coates, John/ Yellow Bird, Michael (eds.): Indigenous Social Work around the World. Towards Culturally Relevant Education and Practice. Southhampton: Ashgate, 203–217.

Polanyi, Michael (1985): Implizites Wissen. Suhrkamp, Frankfurt am Main.
Rehklau, Christine/Lutz, Ronald (2009): Partnerschaft oder Kolonialisation? In: Wagner, Leonie/Lutz, Ronald (eds.) (2009): Internationale Perspektiven Sozialer Arbeit, Wiesbaden: VS- Verlag, 33–53.
Rinke, Stefan/Fischer, Georg/Schulze, Frederik (eds.) (2009): Geschichte Lateinamerikas vom 19. bis zum 21. Jahrhundert. Stuttgart [et.al.]: Metzler.
Ross, Rupert (2014): Indigenous Healing – Exploring Traditional Paths. Toronto: Penguin Random House Canada.
Schilling-Vacaflor, Almut (2010): Recht als umkämpftes Terrain. Die neue Verfassung und indigene Völker in Bolivien. Baden-Baden: Nomos.
Schirilla, Nausikaa (2018): Dekolonialisierung des Wissens. In: Spatschek, Christian/ Steckelberg, Claudia (eds.) (2018): Menschenrechte und Soziale Arbeit. Opladen, Berlin, Toronto:Verlag Barbara Budrich, 109–129.
Straub, Ute (2020b): Spiritualität und Religion – eine politische Dimension in der Sozialen Arbeit. In: Straub, Ute/ Rott, Gerhard/ Lutz, Ronald (eds.): Indigenous and Local Knowledge. Volume Nr IX Social Work of the South. Opladen: Paulo Freire- Verlag, 347–366.
Straub, Ute (2015): Machtungleichgewichte - Konflikte in der Internationalen Sozialen Arbeit. Die neue Globale Definition und indigene Soziale Arbeit. In: Stövesand, Sabine/ Röh, Dieter (eds.) (2015): Konflikte – theoretische und praktische Herausforderungen für die Soziale Arbeit. Opladen, Berlin &Toronto: Verlag Barbara Budrich, 58–68.
Straub, Ute (2012): „Kreise schließen"- Indigenisierte Soziale Arbeit auf dem Weg in den Mainstream. In: Gisela Thiele (eds): Gesellschaftlicher Wandel - wohin? Innovative Entwicklungen in den Sozialwissenschaften. Berlin, Frankfurt am Main: Peter Lang, 47–63.
Tamburro, Andrea (2013): Including Decolonization in Social Work Education and Practice. In: Journal of Indigenous Social Development, Heft 3 (1), 1–16.
United Nations Permanent Forum on Indigenous Issues: Who are Indigenous Peoples? (https://www.un.org/esa/socdev/unpfii/documents/5session_factsheet1.pdf (retrieved at 28.02.2024).
(2014): Resolution der Generalversammlung, verabschiedet am 22. September 2014 [online]. Ergebnisdokument der Plenartagung der Generalversammlung auf hoher Ebene mit der Bezeichnung „Weltkonferenz über indigene Völker" (A/RES/69/2). New York: Vereinte Nationen, 25.09.2014. https://www.un.org/depts/german/gv-69/band1/ar69002.pdf (retrieved at 28.02.2024).
United Nations (UN) (2007): United Nations Declaration on the Rights of Indigenous Peoples. https://www.un.org/development/desa/indigenouspeoples/declaration-on-the-rights-of-indigenous-peoples.html (retrieved at 28.02.2024).
Walsh, Catherine (2010): Development as Buen Vivir: Institutional arrangements and (de)colonial entanglements, in: Development 53 (1), 15–21.
Zimmermann, Marc (2001): Rigoberta Menchú After the Nobel: From Militant Narrative to Postmodern Politics. In: Rodríguez, Ileana: The Latin American subaltern studies reader. Durham: Duke University Press, 111–128.

II.8 Nothing About Us Without Us: Social Movements of People with Disabilities

Ernst Kočnik, Rahel More & Marion Sigot

3rd December – International Day of Persons with Disabilities

> **Summary**
>
> This chapter is about social movements of people with disabilities and their significance for social work. The phrase *Nothing about us without us* represents the movements' demand for self-determination. The links between human rights and social work with international psychiatry-critical movements, the Independent Living Movement and the People First movement are outlined. This is followed by short portraits of three Austrian activists, who are active in social movements, and the introduction of local initiatives lead by people with disabilities, including a peer-counselling centre, a self-advocacy group of people with learning difficulties and a project on personal assistance by people with learning difficulties.

1. Human rights and social movements of persons with disabilities

Since the 1960s, people with disabilities have increasingly organised themselves and mobilised protest movements. The central concern of various social movements of people with disabilities is to demand the implementation of human rights and to put an end to human rights violations. Along these developments, the theory and practice of social work also increasingly refer to human rights and human dignity as their normative framework. At the same time, the social movements of people with disabilities are critical of rehabilitation-, problem- and deficit-focused approaches, which violate human rights and are widespread in social work organisations and practice.

1.1 The UN Convention on the Rights of Persons with Disabilities

The United Nations' (UN) *Convention on the Rights of Persons with Disabilities*[62] is currently the most relevant international reference framework for the implementation of *the rights of persons with disabilities*. Its history goes back to the commitment and activism of persons with disabilities (Degener 2016).

> **UN Convention on the Rights of Persons with Disabilities (CRPD)**
>
> The States Parties to the UN CRPD, which also include Austria (ratification 2008) and Germany (ratification 2009), have made a binding commitment to the inclusion and equality of persons with disabilities in all areas and phases of life. The UN CRPD contains 50 articles on specific topics, such as childhood,

---

[62] https://social.desa.un.org/issues/disability/crpd/convention-on-the-rights-of-persons-with-disabilities-crpd (retrieved 28.02.2024).

> family, education and the right to self-determination, and an optional protocol. The latter includes specific types of procedures for implementing the CRPD in the states concerned and thus provides a more comprehensive human rights basis than the CRPD alone. As of May 2022, 185 states worldwide have ratified the CRPD, 100 of them including the optional protocol. 164 states have signed (but not ratified) the CRPD, 94 of which have also signed the optional protocol. Ratification means that states adapt their national legislation to the content of the CRPD and is therefore a stronger commitment than only signing the convention. Human dignity, self-determination, non-discrimination and inclusion are among the central principles of the CRPD.

The CRPD is an important human rights framework for social work because of its comprehensive claim for inclusion in all areas of life. Its relevance is also evident in its fundamental critique of power and oppression, which is closely linked to a society-critical view of disability (Dannenbeck 2021).

The CRPD is based on an understanding of disability as an interaction between a person and environmental conditions (e.g. different forms of barriers). At the same time, the convention encompasses the rights of *all* people "who have long-term physical, mental, intellectual or sensory impairments" (see: Article 2 - Purpose). This means that the CRPD does not exclude people with a certain type of disability and explicitly strengthens and highlights the position of persons with psychological disabilities and people with learning difficulties[63] (Degener 2009).

From a global perspective, social movements of persons with disabilities have made demands for transnational justice in recent decades, uniting movements from the Global North and the Global South (Soldatic 2013). However, one of the central criticisms regarding the CRPD is its focus on the nation-state level and the accompanying neglect of transnational justice issues. Especially from a post-colonial perspective it would be important to address the transnational causes of disabilities (ibid.).

1.2 Further (human) rights frameworks

Previous to the CRPD, the *Convention for the Protection of Human Rights and Fundamental Freedoms*, (also known as the *European Convention on Human Rights*), adopted by the Council of Europe in 1953, was particularly relevant in Europe for the rights of persons with disabilities and psychiatric diagnoses. This convention provided a binding and enforceable protection of fundamental human rights under international law and begins with the frequently quoted sentence "All human beings are born equal in dignity and rights", which in turn is based on the *Universal Declaration of Human Rights* of the United Nations from 1948 (Schulze 2011).

Important milestones in the history of the human rights of people with disabilities were the so-called *UN Declaration on the Rights of Mentally Retarded Persons*[64]

---

[63] Self-advocacy movements adopted the term "persons with learning difficulties" as a dignified term to replace other, more stigmatising labels (Goodley 2001).
[64] This terminology is now considered offensive.

in 1971 and the *UN Declaration on the Rights of Disabled Persons* in 1975. However, these two human rights treaties still contained legitimations for the withholding of human rights from persons with disabilities (Degener 2015). The beginning of a stronger human rights orientation, as we know it today, had its origins around the "International Year of Disabled Persons" in 1981, but what was central in the German-speaking world was first and foremost the criticism on the "Year of Disabled Persons" that was voiced by disability rights movements (Köbsell 2012). Following the "Year of Disabled Persons", the "UN Decade of Disabled Persons", the "World Programme of Action concerning Disabled Persons" in 1982 and the "Standard Rules on the Equalization of Opportunities for Persons with Disabilities" in 1993 were adopted (Degener 2016).

From a global perspective, however, it was mainly the countries of the Global North that benefited from the "UN Decade of Disabled Persons". On the African continent, for example, hardly any noticeable improvements in the human rights of persons with disabilities could be evidenced as a result of the global decade (Chataika/McKenzie 2016). Accordingly, in 1999 the African Union initiated the first, and subsequently the second, "African Decade for Persons with Disabilities" (ibid.). The Asia-Pacific, Latin America and Caribbean, and West Asia regions have also launched international human rights-oriented strategies (Mittler 2015).

Because this chapter is written by authors situated in an Austrian context, the following sections have a specific focus on Austrian developments and initiatives in the light of the international human rights strategies and social movements of people with disabilities. In the course of European developments, there have been national reforms in Austria, some of which have led to significant improvements regarding the legal status of persons with disabilities and psychiatric diagnoses. However, it is not uncommon for human rights strategies to lack in their implementation, even in countries that have ratified the CRPD. This is for instance evident in the recently completed combined second and third state report procedure in Austria (Committee on the Rights of Persons with Disabilities 2023).

Important national legislative reforms in Austria

The Compulsory Admission Act (Federal Law No. 155/1990) restricted the involuntary placement of people with psychiatric diagnoses to the presence of a danger to themselves or others. This brought about changes in the living situation of adults with "mental disabilities", as this attribution was no longer a justification for placement in psychiatric institutions. The Parent Child Relation Amendment Act (Federal Law I No. 135/2000) strengthened the human rights of children and adolescents with disabilities with a general ban on the sterilisation of minors. The Residential Homes Act (Federal Law I No. 11/2004) further regulated restrictions on freedom. Finally, a new Adult Protection Law (Federal Law No. 59/2017) reformed the representation of people with learning difficulties and mental disabilities and was positively acknowledged by the UN (Committee on the Rights of Persons with Disabilities 2023).

1.3 Psychiatry-critical movements, the Independent Living Movement and People First

Demands to improve the legal status of people with disabilities and psychiatric diagnoses came and still come primarily from their social movements. Internationally, various movements critical of psychiatry developed around the 1960s, which were pivotal for later psychiatric reforms (Lüthi 2022). For example, the psychiatric reform originating in the Italian city of Trieste resulted in the opening of closed psychiatric institutions, first in Italy (Jantzen 2016; Sigot 1998) and later also in Germany (Finzen 2015: 1). Despite the revolutionary implications of the Italian reform, there is scant literature on its further international relevance, particularly regarding its continuing effects on policy and practice (Di Lorito et al. 2017).

> **Legge Basaglia and the Psychiatry Enquête**
>
> The *Legge Basaglia,* an Italian law named after the important representative of democratic psychiatry, Franco Basaglia (1924–1980), reformed voluntary and compulsory psychiatric treatment in 1978. As the new director of the psychiatric institutions in the areas of Gorizia, Colorno and Trieste, Basaglia criticised their inhumane conditions in the 1960s and involved professionals and residents in the reform processes. The main improvements included the opening of closed wards, the ending of coercive measures and the establishment of decentral mental health centres. Psychiatric reform then spread to other European countries. The 1975 so-called Psychiatry Enquiry in Germany was also an important milestone in the improvement of the conditions in psychiatric institutions and had the goal of guaranteeing the human rights within psychiatric reform. In Germany, too, a decentralised system of diverse health services was to replace the previous institutional psychiatry.

Numerous organisations and initiatives developed from psychiatry-critical movements in Germany and Austria. These included approaches for Democratic Psychiatry in orientation of Basaglia (Lüthi 2022). New democratic concepts such as community work were based on "professionals from the institutions and welfare associations, citizen helpers, relatives, people with psychiatric experience" having a say (Schwendy 2015: 21, translated by authors). However, the restructuring of psychiatric services is still considered an incomplete forthcoming process.

The *Independent Living Movement* of people with disabilities has its roots in 1960, when disabled students protested and claimed their right to independent living in Berkley, California. Similar Independent Living Movements began to emerge in Europe from the 1970s onwards. The main underpinnings of the Independent Living Movement today as well as in the past include the control of people with disabilities over support services in the form of personal assistance, accessibility and assistive technology, inclusive education, access to employment, independent advocacy and peer counselling, and accessible healthcare (Mladenov et al. 2023). In Austria, as elsewhere, the movement's vehement political advocacy has "reinforced an international paradigm shift that promotes self-determination, inclusion, de-institutionalisation, and the empowerment of people with disabilities" (Schönwiese 2019: 82, translated by authors).

The roots of *People First* as a self-advocacy movement of people with learning difficulties reach back to 1968, when people with learning difficulties formulated requests for change to service providers at a conference organised by a Swedish parents' organisation (People First 2004). At the first conference organised by people with learning difficulties in the US in 1974, the name "People First" was coined and became known as "Mensch zuerst" (a direct translation of People First) in Germany (Haake 2000). In Austria, similar developments only started after the turn of the millennium (Kočnik et al. 2022).

People First or similar self-advocacy initiatives exist in many regions and states worldwide (see: www.inclusion-international.org/news-item/global-self-advocacy-summit-2020/). Despite efforts of international networking such as the Global Self-Advocacy Summit in 2020, People First remains a fragmented movement with funding difficulties in many areas (e.g. in England: Walmsley/The Central England People First History Project Team 2014). The self-advocacy groups of people with learning difficulties may have different focal points, but they all advocate for equality and inclusion. People First in England and Wales[65], for example, declare three pillars for access to independent living: self-advocacy and speaking up, accessible information and easy read, and local community advocacy and support. According to Wibs, a local Austrian People First organisation, their central demands include equality in the areas of work, housing, leisure, education and partnership[66].

1.4 Social movements and their academic fields: Disability Studies and Mad Studies

Based on the Independent Living Movement and the psychiatry-critical movements, anti-hegemonic research and scholarship traditions have evolved: Scholars in the fields of Disability Studies and Mad Studies question previously established academic traditions and the objectification of people with disabilities through research.

Disability Studies, an international and interdisciplinary field, explore social norms and power relations to contest "the popular view that disability equates with human failing"(Goodley 2017: xi). The critique expressed by Disability Studies and the social movements of people with disabilities of deficit-oriented views, theories and concepts offers- important impulses for social work in the context of disability (Kočnik et al. 2022). In the context of social work as well as in other disciplines and professions that focus on human rights, the widespread individualistic understanding of disability (often referred to as the "medical model") is increasingly being questioned in favour of social, cultural and human rights perspectives on disability.

Mad Studies are an international field of research that has its origins in Canada and has emerged since the 2000s out of movements critical of psychiatry and from activist knowledge. Mad Studies are "committed to a praxis for radical

---

65 www.peoplefirstltd.com/pages/our-campaigns (retrieved 28.02.2024).
66 www.wibs-tirol.at/ (retrieved 28.02.2024).

survivor-led change that seeks to unify learning and action" as well as "to remain accountable to the mad community and to stay connected with their struggles" (Beresford 2021: 6). In the German-speaking world, Mad Studies are becoming increasingly established due to their growing academic presence (Lüthi 2022). Representatives of Mad Studies work on a social, legal and scholarship level against stigmatisation, discrimination and exclusion of people with psychiatric diagnoses and plead for "alternative forms of helping people experiencing mental anguish [that] are based on humanitarian, holistic perspectives where people are not reduced to symptoms but understood within the social and economic context of the society in which they live" (Menzies et al. 2013: 2).

Disability Studies as well as Mad Studies focus on the empowerment of people with disabilities, and both fields criticise hegemonic modes of knowledge production in the academic context and call for the recognition of activist knowledge (Lüthi 2022). As we discuss in the following section, the knowledge from social movements and their academic fields is important for human-rights-based social work.

1.5 Links of social movements and their knowledge with social work

Along the timelines of the social movements described above and their human rights achievements, as well as of other movements, the theory and practice of social work also evolved and took up theoretical impulses from social movements (Thompson 2002). As evident in the global definition of social work by the *International Federation of Social Workers* (IFSW), human rights are a core element of the professional self-understanding of social workers.[67] However, despite its increasing human rights orientation (Staub-Bernasconi 2019), social work was (and still is) significantly involved not only in supporting people with disabilities but also in their exclusion, for example through segregated housing and employment facilities, such as sheltered workshops, and through deficit-focused assessment and intervention (Wesselmann 2022) and their oppression within mental health services (Cranford/LeFrançois 2022).

According to Wesselmann (2022), social movements of people with disabilities as well as Disability Studies have contributed to shaping the frameworks and methods of social work. Nevertheless, social work has failed to consider various impulses from the movements of people with disabilities for a long time. The reason for social work's lack of engagement with Disability Studies may lay in the professional interests and entanglements of social work, which Disability Studies criticise from a power-analytical perspective. Particularly against the backdrop of social policy developments that minimise social rights and security, and where social work is tied to capitalist differentiations of non/deservingness, the domination of medicalised approaches to disability and the orientation of interventions in favour of the normative, profitable body are evident (Stafford 2020).

---

[67] See: www.ifsw.org/what-is-social-work/global-definition-of-social-work/ (retrieved 28.02.2024).

Human-rights-based social work (not only) with people with disabilities benefits however immensely from ideas such as user-led services and addressee participation in the creation, organisation and implementation of services, which can be traced back to the achievements of social movements (Thompson 2002). With their demand for academic recognition of activist knowledge, Mad Studies also provide an important impetus for social work as a discipline and profession (Cranford/LeFrançois 2022), including, but not limited to, for the education of social workers (Snyder et al. 2019). In the following section, the significance of different social movements for social work is specified from the perspective of three Austrian women who are activists with disabilities.

2. Short portraits of three activists from social movements

In order to concretise the described developments and demands of the social movements in the context of social work, we conducted short written interviews with activists in April 2022 and asked about their approaches to, and experiences with, the respective movement. The interviews were written in German language and translated with permission from the three activists for the purpose of this publication.

2.1 Oana Iusco: experiential expert and human rights activist

Oana Iusco calls herself an expert by experience and is part of the international voice hearing and *recovery* movement. She is founder and managing director of the company *Littlevoice*, a peer counsellor at the regional counselling centre for people with disabilities in the Austrian city of Graz, board member of the *Styrian Monitoring Committee for People with Disabilities* as well as a group leader for self-help groups and board member at the association *Achterbahn* (Engl. "rollercoaster") in Graz. She is (co-)author of several publications and regularly gives lectures and leads trainings, e.g. on the topic of hearing voices and the efc approach together with the efc institute. efc stands for *Experience Focussed Counselling*, a psychosocial counselling approach that was developed based on the findings of voice hearers (see: www.online efc-institut.de). Oana Iusco reports:

> "As with many experts by experience in movements critical of psychiatry, my activism and activities have arisen from my personal, intense and often not positive experiences of psychiatry.
>
> After a long period of self-stigmatisation, I now want to help shape the system through these experiences and my own *recovery journey*, so that others can be spared similar experiences as I had back then and can be given appreciative support on an equal footing."

> **Short interview with Oana Iusco**
>
> *How is your activism related to movements critical of psychiatry?*
> O.I.: I find some psychiatry-critical considerations interesting, but my activism is mainly related to human rights. Because in all my activities, and especially as part of the international voice-hearing and recovery movement, the focus is on the human being in his or her wholeness and thus as a meaning-making and resource-rich being, and not on pathology. This is primarily about understanding individual suffering rather than general stigmatisation in the form of societal assessments as well as norms. My focus is to live, manifest and pass on this positive activism of humanity in all my activities.
>
> *In your view, what are the most important demands and goals of the movement?*
> O.I.: In general, the most important factors for me are transparent and competent information about treatment alternatives, access and options, also beyond the often one-sided and pathologising mainstream offers, in order to find recovery-promoting ways forward. This requires self-determined choices in the form of support, whether medication or not, whether residential or ambulatory, home-based outreach or whether counselling/therapy or another approach, as well as encouragement of one's own lifestyle.
>
> *What is the significance of psychiatry-critical movements for social work?*
> O.I.: My vision of the fusion of some psychiatry-critical considerations with social work is that the increased focus on human rights enables a process-oriented further development of the system towards a client-centred and client-led range of services at eye level. Away from any stigmatisation towards a truly appreciative, open interaction, which is also experienced as such by clients and therefore generates a basis of trust. On this basis, the support provided by social workers can not only be more successful but also lead more efficiently to the individual goals of the clients.

2.2 Monika Rauchberger: project manager of the Wibs Counselling Centre

Monika Rauchberger is a woman with learning difficulties and has been running the counselling centre Wibs in Tyrol, Austria, together with a support person for 14 years. She is the author of numerous (German-language) publications on the topic of self-determination in different areas of life (see e.g.: https://bidok.uibk.ac.at/bibliothek/index.html). Monika Rauchberger is, among other things, co-author of the so-called "Equality Book" (2005) and the "Network Book" (2016), both published in German. In her life story, she writes:

> "When I was 18, I also started working in a rehab workshop. There I was occupied with different activities; e.g., I had to sand pieces of wood or tear tissue paper. Over time, I realised that the workshop was not for me in the long run. I decided to look for another job. Since 4.11.2002 I have been working at Wibs, which is a People First project. Here I earn real money, I have a pension and social security. I am responsible for public relations, give lectures and courses with the speech computer. My work is important for many people with learning difficulties" (Rauchberger 2006/2020: n.p., translated by authors).

> **Short interview with Monika Rauchberger**
>
> *What do you do at People First?*
> M.R.: I do the content-related project management. I have had a real job at Wibs for 20 years. Wibs is a counselling centre for and by people with learning difficulties. Wibs is funded by the Social Ministry Service in Tyrol. Independent Living Innsbruck (in the same region) is our supporting association. The counselling centre Wibs is independent. Wibs (Germ. wir informieren beraten und bestimmten selbst) means that we inform, advise and decide for ourselves. A total of 4 counsellors with learning difficulties and 3 support persons work at the counselling centre Wibs. I am currently the only woman with learning difficulties in Tyrol who is in charge of the project. We work according to the rules of People First. The responsibility lies with the people with learning difficulties and not with the support persons.
>
> *What does People First want to achieve for people with learning difficulties?*
> M.R.: We, the counsellors at Wibs, encourage people with learning difficulties. So they can change something in their lives and that they are less afraid to try something new. To do this, we inform them about their choices. For example, what different jobs are available. And also about work that is subject to social insurance and about pensions. So all people with learning difficulties can retire when they no longer want to work or when their working years are fulfilled.
>
> *Why is People First important for social work?*
> M.R.: It is very important that people with learning difficulties educate themselves about how it is with us people with learning difficulties. That we are just normal people. That people without disabilities know how they can and should deal with us. And also what we need. For example, easy language and slow speech. It is also important that people with learning difficulties no longer automatically come from school to the sheltered workshops in the future. People with learning difficulties are very often in special schools. Therefore, they do not have a qualification after school with which they can pursue a real profession. Before people with learning difficulties finish school, it is important that they find out themselves, or with support, what they would like to do. It is important to ask people with learning difficulties what their ideas are about work. It is important that people with learning difficulties have the chance to get a proper job. They need support for that.

2.3 Bernadette Feuerstein: chairwoman of the Independent Living Initiatives in Austria

Bernadette Feuerstein has been involved in the Independent Living Movement for over 40 years. She is a peer counsellor and has been chairperson of the umbrella organisation of the Independent Living Initiatives in Austria (SLIÖ) for several years. Bernadette Feuerstein is the author of numerous publications, was involved in the project History of the Disability Movement in Austria (see: www.bidok.uibk.ac.at/projekte/behindertenbewegung[68]), regularly gives expert lectures and is a lecturer at various Austrian universities. She reports:

---

[68] There are some English resources on this website, including an introductory text with the title "Digital Archive of the Disability Rights Movement in Austria".

"For me, the fight for disability rights is synonymous with the fight for human rights. The most important task in my disability policy work is the realisation of equal and self-determined living."

Short interview with Bernadette Feuerstein

How is your activism related to the Independent Living Movement?
B.F.: In 1980 I was a co-founder of the *Disabled and Crip Initiatives*, which developed into SLIÖ after a few intermediate stages. Intermediate stations included the founding of Bizeps – Centre for Independent Living in 1990, where I was also on the board until 1997. The WAG assistance cooperative emerged with several committed colleagues from the Independent Living Movement in Vienna and soon became an independent cooperative because it was very successful. Together with many colleagues, also from the other provinces, we have achieved a lot. One of our successes is the amendment of the constitution as an achievement with regard to the equality of people with disabilities; *Article 7(1): All citizens are equal before the law. Privileges of birth, sex, status, class and creed are excluded.* **No one may be disadvantaged because of his or her disability**. Furthermore, in the introduction of the care allowance, the work on a Disability Equality Act, in standardisation committees, in the creation of equal cultural opportunities, in the newly created Human Rights Advisory Board at the Ombudsman Board and the establishment of personal assistance throughout Austria, unfortunately in very different models and quality. In my work in the Independent Monitoring Committee for the Implementation of the UN CRPD, the National Action Plan on Disability 2022–2030 and in the exchange of disability organisations on Covid-19 at the Ministry of Social Affairs, equal treatment and equality have always been my goal.

In your view, what are the most important demands and goals of the movement?
B.F.: Despite the improvements that have been made over the decades, we are still a long way from reaching our goal. In many areas of life, people with disabilities are still discriminated against; in education, the labour market, mobility, barriers, etc., disadvantages are still our everyday life. Conservative tendencies in politics and the powerful economic constraints even lead to regressions, clearly noticeable, e.g., in some building regulations. This means that we have to put a lot of energy and work into maintaining the status quo. I also see a great challenge for society and a vision for the future in the fact that all people with disabilities, regardless of their characteristics, should have the same rights and receive the individually required support. One of our core issues continues to be self-determined living with personal assistance. We are not losing sight of our goals of living in the middle of society on an equal footing with others and de-institutionalisation.

What is the significance of SLIÖ for social work?
B.F.: The Independent Living Movement has (hopefully) fundamentally changed social work. People with disabilities are no longer seen as charity recipients or helpless 'cases' but increasingly as equal members of our society. The realisation that disability rights are also human rights is slowly seeping into the contact with clients. The slogan of the Independent Living Movement "Nothing about us without us" is leading to a new understanding of roles and improved cooperation on an equal footing.

3. Counselling, Mobility and Competence Centre (an Independent Living initiative)

"Every person must have the right to determine his or her own life!"[69]

The so-called Counselling, Mobility and Competence Centre (BMKz) was founded in 2002 at the University of Klagenfurt, in the South of Austria, by people with disabilities as a non-profit association. It defines itself as an independent living initiative and is a member of the umbrella organisation of independent living initiatives in Austria[70]. The BMKz is committed to the principles of the movement and the motto "Nothing about us without us!".

A decisive factor for the emergence of the BMKz was the "dissatisfaction with the representation of disabled people in Carinthia", which was characterised by outdated structures of individual disability associations (Kočnik 2005: 100, translated by authors). However, the most essential role for the foundation of the BMKz was the desire to finally establish and implement the Independent Living Movement in Carinthia. As mentioned above, one of the pillars and main demands of the Independent Living Movement is personal assistance for people with disabilities, which is viewed to be the underpinning of empowerment and participation. According to Ratzka (2004: 3), one of the most central figures in the fight for independent living, the model of personal assistance is based on user-control, that is the "funding of services follows the person and not the service provider", but this also contains users' free choice over "their preferred degree of personal control over service delivery according to their needs, capabilities, current life circumstances, preferences and aspirations." Important is first and foremost "the right to custom-design their own services, which requires that the user decides who is to work, with which tasks, at which times, where and how." (Franz 2002: 37)

The fundamental goal of the BMKz association is the full, unrestricted participation of all people in all areas of life, for which the observance of human rights is seen as a prerequisite. The mediation, organisation and qualitative improvement of personal assistance in the sense of the quality standards of the Independent Living Movement and the implementation of a nationwide regulation for needs-based personal assistance, independent of income and care allowance level, are as much part of the association's goals as the implementation of a needs-based personal budget. Naturally, the activities of the association also include information and counselling with regard to accessibility, whereby the counselling is based on the principle of peer counselling. The BMKz aims to achieve its goals through the organisation and implementation of public events and projects, public relations work as well as further training and workshops.

In the 20 years since its foundation, the BMKz activists have launched numerous projects and initiatives, many of them in close cooperation with the unit of Social Pedagogy and Inclusion Research at the University of Klagenfurt. In addition to

---

69 www.bmkz.at (retrieved 28.02.2024).
70 www.slioe.at (retrieved 28.02.2024).

lectures, this includes publications and conferences on topics such as inclusive education, self-determination, personal assistance and personal budget. The activists of the BMKz were and are also active in various regional expert committees as representatives of the interests of people with disabilities, such as currently in the local Equal Opportunities Advisory Board, in the Expert Committee on Equal Opportunities of the Province of Carinthia (Austria), in the Steering Group of the Carinthian Provincial Step-by-Step Plan (LEP) and in the Carinthian Monitoring Committee to monitor the implementation of the *UN Convention on the Rights of Persons with Disabilities*. There they represent an image of people with disabilities that does not portray them as helpless and poor but as persons who determine their own lives.

Many BMKz initiatives deal with accessibility, which is essential for people with disabilities. It is often assumed that a building that is accessible to wheelchair users is accessible to everyone. However, this does not take into account the needs of blind, hearing impaired or deaf people or of people with learning difficulties, allergies or chronic illnesses. For the BMKz activists, it is therefore very important to really consider all facets of accessibility and the needs of people with different disabilities. It is also the fundamental intention of the BMKz to consider inclusion of all people as indivisible (Dederich, 2013).

One of the successes of the BMKz is that since 2004 it has been possible for people with disabilities in Carinthia to claim Personal Assistance at Work (PAW). Since 2007, it has also been possible for people with disabilities in Carinthia to claim Personal Assistance (PA) in the private sphere, and since 2009 it has been possible for pupils in federal schools to claim Personal Assistance in Education (PAE). Funding for Personal Assistance is provided by the province of Carinthia (PA) and the federal government (PAW by the Ministry of Social Affairs and PAE by the Ministry of Education), depending on the responsibility. The access regulations differ: for PAW and PAE, which are financed by the federal government, the prerequisite is the receipt of a care allowance from level 3 (more severe needs); for PA, which is financed by the province of Carinthia, receipt has already been possible from care level 1 (less severe needs) from the beginning, and in the meantime the link of PA to the receipt of care allowance has been dropped altogether.

Personal assistance can only be used by people with physical and sensory disabilities; people with learning difficulties and people with mental illnesses/disabilities are excluded from receiving it. Currently, about 70 persons with disabilities are supported by about 130 assistants with personal assistance in Carinthia in the areas of PA, PAW and PAE.

3.1 People First Carinthia

Since February 2020, the BMKz has been the responsible body for the measure "Independent self-representation of persons with disabilities" anchored in the

Carinthian LEP[71] in guideline 7 "Self-determined life".[72] In working group meetings within the framework of the LEP, it was determined that, although there are self-representation initiatives in some housing and employment facilities, these primarily relate to their own sphere of activity, but that independent self-representation of people with disabilities was lacking in Carinthia. On the initiative of the BMKz, an inclusive working group was constituted in 2018 to establish a People First initiative in Carinthia. The concept developed by this group was finally approved for implementation by the province of Carinthia and provides for the establishment of the initiative in close cooperation with the BMKz, but at the same time it was guaranteed that the People First initiative should subsequently act completely independently and become its own association, its own legal entity.

The main focus is to represent the rights and interests of people with learning difficulties. The independent self-advocacy is intended to be a contact point for questions on the topic of disability, whereby the concept of peer counselling and peer support are considered a central aspect in the struggle for independent living (Barnes/Mercer 2006). Since 2020, four people with learning difficulties have been employed in the project on a paid basis, plus two people as project management and support. People First Carinthia is supported and financed by the province.

The self-advocates with learning difficulties were trained extensively for two years by BMKz activists and others. Due to the Covid-19 pandemic, much of the training had to be delivered virtually, but the training phase was completed on time in early 2022. The training content included, among other things, working as a self-advocate, self-determined living and personal assistance, teamwork, basics of communication, dealing with conflicts, legal basics in connection with disabilities in Austria, dealing with one's own disability, self-confidence, personality development, basics of labour law, work attitude, computer training, presentation techniques and awareness raising.

> **Goals of the self-advocates of People First Carinthia** [73]
>
> "The UN Convention on the Rights of Persons with Disabilities sets out the rights of persons with disabilities. We stand up for these rights.
> We are committed to accessbility. Accessible means without obstacles. We want fewer obstacles in buildings and in public transport.
> For people with learning difficulties, difficult language is an obstacle. That is why easy language is very important for us. We want information, documents and contracts to be easier to understand. We need consultations in easy language.
> We are committed to equal treatment. All people should be able to participate and take part everywhere.
> We are against discrimination.
> We want encounters without prejudices.

---

71 www.ktn.gv.at/Service/Formulare-und-Leistungen/GS-L71 (retrieved 28.02.2024).
72 www.portal.ktn.gv.at/Forms/Download/GS159, (retrieved 11.12.2022).
73 www.mz-ktn.at (retrieved 28.02.2024, translated by authors).

> We are committed to respectful interaction. We want to work together and not against each other.
> We support self-determination in leisure time, at home and at work. People with learning difficulties should be able to live the way they want.
> We want to encourage people with learning difficulties to find their own way.
> We advocate for wages instead of allowance (e.g. in sheltered workshops). People have to be paid fairly for their work."

Already during the training phase numerous contacts were established with other People First initiatives in Austria and internationally, and several project presentations were made at universities. In accordance with the objectives, the self-advocates will in the future establish more contacts with other people with learning difficulties locally and present People First Carinthia in residential facilities and workshops for people with disabilities. The focus will be on information on self-determination, participation and equality in the sense of the UN CRPD. Of course, awareness-raising for the concerns of people with learning difficulties will also take place beyond the institutional sphere through public appearances.

3.2 Personal Assistance Inclusive

Just like People First Carinthia, the project Personal Assistance Inclusive (PAi) is based on a measure in the LEP: Guideline 8 "Participation in social life", Measure "Project Question Mark – Assistance of a different kind". The aim of this measure is to train two people with learning difficulties as personal assistants in a pilot phase.

In the numerous discussions that took place within the framework of the guideline it was determined that there are still many people with disabilities in Carinthia in various institutions such as sheltered workshops. The lives of these people are for the most part determined by others. Among other things, they are usually not free to decide what they want to do for work; instead, they are tested for their suitability for various employment offers by means of test procedures and assigned to an activity according to the results. There they do valuable work, which is, however, only compensated with a small allowance that does not meet the legal requirements of gainful employment.

The BMKz was entrusted with the implementation of the measure designated in the LEP. The project was launched in 2020 with the paid employment of two people with learning difficulties and one person as project leader and supporter.

As there are many synergies between the PAi project and People First Carinthia, the training measures were interlinked. In the first phase, the participants of PAi trained together with those of People First. Only in a later phase the training contents for the participants of both projects were differentiated and those of the PAi participants specifically oriented towards their work as personal assistants. To recognise what is important with regard to personal assistance for people with different disabilities was an essential part of the training. It was important that this content was taught by people who were affected themselves. Personal assistance for elderly people was also a topic of the training. Internships were already carried out during the training phase. The internship phase is accompanied by the project leader or supporter, and the same is planned for the first phase when the two PAi participants begin their work as personal assistants.

The PAi project aims to give "classic workshop clients" with learning difficulties a perspective for their lives with paid employment. By working as a personal assistant, they are enabled to expand their competences, and with this measure people with disabilities evolve from welfare-recipients to equal members of civil society. They have a job and are covered by social security. The aim is for them to pursue an employment in the first labour market. Furthermore, this measure is an important step in the direction of de-institutionalisation because people with learning difficulties are given the opportunity to being able to afford having their own home through employment.

After an evaluation of the pilot project towards the end of 2022, a continuation of the project with further training participants is planned. The successful course of the project so far makes this seem realistic, and there are already positive signals from the province of Carinthia for a continuation of the project. As the evolvement of these projects shows, social movements of people with disabilities and their initiatives have an important role in transforming local policy and practice, which also affects the broader context of social work through the transformation of structures and support measures such as personal assistance instead of institutions.

4 What can social work learn from social movements of people with disabilities?

Psychiatry-critical movements, the Independent Living Movement and the People First movement have given significant impulses for the theory and practice of social work (Thompson 2002; Kočnik et al. 2022) – which social work has picked up to a varying degree. These movements have demanded human rights and have also had an international impact, for example through their contribution to the establishment (and now the monitoring of the implementation) of the UN CRPD. The principles demanded by the movements, such as self-determination, inclusion, participation, empowerment and accessibility, are increasingly taken up and reflected in social work. The social critique and impulses of social movements are indispensable for human-rights-oriented social work.

As Schmitt (2022) argues, this should not stop at national borders, which are still central control instances that the implementation of internationally negotiated human rights treaties such as the CRPD is dependent on. Staub-Bernasconi (2019), one of the most prominent representatives of human-rights-based social work in the German-speaking world, sees global or transnational approaches to changing hegemonic power structures and unequal distribution of resources as a central future perspective.

Particularly with regard to poverty and flight, but also regarding gender, activist knowledge from the social movements of persons with disabilities is also needed at the international political level. In this regard, as Grech (2016) notes, it is important to implement the demands of Article 32 of the CRPD for international cooperation in an inclusive manner, to decolonise it and to include disability in all international agendas.

> **Reflective questions**
>
> - Which international treaties and laws have been relevant to the human rights of persons with disabilities?
> - To what extent are psychiatry-critical movements and psychiatric reforms related?
> - Which demands and criticisms are characteristic of the fields of Disability Studies and Mad Studies?
> - What are the goals of the three activists with disabilities that were introduced in this chapter?
> - What are the aims and responsibilities of the self-advocates of the BMKz and People First Carinthia?
> - What connections are there between the social movements of people with disabilities and social work?

Introductory literature (in English)

Barnes, Collin/Mercer, Geoffrey (2006): Independent futures: Creating user-led disability services in a disabling society. Bristol: Policy Press.

Beresford, Peter (2021): Introduction. In: Beresford, Peter/Russo, Jasna (eds.): The Routledge International Handbook of Mad Studies. Abingdon: Routledge, 1–16.

Degener, Theresia (2016): Disability in a human rights context. In: Laws 5, 35. https://doi.org/10.3390/laws5030035 (retrieved at 28.0.2024).

Goodley, Dan (2017): Disability Studies: An interdisciplinary introduction (2. edition). London: Sage.

Mladenov, Teodor/Cojocariu, Ines Bulic/Angelova-Mladenova, Lilia/Kokic, Natasa/Goungor, Kamil (2023): Special Issue Editorial. Independent Living in Europe and Beyond: Past, Present, and Future. In: International Journal of Disability and Social Justice. http://doi.org/10.13169/intljofdissocjus.3.1.0004 (retrieved at 28.0.2024).

Ratzka, Adolf (2004): Model National Personal Assistance Policy. A project of the European Center for Excellence in Personal Assistance (ECEPA). https://www.independentliving.org/docs6/ratzka200410a.pdf (retrieved at 28.0.2024).

Soldatic, Karen (2013): The transnational sphere of justice: disability praxis and the politics of impairment. In: Disability & Society 28, 6, 744–755.

Thompson, Neil (2002): Social movements, social justice and social work. In: British Journal of Social Work 32, 711–722.

Walmsley, Jan/The Central England People First History Project Team (2014): Telling the History of Self-Advocacy: A Challenge for Inclusive Research. In: Journal of Applied Research in Intellectual Disabilities, 27, 34–43.

Further reading (in English and German)

Chataika, Tsitsi/McKenzie, Judith A. (2016): Global Institutions and their engagement with disability mainstreaming in the south: Development and (dis)connections. In: Grech, Shaun/Soldatic, Karen (eds.): Disability in the Global South. Cham: Springer, 423–436.

Committee on the Rights of Persons with Disabilities (2023): Concluding observations on the combined second and third reports of Austria. Geneva: United Nations.

Cranford, Jennifer M./LeFrançois, Brenda A. (2022): Mad Studies is maddening social work. In: Zeszyty Pracy Socjalnej 27, 3, 69–84.

Dederich, Markus (2013): Inklusion und das Verschwinden der Menschen. Über Grenzen der Gerechtigkeit. In: Behinderte Menschen 1/2013. https://bidok.uibk.ac.at/library/beh-1-13-dederich-inklusion.html (retrieved at 28.0.2024).

Degener, Theresia (2009): Die UN-Behindertenrechtskonvention als Inklusionsmotor. In: Recht der Jugend und des Bildungswesens 57, 2, 200–219. www.inklusion-als-menschen recht.de/gegenwart/zusatzinformationen/die-un-behindertenrechtskonvention-als-inklusi onsmotor/ (retrieved at 28.0.2024).

Degener, Theresia (2015): Die UN-Behindertenrechtskonvention – ein neues Verständnis von Behinderung. In: Degener, Theresia/Diehl, Elke (eds.): Handbuch Behindertenrechtskonvention. Teilhabe als Menschenrecht – Inklusion als gesellschaftliche Aufgabe. Bonn: Bundeszentrale für Politische Bildung, 55–74.

Di Lorito, Claudio/Castelletti, Luca/Lega, Ilaria/Gualco, Barbara/Scarpa, Franco/Völlm, Birgit (2017): The closing of forensic psychiatric hospitals in Italy: Determinants, current status and future perspectives. A scoping review. In: International Journal of Law and Psychiatry 55, 54–63.

Finzen, Asmus (2015): Auf dem Wege zur Reform: Die Psychiatrie-Enquete wird 40. www.finzen.de/pdf-dateien/psychiatriereform.pdf (retrieved at 28.0.2024).

Goodley, Dan (2001): 'Learning difficulties', the social model of disability and impairment: Challenging epistemologies. In: Disability and Society 16, 2, 207–231.

Grech, Shaun (2016): Disability and development: Critical connections, gaps and contradictions. In: Grech, Shaun/Soldatic, Karen (eds.): Disability in the Global South. Cham: Springer, 3–20.

Haake, Doris (2000): People First Deutschland – eine Organisation für Menschen mit Lernschwierigkeiten, die auch von Menschen mit Lernschwierigkeiten geleitet wird. In: Hans, Maren/Ginnold, Antje. (eds.): Integration von Menschen mit Behinderungen – Entwicklungen in Europa. Neuwied: Luchterhand, 292–298.

Jantzen, Wolfgang (2016): Franco Basaglia und die Freiheit eines jeden. Oder: „Die Suche nach der verlorenen Psychiatrie". In: Lanwer, Willehad/Jantzen, Wolfgang (eds.): Jahrbuch der Luria Gesellschaft 2015. Berlin: Lehmanns, 66–75.

Köbsell, Swantje (2012): Wegweiser Behindertenbewegung: Neues (Selbst-)Verständnis von Behinderung. Neu-Ulm: AG Spak.

Köbsell, Swantje/Hermes, Gisela/Kuppers, Petra/Schönwiese, Volker/Wehrli, Peter (2020): Wie war das damals eigentlich? Wie die Disability Studies Deutsch sprechen lernten. In: Brehme, David/Fuchs, Petra/Köbsell, Swantje/Wesselmann, Carla (eds.). Disability Studies im deutschsprachigen Raum. Zwischen Emanzipation und Vereinnahmung. Weinheim: Beltz Juventa, 24–40.

Kočnik, Ernst (2005): Krüppel aus dem Sack. Das Beratungs-, Mobilitäts- und Kompetenzzentrum an der Universität Klagenfurt. In: Kaiser, Herbert/Kočnik, Ernst/Sigot, Marion (eds.): Vom Objekt zum Subjekt. Inklusive Pädagogik und Selbstbestimmung. Klagenfurt: Hermagoras, 99–108.

Kočnik, Ernst/More, Rahel/Sigot, Marion (2023): Die Selbstbestimmt-Leben-Bewegung und ihre Impulse für die Soziale Arbeit. In: Scheipl, Josef/Heimgartner, Arno (eds.): Beiträge zur Geschichte der Sozialen Arbeit in Österreich. Münster: LIT Verlag, 611–636.

Lüthi, Eliah (2022): Mad Studies und Disability Studies. In: Waldschmidt, Anne (ed.): Handbuch Disability Studies. Wiesbaden: Springer VS, 435–452.

Menzies, Robert/LeFrançois, Brenda A./Reaume, Geoffrey (2013): Introducing Mad Studies. In: LeFrançois, Brenda A./Menzies, Robert/Reaume, Geoffrey (eds.): Mad matters: A critical reader in Canadian Mad Studies. Toronto: Canadian Scholars' Press, 1–22.

Mittler, Peter (2015): The UN Convention on the Rights of Persons with Disabilities: Implementing a paradigm shift. In: Journal of policy and practice in intellectual disabilities 12, 2, 79–89.

People First (2004): Was ist Selbstvertretung? https://bidok.uibk.ac.at/library/peoplefirst-sel bstbestimmung.html#~:text=Selbstvertreter%20werden%20eigenm%C3%A4chtig%3A

-,Mit%20Selbstvertretung(%2Dsgruppen)%20meinen%20People%20First%20Mitglieder%3A,und%20die%20gegen%20Diskriminierung%20k%C3%A4mpfen (retrieved at 28.0.2024).

Rauchberger, Monika (2006/2020): Meine Lebensgeschichte. Von Monika Rauchberger. www.wibs-tirol.at/wp-content/uploads/2020/08/Meine_Lebensgeschichte.pdf (retrieved at 28.0.2024).

Schmitt, Caroline (2022): Mobilität und Migration. Soziale Arbeit auf dem Weg zu einem neuen Paradigma? In: Diwersy, Bettina/Köngeter, Stefan (eds.): Internationale und Transnationale Soziale Arbeit. Hohengehren: Schneider Verlag, 89–115.

Schönwiese, Volker (2019): Geschichte der Behindertenbewegung. Selbstbestimmt Leben Bewegung in Österreich. In: Biewer, Gottfried/Proyer, Michelle (eds.): Behinderung und Gesellschaft: Ein universitärer Beitrag zum Gedenkjahr 2018. Wien: Institut für Bildungswissenschaft, 72–84.

Schulze, Marianne (2011): Menschenrechte für alle: Die Konvention über die Rechte von Menschen mit Behinderungen. In: Flieger, Petra/Schönwiese, Volker (eds.): Menschenrechte – Integration – Inklusion. Aktuelle Perspektiven aus der Forschung. Bad Heilbrunn: Klinkhardt, 11–25.

Schwendy, Arndt (2015): Bürger und Irre: Der Beitrag der Zivilgesellschaft zur Psychiatrie-Reform. In: Görres, Birgit/Anssen, Ludwig (eds.): 40 Jahre Psychiatrie-Enquete, 40 Jahre Dachverband Gemeindepsychiatrie. Cologne: Psychiatrie Verlag, 16–21.

Sigot, Marion (1998): Die Integrationspädagogik als Wegbereiterin einer allgemeinen integrativen Pädagogik? Eine wissenschaftliche Analyse der Integrationspädagogik im Rahmen ser Pädagogik. Klagenfurt: Dissertation.

Snyder, Sarah N./Pitt, Kendra-Ann/Shanouda, Fady/Voronka, Jijian/Reid, Jenna/Landry, Danielle (2019): Unlearning through Mad Studies: Disruptive pedagogical praxis. In: Curriculum Inquiry 49, 4, 485–502.

Stafford, L. 2020. Disrupting ableism in social work pedagogy with Maurice Merleau-Ponty and critical disability theory. In Morley, Christine/Ablett, Phillip /Noble, Carolyn/Cowden, Stephen (eds.): The Routledge handbook of critical pedagogies for social work. Abingdon: Routledge, 359–372

Staub-Bernasconi, Silvia (2019): Menschenwürde – Menschenrechte – Soziale Arbeit: Die Menschenrechte vom Kopf auf die Füße stellen. Opladen: Budrich.

Waldschmidt, Anne (1998): Flexible Normalisierung oder stabile Ausgrenzung: Veränderungen im Verhältnis Behinderung und Normalität. In: Soziale Probleme 9, 3–25.

Wesselmann, Carla (2022): Disability Studies und Soziale Arbeit. In: Waldschmidt, Anne (ed.): Handbuch Disability Studies. Wiesbaden: Springer VS, 305–320.

II.9 Divided Humanity, Divided World
– Questions and Perspectives for a Peace-oriented Diversity Education as Global Citizenship

Hans Karl Peterlini

21st September – International Day of Peace

Summary
This chapter deals with the question of the destructive behaviour of humans towards themselves, the environment and the planet. The contribution discusses fundamental questions of an international peace movement, such as "How do violence and war arise in thought and structures? What does positive and negative peace mean? What does peace mean as a process?" The chapter highlights the power of dichotomous divisions between 'us' and the 'others', between genders and between humans, animals and nature, resulting in a loss of empathy for the respective split-off other. The chapter examines Global Citizenship as a counter-model in the sense of planetary responsibility. Portraits of the pioneer of *Citizenship of the Earth*, Edgar Morin, and the peace and human rights activist Sima Samar reveal lived examples of such a consciousness. The *UNESCO Chair for Global Citizenship – Culture of Diversity and Peace* and its project Global Campus Online will be presented as a project and academic practice. In social work, diversity education and *global citizenship education* are proposed as approaches for an exchange that may challenge, stimulate and, in the best case, enrich both pedagogical research and practice.

1. Introduction to the topic: A peace that is not peace

With Russia's military attack on Ukraine in 2022, a supposed peace of the century came to an abrupt and shocking end for generations of people (cf. Ash 2022). Europe, which had sworn 'never again war' after the two world wars and the Holocaust, was immediately exposed to the horror of unrestrained armed violence, targeted destruction of life, flight and expulsion, with the danger of a new, possibly nuclear world war. As understandable as the consternation associated with this is, it ultimately represents the awakening from a state of repression. The development since the Iron Curtain's opening and the Berlin Wall's fall in 1989/90 with the hope for a new world order based on solidarity was soon accompanied by disillusionment. In 1991, Europe experienced war again in Yugoslavia, which was falling apart, and in Crimea, occupied by Russia in 2014, war was just avoided by accepting the seizure of land. The East-West conflict creepingly returned in the planned NATO expansion to the East and the neo-totalitarian tendencies in Russia. National hardening also became apparent in the European democracies. The flight movements from war zones such as Syria and Afghanistan were answered with the renationalisation of internal borders and tightened border regimes towards the outside. Populist fear politics also seduced progressive parties into inhuman rejectionist attitudes; democratic standards came under pressure from authoritarian regulatory policies not only in the new EU states in the East (cf. Peterlini 2023a; Peterlini 2017: 175–178). Even the urgently needed ecological turnaround is permanently promised rhetorically but undermined (cf. Peterlini 2023b; Peterlini 2019).

The perceived golden era after the Second World War, accompanied by growing prosperity, a levelling-off of social disparities, socio-political openings and a sense of ecological responsibility, for instance, through the Club of Rome (cf. Meadows et al. 1972), has, strictly speaking, only come to an end from a reality-denying Eurocentric and US-oriented perspective. In many parts of the world, it never took place. Furthermore, even in the so-called West, peace was obscured by the *Cold War*. This term was coined by George Orwell, the famous author of "1984" and "The Animal Farm", already 1945 in the essay "You and the Atomic Bomb" (Orwell 1968). The dropping of American atomic bombs on Hiroshima and Nagasaki on 6 and 9 August 1945 were sure signs for Orwell that East and West would entangle each other in an atomic threat posture that would (hopefully) keep them from striking each other with destruction but would only allow a "peace that is not peace" (ibid.).

The struggle for spheres of influence continued in proxy wars in sometimes shifting and contradictory alliances, including in Korea (1950–1953), Vietnam (1964–1974), Angola (1975–2002), Ethiopia (1977–1978), Afghanistan (from 1979), Syria (from 2011). In Yemen (from 2004), the warring parties are supported by Saudi Arabia on the one side and Iran on the other, which are related to the superpowers (cf. Greiner et al. 2006). Their confrontation has had a destabilising effect on the European states. The 1968 movement perceived US imperialism as so oppressive that isolated groups believed they could only rise against it by force. Examples include the *Rote Armee Fraktion* (RAF) in Germany and the *Brigate Rosse* (BR) in Italy (cf. Rossi 1993). They understood the terrorism against targets in their own countries as a fight for solidarity with oppressed groups in the world (mainly South America and Palestine) and against international imperialism (cf. Rote Armee Fraktion 1997). Both groups, whose initial activism led to terrorism, were also caught up in the hegemonic power struggle between East and West, between capitalism and communism.

This correlation can be seen particularly well in the case of Italy. Left-wing and right-wing terror domestically reflected the hegemonic struggles for world supremacy (cf. Peterlini 1993: 43–49). Thus, under NATO orders, secret sabotage troops were created in many European countries, even in neutral Austria, to defend against a feared Soviet invasion (cf. Schmidt-Eenboom/Stoll 2015). At the same time, fascist attacks, attributed to the political left through misguided investigations by the intelligence services, served in Italy to curb the strengthening of the Communist Party through criminalisation (cf. Hof 2011). The *asymmetric war* (due to terrorist acts and political destabilisation no longer on clear front lines but within states) finds its precursors here. In this sense, the European peace of the century was a pseudo-peace.

2 Peace, what is this?

For recent peace research, the absence of manifest war is a *negative peace*. Such a condition can be a prerequisite for *positive peace*, but it is not yet *real peace*. The two key concepts of negative and positive peace go back to the peace researcher Johan Galtung (1998: 17f.). The origins go a long way. In his analysis of war, Thomas Hobbes starts from pre-political conditions in which, in the absence of a state monopoly on the use of force, the 'war of each against each' could prevail. Only when the state secures peace internally and maintains it externally, there can be talk of peace as the *negation of war* (cf. Hobbes 1984/1651/1984: 96). Immanuel Kant (1975/1999), in his essay "On Perpetual Peace", committed the state to the granting of civil co-determination (ibid.: 353) and the preservation of human rights internally and externally (ibid.: 380). In the struggle against racial discrimination in the USA, Martin Luther King took up the idea of *true* peace, which is only given through justice: *"True peace is not merely the absence of tension; it is the presence of justice"* (King 1964: 30).

Galtung intertwined these approaches with a differentiation of the concept of violence. In addition to visible *direct violence*, positive peace is impaired by *cultural* and *structural* factors (Galtung 1975). In contrast to direct violence, structural violence cannot be attributed to a personal perpetrator but is rooted in social structures of inequality and discrimination. It has the effect of limiting the quality of life opportunities for participation and development. It is always present when the actual realisation of people is "less than their potential realisation" (ibid.: 9). Galtung's concept of violence thus encompasses economic inequality, limited political participation and all forms of discrimination. The almost synonymous use of the concept of violence for "social injustice" (Galtung 1971: 62) is also viewed critically, as it entails a "delimitation of the concept of violence" (Bonacker/Imbusch 2010: 88), which could both relativise direct violence and subordinate social hardship such as "poverty, oppression and alienation" (ibid.) to the concept of violence, thus making other perspectives difficult. What is productive about Galtung's concept of violence is that violence dynamics become visible in any discrimination, which means suffering and injustice for people and is not caused by fate but by social, economic and political factors. The concept of *cultural violence* refers less, as is sometimes misunderstood, to violence as a consequence of cultural practices but rather to hegemonic discourses, religions, ideologies and sciences that conceal both direct and indirect forms of violence (cf. Galtung 1993: 473–476). That in such discursive way oppression and deprivation of rights are rendered invisible and unconscious is more clearly captured by the concept of *epistemic violence* as a "contribution to violent social relations that is inherent in knowledge itself, in its genesis, formation, organisation and effectiveness" (Brunner 2015: 39; cf. Brunner 2021). The hierarchisation of forms of knowledge, the dominance of prestigious, elite or specialised languages, the definition of gender roles, the privileging of particular identities and lifestyles while devaluing all others can thus restrict individuals and groups in their possibilities of self-constitution and shape the world in such a way that they do not even become aware of their disenfranchisement, degradation and incapacitation, let alone stand up against it. Gayatri Chakravorty Spivak (1988) described this as the speechlessness of the *subaltern*. In doing so, she took up a term coined by Antonio Gramsci, a Marxist theorist and pacifist activist in fascist Italy, for the rural population of the South. Unlike the urban proletariat, they could hardly be reached for a struggle for their rights because they had no language for their disenfranchisement (cf. Steyerl 2008: 8f.).

The "violent constitution of the world society" (Bonacker/Imbusch 2010: 88; cf. Bonacker/Kowalewski 2014), as structural violence can be understood, makes peace seem like a utopia, which has to be wrested from the impossibility in the sense of Jacques Derrida (1998). Derrida's supposed paradox, "I distrust utopia, I want the impossible" (ibid.), opens the possibility of political-emancipatory discourse based on the insight that life is not fixed but eventful. The paradox makes the impossible possible "to let something happen through speaking" (Derrida 2003: 24). This is followed by pedagogical and performative approaches that aim to stimulate problem awareness and change, such as the pedagogy of the oppressed (Paulo Freire 2007), forum theatre as a staging and testing of change (Augusto Boal 1993) or more recent participatory methods such as *PhotoVoice* and *community mapping* (Unger 2014: 69–83). These approaches have in common that they open up alternative forms of speaking beyond the constraints of cultural/epistemic limitation and, thus, potentially empower transformative learning. The methods are oriented towards the postcolonial approach that science does not only speak *about* and not only *for those* affected but must let them speak for themselves (cf. Peterlini 2016: 226). Such a turn from determination to eventfulness needs an understanding of peace neither as a utopia nor as a state but as a process – as a gradual progression from "decreasing violence" to "increasing justice", which is always in danger of backlash and has to be encouraged continuously (Jäger 2010: 539; cf. Jäger 2014).

In this conception of peacebuilding, we find a viable starting point for social work. Peace is a topic that has received little attention in social work so far. Against the backdrop of the war in Ukraine, however, more and more search movements can be discerned that ask how peace policy and peace education perspectives are related to social work. For example, the position paper "No war in Ukraine" (Kein Krieg in der Ukraine) by the specific section of the German Society for Social Work (DGSA) states that social work, in particular, must work for peace and justice beyond national borders (DGSA 2022). Similar positions appear also in the statements of the *International Federation of Social Work* of 24th February 2022 and the *International Association of Schools of Social Work* of 26th February 2022.

2.1 Peace in and with the world

If we ask people whether they prefer to live in war or peace, the answers should be obvious. There could be arguments about why someone might sometimes consider war unavoidable. However, it is hard to imagine that anyone would prefer to live under life-threatening conditions of violence than under peaceful, fair, life-friendly conditions.

Why then war? Albert Einstein asked this question in a famous letter to Sigmund Freud in 1932: "Is there a way to free humanity from the doom of war? The realisation that this question has become a question of existence for civilised humanity through the progress of technology has fairly generally penetrated. However, efforts to solve it have failed to a frightening degree" (Einstein/Freud 1932/1972: 15).

Einstein's reflections on individual psychological and political motives for war are timeless. On the one hand, he recognises that there was (and is) no efficient jurisdiction at the international level that could resolve disputes with authority (cf. ibid.: 17f.). Within states, he recognises the power of lobbies that earn economic and political money from war (ibid.: 18). However, Einstein cannot understand why this small, albeit powerful, "minority can make the mass of the people subservient to its desires, which only has to suffer through a war" (ibid. 18f.). Einstein finds an explanation in the fact that the "minority of the respective rulers [...] has above all the school, the press and usually also the religious organisations in their hands" (ibid.: 19). This would guide the "feelings of the great masses". Up to this consideration, Einstein has ultimately named structural causes for war; now he turns to psychological questions. The experience that "the masses can be inflamed to the point of frenzy and self-sacrifice by the means mentioned" leads Einstein to the assumption of a destructive disposition of humanity: "In man lives a need to hate and to destroy" (ibid.: 19). If this disposition could be suppressed in calm times, it could easily increase to mass psychosis in a state of emergency – and explicitly not only among the "so-called uneducated" but also among the "so-called intellectuals" (ibid.: 20). This was a realisation from the war enthusiasm of the intellectual elite at the outbreak of the First World War.

In his answer, Freud also introduces the problem of political orders, with the restriction that these, like the "law" they constitute, were originally brute force, and still today the law cannot do without the support of violence (ibid.: 36). Only after this premise does Freud turn to the libidinal tendency to violence. According to this, "destructive strivings are often so intertwined with other erotic and idealistic ones" that they are challenging to deal with (ibid.: 38). Through repression, suppression and splitting-off of the destructive disposition they often become even more vital. The only way to counteract Thanatos's violent, destructive and deathly instinct is to call upon the antagonist *Eros* or love: "Everything that creates emotional bonds between people must counteract war" (ibid.: 40f.).

Freud thus addresses an approach that focuses on a critical moment not only for war among humans but also for the destructive behaviour of humans towards nature, the animal world and, ultimately, the entire planet. The reliance on creating "emotional bonds" points to the fundamental problem of perceptions and orders that divide and separate. Political and social orders emerge from demarcations that collective we-containers (state, nation, culture, social class, gender, age group, generation, elite) create by distinguishing one's 'own' from an imagined or real 'other'. For Habermas, groups and communities develop their "normative core" (Habermas 1976: 25) precisely through such demarcations, with the consequence that they "perceive every destruction or violation of this normative core as a threat to their own identity" (ibid.). In many cases, the demarcations are based on a dichotomous division of reality, as the Italian philosopher Giorgio Agamben sees in the division between man and animal. For Agamben, "the definition of the boundary between the human and the animal" is not a scientific division but "a fundamental metaphysical-political operation through which alone something like a 'human' can be determined and produced" (Agamben 2003: 31). This has created a line of difference between higher-order and lower-order life, which, as a figure of thought, reproduces itself within humanity and constructs there animalised groups that are denied humanity and can consequently be treated like animals. Examples are enslaved people, camp prisoners, opposing warring parties and refugees.

2.2 "Us and them" – the power of division

Dichotomies – from the Greek word for cutting in two – divide reality into pairs of opposites such as human–nature, human–animal, mind–body, reason–drive, man–woman, white–black, normal–disabled, belonging–foreign. They thus enable tailored social orders at the price of fading out ambivalences, ambiguities and connections between the separate halves. Almost inevitably, the dynamic of hierarchisation is inherent in every division into two halves. One half is set as normality, from which the other is only a deviation, so that 'black' becomes a deviation from 'white' as the norm colour of humanity, and "a black is not a man", as the postcolonial theorist Frantz Fanon puts it (2008: xii). The racist chain of thought of blackness-nature-wildness exemplifies the underlying matrix of the human-animal dividing line. Similarly, it underlies the repression of human sexuality and even more so in the patriarchal control of female sexuality, which ranged from witch hunts to murderous demonisation and can lead to femicides (cf. Lohrenscheit's contribution in this volume) right up to the present day, when abandoned husbands avenge the loss of their 'property'.

The question of why war, violence and destruction override the far closer desire for peace and harmony cannot be answered mono-directionally, not from the side of a violent human disposition but also not from the structural, institutional side. Belonging to a 'we' also implies demarcation from 'the others' as a matrix for producing social orders. According to psychoanalytic theory, attitudes toward destruction relate to the repression of vulnerability (cf. Berghold 2007: 104–108). Through our consciousness, we know about our existential distress but find it difficult to bear, so we try to split it off from ourselves or repress it, such as the knowledge of mortality and exposure to illness, failure, social decline and economic hardship. The projection of these repressed insecurities onto real or fictitious enemy images (ibid.: 94) or an outside world separate from us makes it possible to *dispose of* our own problems. This can manifest itself on different levels, for example, in everyday or professional situations in forms of subtle psychological violence such as mobbing or sadistic leadership styles, or politically from discrimination against minorities to self-harming war affirmation.

In tandem with the dichotomous structuring of belonging and non-belonging, the suffering of all those we have mentally split off from our 'us' can easily be ignored. The tendency to think of 'others' as so different and to put them into categories as so different that they no longer have anything to do with us legitimises deep socio-economic injustices, racism, sexism, gender inequality, discrimination against others, the refusal to show solidarity with refugees, the murder of 'enemies' in war. The dichotomies cut the bond of interconnectedness and, thus, of compassion as a prerequisite for acting in solidarity or at least with care. The same applies to the destructive treatment of nature and the ignoring of animal suffering, for example, in factory farming.

European colonialism shows how psychological, political, economic and epistemic dynamics intertwine. The violent subjugation and unscrupulous exploitation of other continents were made possible by the dichotomous division of humanity into 'civilised' and 'savage' peoples. The so-called civilisation was constituted by the construction of the uncivilised, in an interaction with similar divisions within the 'civilised'. Thus, the subjugation of the 'savage' is related to the construction of the 'savage child', who was to be made human through education in the first place. Behind the pedagogical impetus of the Enlightenment epoch with its excesses of black pedagogy is the assumption, prominently advocated by Immanuel Kant, that children must be saved from their savagery through coercion in a similar way to the savages in the world, whose level of development was admittedly regarded as even more animalistic:

> "Man can only become man by education. He is merely what education makes of him. [...] Discipline changes animal nature into human nature. [...] It can also be seen in the savage nations. [...] With them, however, it is not the noble love of freedom which Rousseau and others imagine but a kind of barbarism – the animal, so to speak, not having yet developed its human nature" (Kant 1803[1900]).

Thus, "education becomes a model of colonisation and national integration" (Richter 1987: 151): "The little 'savages' must stand in for the 'big ones': for the natives of the overseas countries and the 'uncivilised' parts of Europe, the 'people'" (ibid.). What for the European educational science of the time, as a consequence of initially epistemic violence, also legitimises psychological and physical violence through draconian educational measures on children justifies murder, disenfranchisement, degradation and exploitation of people and countries in the colonies. Agamben's analysis that the human-animal distinction reproduces itself as a matrix for discrimination within humanity can be understood here in an oppressive way.

3. Perspectives of a diversity-reflexive pedagogy also for social work and social pedagogy

Against this backdrop, a dichotomy-critical, diversity-reflective examination of divisions and the resulting (in-)orders becomes a primary pedagogical responsibility, which poses fundamental questions and can offer foundations for social work and social pedagogy. Which mental and structural divisions produce which subject of education? Which attributions and delimitations of a child, a young person or an adult lock them into which category, in which they are reduced to a few, mostly deficiently perceived distinguishing characteristics? How can sharply cut classifications – and thus generated orders – be subjected again to a *blurring* that does more justice to the concrete person, the concrete situation and the concrete problem?

First and foremost, this means perceiving diversity *on this side* of dichotomous and mostly hierarchical notions of normality as constructed and stabilised by categories such as language, social and territorial origin, socio-economic status, gender, skin colour, sexual orientation, aptitude, disability, religious and ideological affiliation. 'This side' means perceiving concrete persons in their response to the world and history even before they are categorised and diagnosed on the basis of isolated diversity characteristics. At the same time – and this is not a contradiction but a challenging ambivalence – subjects (in the plural) often define themselves through precisely those differences exposed to discrimination. This is not necessarily so, but it is often *necessary for* them to be able to stand up for their rights in social movements, be it as a linguistic-ethnic minority, as a disadvantaged gender, as a religious group, as a person affected by social disability, as a diaspora community or as a person affected by socio-economic inequality. Here lies the potential of difference and diversity, which is as susceptible to discrimination as it is empowering.

As a method of choice for a peace-oriented and socially engaged pedagogy, the phenomenological attitude refrains from safe definitions and categorisations in favour of an open description of what is revealed by open looking, listening and feeling (cf. Peterlini 2020). The ostensible usefulness of dichotomous distinctions in everyday life obscures differentiations within the categories and transitions between them in favour of a dichotomous absolutisation of the distinguishing features. As a result, deviating forms or intermediate forms of masculinity–femininity, for example, are lost, as are the characteristics of impaired people and the unique features of the so-called normal; the talents of people with learning difficulties, as well as the non-talents of the gifted, escape the pedagogical gaze; linguistic achievements of multilingualism become devalued as a deficit compared to the dominant national language; people are fixed to their origins and deprived of their future. Such distortions are challenging, especially for social pedagogical approaches and social work.

From a broader perspective, the so-called Global North believes it can seal itself off from the Global South by ignoring its planetary interconnectedness and its historical and contemporary co-responsibility. This division of the world serves to artificially maintain an outside, into which internal contradictions, social problems, and economic and ecological burdens can be disposed of. The externalisation goes from outsourcing labour and social costs to low-wage countries to the export of waste and unhealthy production methods. This externalisation strategy (cf. Lessenich 2016) has long nourished the illusion of ideal conditions in the Global North. However, the impoverishment of biodiversity and climate change, which threatens the world's existence, are coming back like boomerangs and demand a profound confrontation instead of the previous attitudes of non-solidarisation and isolation. Analysing and dealing with these contexts and their effects on people's lives is the task of peace education within a diversity education made fruitful for social work.

3.1 Peacebuilding and Global Citizenship Education

Global Citizenship Education is a pedagogical concept suitable for international social work in this framework, which integrates dichotomous divisions locally and globally. The approach means neither a globetrotting fancy nor an escape into romantic world concepts but a concrete confrontation with the divisions of this world and in this world. Reflecting global problems on one's way of life and vice versa, putting one's own structural and personal conditions into a relationship with higher-level questions ultimately means becoming aware of the fading-out and outsourcing and taking responsibility for one's behaviour and political order.

UNESCO, the educational organisation of the United Nations, sees *Global Citizenship Education* as "the" response to global inequalities and injustices:

> "While the world may be increasingly interconnected, human rights violations, inequality and poverty still threaten peace and sustainability. Global Citizenship Education [...] works by empowering learners of all ages to understand that these are global, not local issues" (UN 2015).

Often mentioned alongside or with other political pedagogies such as peace education or education for sustainable development, *Global Citizenship Education* might not be a competitor to these approaches. Instead, the concept attempts to think of all the other political pedagogies together. How can humans learn to "rethink ourselves and the world" (Wintersteiner 2021) to escape those orders that separate us from the consequences of our actions and our political responsibilities and thus also prevent urgently needed change?

The *machine of division*, as Agamben describes dividing dichotomies because of their inevitability, fails its service on a global level. Here, there is no outside to which we can relocate our divisions. Globally understood *citizenship*, as outlined by Edgar Morin (see portrait), requires efforts to re-establish connections in a divided world, which not only hypothetically – or as political marketing – invoke being part of a shared responsibility but also make it concrete. Dichotomous categorisations prevent co-experience and empathy. Empathy is also nationally tuned and limited in a world divided by nations, power hierarchies, weapon strengths and wealth disparities.

Global Citizenship Education inevitably raises questions about the structuring of education: Can such learning succeed in educational settings shaped by national thinking and structured hierarchically, settings that stem from colonial understandings of the 'wild child', which reproduce patriarchal patterns of domination and in which learning is not appreciated as an experience in its processuality but is measured and evaluated by the output of predefined performance categories? Such learning spaces are not experiential but permeated by dichotomous categories of right–wrong, reward–punishment, gifted–minor gifted, normal–disabled. Accordingly, the latest UN and EU strategy papers call for new understandings of learning and education. So far, the paper calling for such perspectives has been very patient. The constant of war, the now globally perceptible consequences of inequality, and the threat to biodiversity, the climate and thus also human existence simply no longer allow for such patience.

In the following, we present two portraits of peace activists who intervene in the conditions of our world and make peace visible as a practice.

Portrait: Edgar Morin – "in solidarity with this planet"

The philosopher Edgar Morin was born Edgar Nahoum in Paris on 8th July 1921. The child of a Jewish Sephardic family that had moved to France from Thessaloniki, he was born into a world of dislocation and loss, of fissures and rifts. *Sephardic* is the name given to descendants of the Judeo-Spanish community displaced from the 15th to the 16th century, who settled mainly in south-eastern Europe. Morin lost his mother at an early age. At 20, as a member of the French Communist Party (PCF), he was active in the Résistance against the National Socialist occupation forces. He kept the code name *Morin*, which he adopted for this purpose for the rest of his life. However, as early as 1949, he was expelled from the Communist Party because he opposed its Stalinist orientation. In 2002, his criticism of the attitude of the State of Israel towards the Palestinian population earned him a charge of anti-Semitism, from which he was acquitted only in the last instance. Although an avowed atheist, he and Pope Francis maintained an intensive exchange, and the basic features of his life's work shine through unmistakably in the papal writings on the reconciliation of people with each other and the earth. On the occasion of his 100th birthday in 2021, the Pope congratulated Morin with a telegram in which he underlined the commonalities of Morin's anti-capitalist social stance, shared his concerns about the "risks and dangers" of current developments and thanked the jubilarian for having "worked out the hopeful aspects of this development" (Vatican News 2021).

The critical question in Morin's scientific work is how people relate to each other and the world. In doing so, he starts from a twofold dimension of the human being as a natural and cultural being (Morin/Kern 1993: 62). In contrast to conventional dichotomous understandings, he does not assign culture to people's ability to reason and nature to their instincts. Instead, he sees rationality and irrationality as intertwined in a complex way. By developing out of their natural status, people lose themselves in "error", which can be understood as an uncertainty of natural integration and instinctuality. By transcending this embeddedness, people develop "hubris": "The violence limited in animals to defence and the capture of food is unleashed in man beyond what is necessary" (Morin 1974: 131). Thus, on the one hand, man is "capable of and tempted to lust, intoxication, ecstasy, on the other hand to anger, rage, hatred" (ibid.: 129). For Morin, the fact that humanity has not failed in this (so far) but has placed itself in a position of dominance over the planet is, on the one hand, possibly a consequence of this complex combination of rationality and irrationality, but on the other hand it is also self-endangering. If humanity is to preserve itself, it must continue in the "continuation of becoming human" (Morin/Kern 1993: 117), in the sense of *civilising the civilisation*, as Morin's call for a *civilisation policy* likes to describe it (cf. Ley 2005: 7). For Morin, it is central that societies find a good way of dealing with their complexity, and that complexity also means freedom, autonomy and community (Morin 1999; cf. Morin 2012: 66). This is only possible through an increase in solidarity. Otherwise, the complexity of society gets increased by inequalities, discrimination, different interests and migration, and it promotes anti-minority tendencies in the deceptive hope of reducing complexity. For convivial living together, according to Morin and Ivan Illich, it is therefore essential to "restore solidarities, make cities human again, revitalise rural regions" (ibid.: 68); likewise, a civilisation policy would have to "reverse the hegemony of the quantitative in favour of the qualitative and give priority to the quality of life" (ibid.). For Morin, the city becomes a model beyond divisive orders (cf. Schmitt's contribution in this volume); it undermines the concept of national citizenship bound to rights of birth and origin in favour of local and global *citizenship* since it develops itself in practices of living together and, already on the level of the nation-state, transcends it to a "planetary height" (ibid.). On his 100th birthday in 2021, Morin was as motivated as ever. He carried a campaign of the *Austrian Centre for Peace and Conflict Resolution* ASPR Schlaining on *"Homeland Earth"* with a video message.[74]

In addition to Morin, Sina Samar, another actor who intervenes in the conditions of the world for the sake of peace, is presented below.

Portrait: Sima Samar from Afghanistan – activist for peace and human rights and winner of the Alternative Nobel Prize

The United Nations lists Sima Samar as a peacemaker;[75] numerous international media and organisations rank her among the world's most influential and powerful women (e.g. Forbes 2006).[76]
The doctor, activist, social worker, women's rights and peace campaigner Sima Samar was born on 3rd February 1957 in Jaghori, Afghanistan, as a member of the Hazara. This Shiite minority has been persecuted for centuries. She dedicated her life to the education and promotion of marginalised groups and the defence of women's and human rights, according to the jury of the Alternative Nobel Prize, which was ceremoniously awarded to Sima Samar in 2012:
"Doctor for the poor, an educator of the marginalized and defender of human rights for all in Afghanistan. She established and nurtured the Shuhada Organization, which 2012 operated more than one hundred schools and 15 clinics and hospitals dedicated to providing education and healthcare, mainly focusing on women and girls. She served in the Interim Administration of Afghanistan and established the first-ever Ministry of Women's Affairs. Since 2004, she has chaired the Afghanistan Independent Human Rights Commission, which holds human rights violators accountable, a commitment that has put her own life at significant risk."[77]

---

74 Re-listen to the ASPR Schlaining website on the Campaign for Planetary Awareness: https://www.aspr.ac.at/bildung-training/aspr-kampagnen/heimatland-erde#/ (retrieved at 28.02.2024).
75 https://peacemaker.un.org/node/3207 (retrieved at 28.02.2024).
76 https://images.forbes.com/lists/2006/11/06women_Sima-Samar_C7J2.html (retrieved at 28.02.2024).
77 For more information on The Right Lively Hood Award for Outstanding Vision and Work of Our Planet and its People for Sima Samar (including a short biography, videos and Dr Samar's acceptance speech), see: https://rightlivelihood.org/the-change-makers/find-a-laureate/sima-samar/ (retrieved at 28.02.2024).

Sima Samar grew up with ten siblings and a father who initially wanted to forbid her from studying to become a doctor. Nevertheless, Samar, who had been interested in women's rights since she was young, found a way. After agreeing to an arranged marriage, she was allowed to attend university. In 1982, she became the first Hazara woman in Afghanistan to complete medical studies at Kabul University. Only two years later, in 1984, she had to flee Afghanistan after her husband was arrested, and her life and the lives of her family were in danger. For the next 17 years, she remained in Pakistan, tirelessly dedicating herself to the social and medical care of refugees, especially Afghan women and children. She set up hospitals in Pakistan, including women's health centres, and developed educational programmes for girls – even against the declared will of the political leadership in Pakistan.

In 1989, Sima Samar founded *Shuhada*, an independent non-governmental organisation (NGO) working for democracy and social justice in Afghanistan, focusing on empowering women and children (see: https://shuhada.org.af/). Catherine Fredette (2017) highlights in her portrait "Ten Facts about Sima Samar and her Impact" that Samar's life was permanently in danger due to the foundation of *Shuhada*. However, despite death threats and public slander, Samar did not let herself be stopped. On the contrary, as Samar herself says (ibid.):

"I've always been in danger, but I do not mind. I believe that we will die one day, so I said, let's take the risk and help somebody else."

After the end of the Taliban regime in 2001, Sima Samar became Afghanistan's first Minister for Women's Affairs. She was responsible, among other things, for getting girls and women back into educational institutions and working life. She became a founding member and chairperson of the Afghanistan Human Rights Commission (https://www.aihrc.org.af/home/members). Since 2005, she has been active in various capacities as an ambassador for peace at the United Nations, including as UN Special Rapporteur on the Human Rights Situation in Sudan and as a member of the *High-Level Advisory Board on Mediation* of the Office of the High Commissioner for Human Rights.

"*Education is the key*", said Sima Samar in a discussion on International Women's Day (translation by the author; cf. The Harvard Crimson 2022). As a peace and human rights activist, she knows that education must always be addressed in all our efforts for peace and social justice (ibid.). Shortly before the return of the Taliban in 2021, Samar left for the USA.

The Alternative Nobel Prize – Right Livelihood Award

The Alternative Nobel Prize, which Sima Samar received in 2012, stands for a just and "right" world. It is an award for individuals and social movements who actively work to shape a better world. Since 1980, the prize, financed by donations, has been awarded annually by the *Right Livelihood Award Foundation* (see: https://rightlivelihood.org/). The name "Alternative Nobel Prize" is not an official designation because there is no institutional connection to the Nobel Prize. The foundation describes the prize, awarded to 186 personalities from 73 countries to date, as a "*Commitment to Peace, Justice and Sustainability for all*" (ibid.). The awarded personalities receive support and networking in their commitment to peace, freedom and justice far beyond the prize money.

4. Presentation of an academic practice project: The "Global Campus Online" (GloCo) at the UNESCO Chair Global Citizenship Education – Culture of Diversity and Peace

Actors like Samar and Morin are significant figures who advocate for more peace and inspire the academic field. In the following, an academic practice project is presented dedicated to peace and unifying thought and action. The *Global Campus Online*, GloCo for short, is a project of the UNESCO Chair at the University of Klagenfurt, supported in a pilot phase by the Province of Carinthia and for the multi-year implementation by the *Austrian Development Agency* (ADA). The idea is an open teaching-learning platform between the Global North and Global South. Global North and South are not only understood as geographical terms but also express global inequalities. In the *Global Campus Online* project, students, NGO staff and stakeholders from different locations exchange views in online dialogue groups on the 17 United Nations Sustainable Development Goals (SDGs) from a global-local (glocal) perspective.

The aim is to learn how gender justice, poverty reduction, social and ecological sustainability, access to education and political participation can be represented from the respective perspectives and questioned about the potential for change. Here, multiple interfaces to topics and concerns of international social work and social movements become effective. Immediately after the start of the project in spring 2022, the *GloCo-Group Pretoria – South Africa* developed three initial concepts that illustrate how social work can be attempted from the perspective of global citizenship and social conviviality. It has linked three selected goals of the 17 SDGs of the United Nations with issues of social precarity: On SDG 1 (no poverty), homeless people are included in a project. For SDG 3 (health and well-being), a case study addresses the lack of recreational activities and open spaces for youth. Furthermore, for SDG 5 (gender equality), ways to facilitate access to essential hygiene products for all genders are explored. Participatory and low-threshold approaches link the three projects. Further projects are in the pipeline.

The overarching goal is to move from talk to action. To this end, a – modest – award called GEPARD (Global Education Project Award) is made available, with which the dialogue groups can carry out small projects. The prize money comes from the GENE Award (Global Education Network Europe), which the University of Klagenfurt received for the Global Citizenship Education III university course, also linked to the UNESCO Chair. The experiences in the project groups are to be compiled and evaluated in a handout as best practice examples for teaching and concrete implementation of the SDGs (information: www.aau.at/en/unesco-chair-global-citizenship-education/gloco/ (retrieved at 28.02.2024)).

UNESCO Schools and UNESCO Chairs

Concrete forms of this strategy are, among others, the UNESCO schools and, for scientific exchange, the UNESCO chairs. Neither the schools nor the universities receive financial support from UNESCO, but UNESCO recognises that these institutions are working in the spirit of UNESCO's goals. 877 Chairs in 117 countries belong to the network (as of 15.12.2021). There are 14 chairs in Germany and 10 in Austria.

> **What is UNESCO?**
>
> UNESCO stands for the United Nations Educational, Scientific and Cultural Organisation. As such it seeks to promote peace, economic justice, social equity, educational opportunity, elimination of all forms of discrimination, gender equality and environmental sustainability through global cooperation. Founded in 1946 under the impact of the Second World War as a peace project, it has 193 member states as of 2022. This broad membership also reflects the problematic balance between vision and realpolitik. UNESCO's membership includes states that disregard human rights and the environment, wage war and maintain structures of economic exploitation. The commitment to the rights of the Palestinian population, for example, led to the temporary withdrawal of the USA and England in the 1970s; Israel withdrew in 2017 for the same reason, and the USA again in 2018 due to the suspicious attitude of then President Donald Trump towards the United Nations. Under the Biden administration 2020-2024, the USA re-established relations with UNESCO.
>
> UNESCO tries to counter the often dystopian realpolitik and real economy with its utopia of a good life for all by bringing together the supportive forces within its member states through cooperation and initiatives in research, science, culture and education. In international social work, UNESCO can become an essential ally of global peace education and educational justice.

The UNESCO Chair Global Citizenship – Culture of Diversity and Peace

The University of Klagenfurt was awarded the *Chair for Global Citizenship – Culture of Diversity and Peace*.[78] The recognition is based on the priorities set at this university, such as the pioneering work of the *Centre for Peace Research and Peace Education*, the development of the only Austrian university course for Global Citizenship Education, the establishment of a Master's programme in Diversity Education and the involvement of the University of Klagenfurt in the field of Global Citizenship, as well as on research and practical projects related to relevant questions of the chair dedication: migration research, peace and conflict research, diversity research, solidarity research, gender research.

The UNESCO label could simply be a proud door sign. To become a 'door to the world', the Chair needs to be actively shaped as a platform for action to bundle and disseminate initiatives that strive to raise awareness of planetary connectedness and responsibility at different levels. The application for the Klagenfurt Chair was also successful because it was supported by many people already active in Austria and internationally. The first few months after the constitution of the Klagenfurt Chair at Christmas 2020 alone reveal the potential of the UNESCO network. What would otherwise remain isolated in a regional university (albeit

---

[78] Key data: Chairholder: Hans Karl Peterlini; Team: Elisabeth Rinne (coordination), Jasmin Donlic, Christiane Faymann, Daniela Lehner, Felix Schniz, Tom Tuček; Scientific Committee: Thomas Geisen (Ch), Heidi Grobbauer (A), Regina Römhild (D), Caroline Schmitt (D), Werner Wintersteiner (A).

with international ambitions), hardly able to find a voice and language, finds worldwide opportunities for networking and visibility. In this way, the Chair can strengthen many things that would also exist without the Chair and inspire many things that would not otherwise exist. However, conversely, the Chair also owes itself only to the life given to it through networking and exchange with the many valuable initiatives.

5 Conclusion and outlook

The starting point of this paper is diversity as a pedagogical challenge and, at the same time, an indispensable task for different pedagogical approaches, especially for social pedagogy and social work. How diversity is constructed, perceived and considered in pedagogical action inevitably influences whether being *different* or *diverse* becomes a target for discrimination or can enable empowerment – of course, also with ambivalent mixtures between the two extremes.

In many cases, diversity constructs emerge from dichotomous divisions, grounded in the history of ideas in the division of man–nature/animal and spirit–body. The dichotomous structure of social orders, which can be explained in simplified terms as 'black-white' thinking, creates pairs of opposites that hardly appear in a balance of power but almost inevitably create hierarchies and thus positions of domination and subordination: man–woman, white–black, normal–disabled. This opens up a wide field for a diversity-reflexive consciousness in all educational fields, especially for social education and social work theory and practice. The peace policy dimension of such a diversity-reflexive approach, which attempts to undermine dichotomous discrimination as far as possible, lies in a transgression of conventional local, regional and national framings of pedagogical action. The dichotomous divisions that promote injustice, such as man–woman, native–migrant, prosperity-winner–prosperity-loser, educated-bourgeois–educated-distant, gifted-learning–weak-learning, are also reflected in the global divisions, which not only make war, social exploitation and externalisation of one's problems at the expense of others disappear from consciousness (because it affects the *very others*, who have nothing to do with *us*) but also cause them and are to blame for them. A diversity-reflective consciousness in pedagogical – and even more so in social pedagogical – thinking and action must always look beyond its own field of action to this more significant dimension of inequality, disadvantage, injustice and rejection.

Reflective questions

- Why is the long period of European peace referred to as a "sham peace"?
- How can negative and positive peace definitions be understood, and what connection do you see here for international social work?
- Following the Einstein-Freud correspondence, how do individual psychological dynamics and structural orders interact in the constant of war?
- What is the significance of dichotomies for discrimination tendencies and lack of solidarity? What tasks, goals and attitudes result from this for international social work?

- What parallels can be identified between colonialism and Black pedagogy?
- Why can Global Citizenship Education answer the central challenges of our time and international social work?

Introductory literature

Bonacker, Thorsten/ Kowalewski, Sina (2014): Peacebuilding and Human Rights, in: Anja Mihr/ Mark Gibney (Eds.): The SAGE Handbook of Human Rights. London: Sage, 875–894.
Brunner, Claudia (2021): Conceptualizing epistemic violence: an interdisciplinary assemblage for IR. Int Polit Rev 9, 193–212 (2021). Open Access: https://doi.org/10.1057/s41312-021-00086-1 (retrieved at 28.02.2024).
Fanon, Frantz (2008): Black Skin, White Masks. Translated from French by Richard Philcox. New York: Grove Press.
Freire, Paolo (2007): Pedagogy of the Oppressed. New York: Continuum.
Jäger, Uli (2014): Peace Education and Conflict Transformation. Berlin: Berghof Foundation. https://berghof-foundation.org/library/peace-education-and-conflict-transformation/ (retrieved at 28.02.2024).
Morin, Edgar (1999): Seven complex lessons in education for the future. Edited by Unesco. Open Access: https://unesdoc.unesco.org/ark:/48223/pf0000117740 (retrieved at 28.02.2024).
Peterlini, Hans Karl (2023a) Dialogue with Adorno. How to Deal with Right-Wing Populism, Racism and Institutional Cruelization. In Peterlini, Hans Karl: Learning Diversity. Wiesbaden: Springer, 139–161. Open Access: https://link.springer.com/chapter/10.1007/978-3-658-40548-9_7 (retrieved at 28.02.2024).
Peterlini, Hans Karl (2023b): Searching for the Lost Paradise. Educational Dilemmas and Potentials for a New Treatment of Nature and Earth. In Peterlini, Hans Karl: Learning Diversity. Wiesbaden: Springer, pp. 163-178. Open Access: https://link.springer.com/chapter/10.1007/978-3-658-40548-9_8 (retrieved at 28.02.2024).
Spivak, Gayatri Chakravorty (1988): Can the Subaltern Speak?, in: Cary Nelson/Lawrence Grossberg (Hg.): Marxism and the Interpretation of Culture, University of Illinois Press: Urbana 1988, 271–313.

Further reading

Agamben, Giorgio (2003): Das Offene. Der Mensch und das Tier. Translated from Italian to German by Davide Giuriato. Frankfurt am Main: Suhrkamp.
Berghold, Josef (2007): Feindbilder und Verständigung. Grundfragen der politischen Psychologie. 3. edition. Wiesbaden: VS.
Boal, Augusto (1993): Theatre of the Oppressed. New York: Theatre Communications Group.
Bonacker, Thorsten/Imbusch, Peter (2010): Zentrale Begriffe der Friedens- und Konfliktforschung: Konflikt, Gewalt, Krieg, Frieden. In: Imbusch, Peter/Zoll, Ralf (Eds.): Friedens- und Konfliktforschung: Eine Einführung. Wiesbaden: VS Verlag für Sozialwissenschaften, 67–142.
Brunner, Claudia (2015): Das Konzept epistemische Gewalt als Element einer transdisziplinären Friedens- und Konfliktforschung. In: Wintersteiner, Werner/Wolf, Lisa (eds.): Friedensforschung in Österreich. Bilanz und Perspektiven, Klagenfurt: Drava, 38–53.
Derrida, Jacques (1998): Ich mißtraue der Utopie, ich will das Un-Mögliche. In: Die Zeit, 5.3.1998, 46–50.
Derrida, Jacques (2003): Eine gewisse unmögliche Möglichkeit, vom Ereignis zu sprechen. Berlin: Merve.
Deutsche Gesellschaft für Soziale Arbeit (DGSA) (2022): Positionspapier „Kein Krieg in der Ukraine – No war in Ukraine".

https://www.dgsa.de/fileadmin/Dokumente/Kein_Krieg_in_der_Ukraine_deutsche_v17_3_22.pdf (retrieved at 28.02.2024).
Einstein, Albert/Freud, Sigmund (1972 [1932]): Warum Krieg? Ein Briefwechsel. Zurich: Diogenes.
Galtung, Johan (1971): Gewalt, Frieden, Friedensforschung. In: Senghaas, Dieter (Hrsg): Kritische Friedensforschung. Frankfurt am Main: Suhrkamp, 55–104.
Galtung, Johan (1975): Strukturelle Gewalt. Beiträge zur Friedensforschung, Reinbek.
Galtung, Johan (1993): Kulturelle Gewalt. In: Zeitschrift für Kulturaustausch, 43 (4), pp. 473–487.
Galtung, Johan (1998): Friede mit friedlichen Mitteln. Opladen: Leske.
Gorton Ash, Timothy (2022): Russia's invasion of Ukraine will change the face of Europe forever. In theguardian.com, 24.2.2022. www.theguardian.com/commentisfree/2022/feb/24/russia-invasion-ukraine-europe-ukrainians (retrieved at 28.02.2024).
Greiner, Bernd/Müller, Christian Th./Walter, Dierk (Eds.) (2006): Heiße Kriege im Kalten Krieg. Hamburg: Hamburger Edition.
Habermas, Jürgen (1976): Einleitung: Historischer Materialismus und die Entwicklung normativer Strukturen. In: Habermas, Jürgen: Zur Rekonstruktion des Historischen Materialismus. Frankfurt am Main: Suhrkamp, 9–48.
Hobbes, Thomas (1984) [1651]: Leviathan oder Stoff, Form und Gewalt eines kirchlichen und bürgerlichen Staates. Ed. by Iring Fetscher. Frankfurt am Main: Suhrkamp.
Hof, Tobias (2011): Staat und Terrorismus in Italien 1969–1982. München: Oldenbourg Wissenschaftsverlag.
Jäger, Uli (2010): Friedenspädagogik - Grundlagen, Herausforderungen und Chancen einer Erziehung zum Frieden. In: Peter Imbusch/Ralf Zoll (eds.): Peace and Conflict Studies: An Introduction. Wiesbaden: VS Verlag für Sozialwissenschaften, 537–556.
Kant, Immanuel (1900 [1795]): Zum ewigen Frieden. Ein philosophischer Entwurf. Gesammelte Schriften, Vol. 23. Berlin: Deutsche Akademie der Wissenschaften.
Kant, Immanuel (1803[1900]): Kant on Education (über Pädagogik). Translated by Anette Churton. Boston: DC Heath & Co.
King, Martin Luther jr. (1964): A Martin Luther King Treasury. New York: Educational Heritage, Yonkers.
Ley, Michael (2005): Zivilisationspolitik: zur Theorie einer Welt-Ökumene. In Zusammenarbeit mit Wilfried Graf. Würzburg: Königshausen & Neumann.
Lessenich, Stephan (2016): Neben uns die Sintflut. Die Externalisierungsgesellschaft und ihr Preis. Berlin: Hanser.
Meadows, Donella/Meadows, Dennis/Randers, Jørgen/Behrens, William W. III (1972): The Limits to Growth. A Report for the Club of Rome's Project on the Predicament of Mankind. New York: Universe Books.
Morin, Edgar (2012): Der Weg. Für die Zukunft der Menschheit. Hamburg: Reinhold Krämer.
Morin, Edgar/Kern, Anne B. (1993): Heimatland Erde. Versuch einer planetarischen Politik. Vienna: Promedia.
Orwell, Georg (1968): You and the Atomic Bomb. In: The Collected Essays, Journalism and Letters of George Orwell, IV. New York: Harvest Book, 3–9.
Peterlini, Hans Karl (1993): Bomben aus zweiter Hand. Zwischen Gladio und Stasi. Bozen: Raetia.
Peterlini, Hans Karl (2016): Lernen und Macht. Prozesse der Bildung zwischen Autonomie und Abhängigkeit. Innsbruck-Vienna: Studienverlag.
Peterlini, Hans Karl (2017): Erziehung nach Aleppo. Pädagogische Reflexionen zu Rechtspopulismus, Rassismus und institutioneller Kälte gegenüber Menschen in Not. In: Gruber, Bettina/Ratković, Viktorija (Eds.): Migration. Bildung. Frieden. Perspektiven für

das Zusammenleben in der postmigrantischen Gesellschaft. Münster: Waxmann, 175–200.

Peterlini, Hans Karl (2019): Über den Abgrund der Dichotomie. Pädagogische Dilemmata und Perspektiven für einen neuen Umgang mit Natur und Erde. In: Dozza, Liliana (Eds.): Io corpo - Io racconto - Io emozione. Bergamo: Zeroseiup, 2019, 31–43.

Peterlini, Hans Karl (2020): Phänomenologie als Forschungshaltung. Einführung in Theorie und Methodik für das Arbeiten mit Vignetten und Lektüren. In: Donlic, Jasmin/Straßer, Irene (Hrsg.): Gegenstand und Methoden qualitativer Sozialforschung. Einblicke in die Forschungspraxis. Opladen: Barbara Budrich, 121–138.

Richter, Dieter (1978). Das fremde Kind. Zur Entstehung der Kindheitsbilder des bürgerlichen Zeitalters. Frankfurt am Main: S. Fischer.

Rote Armee Fraktion (1997): Guerilla, Widerstand und antiimperialistische Front. Mai 1982. In: Martin Hoffmann (Eds): Rote Armee Fraktion. Texte und Materialien zur Geschichte der RAF. Berlin: ID-Verlag, 291–306.

Rossi, Marisa Elena (1993): Untergrund und Revolution: der ungelöste Widerspruch für Brigate Rosse und Rote Armee Fraktion. Zurich: VdF.

Schmidt-Eenboom, Erich/ Stoll, Ulrich (2015): Die Partisanen der NATO. Stay-Behind-Organisationen in Deutschland 1946–1991. Christoph Links, Berlin 201

Steyerl, Hito (2008): Die Gegenwart der Subalternen. In: Spivak, Gayatri Chakravorty (2008): Can the Subaltern Speak? Postkolonialität und subalterne Artikulation. Wien: Turia + Kant, 7–16.

UN (2015): Transforming our World: The 2030 Agenda for Sustainable Development. https://sustainabledevelopment.un.org/post2015/transformingourworld/publication (retrieved at 28.02.2024).

Unger, Hella von (2014): Partizipative Forschung. Einführung in die Forschungspraxis, Wiesbaden: Springer Fachmedien.

Wintersteiner, Werner (2021): Die Welt neu denken lernen – Plädoyer für eine planetare Politik. Lehren aus Corona und anderen existentiellen Krisen. Hrsg. von Hans Karl Peterlini. Bielefeld: transcript.

III. Opportunities, Limits, Perspectives

Outlook:
Making Conditions Dance.
International Social Work and Social Movements as Alliance Partners

Claudia Lohrenscheit, Andrea Schmelz, Caroline Schmitt & Ute Straub

The aim of this volume is to highlight and reflect on the interconnectedness of social movements and international social work. In the previous chapters we have focused on social movements working for human rights, social justice, inclusion, equality and environmental concerns. At the same time we point out that social movements can also take nationalist, racist, anti-Muslim, anti-Semitic, anti-feminist, transphobic and other exclusionary motives as their starting point, which in turn call for strong open-minded alliances.

We see a socio-political and globally urgent need to bundle inclusive voices in their polyphony. That is why we have consciously chosen a path that is inspired by critical social work and has taken you as readers on a journey into the history of international social work from the old social movements in the late 19th century and the first third of the 20th century to the new social movements of the 1970s and 1980s and the "new" new social movements in the 21st century. In doing so, the individual contributions also draw attention to the fact that social movements do not operate in power-free spaces and that they – just like social work – need to be thoroughly examined in terms of their inclusive and exclusive effects.

The movements presented here are united in their concern to work towards more socially and ecologically just, sustainable conditions and to create a sustainable world in intergenerational responsibility. This makes them valuable partners for international social work against the background of increasing global inequalities. In this sense, the volume is also intended as a search for old and new collaborative alliances to solve these problems and as a call to social work to open up its professional perspective.

Dancing together

As with the example of dance, with which we started this volume, international social work has sometimes 'ventured close on' social movements and even helped to promote them, but at other times international social work and social movements have stood many steps apart. They were not and are not always connected to each other in partnership. For example, the proximity of social work to the state was suspicious to the workers' movement. The movement placed little hope in progressive action by social workers and even saw them as accomplices in enforcing bourgeois norms.

But this distance also marks that social work and the movements we are considering are concerned with similar agendas, which is why – according to a central thesis of the volume – they should take note of each other and, in doing so, check whether dancing together wouldn't make a lot of sense.

Such a dance, whether with standard steps, as a circle dance to coordinated rhythms or free style, needs in a first step to get closer courageously and involve with each other. Social movements and international social work have long since proven that joint dances can be possible, productive and enjoyable. Already looking at the old social movements, it became clear how closely social workers were interwoven with these old movements. Many social workers were also closely connected to new social movements – such as those that emerged in the spirit of optimism in the late 1960s – or were part of movements themselves. In the 1970s and 1980s, this interconnectedness opened up a multitude of alternative horizons of thought; old and proven approaches such as group work or community work were taken up again, and new pedagogical concepts and projects emerged – some of which, of course, disappeared again. Others, however, survived and were transferred into institutionalised structures. Central issues, such as living together in an atmosphere of equality, peace and ecological responsibility, were core concerns, which are now being handed down and further developed in the "new" social movements and, in view of the increasing inequalities worldwide, are being addressed today even more than at that time.

In this context, it is indispensable to include the movements of the Global South. These range from the anti-colonial national liberation movements, Indian Gulabi women's gangs against sexualised violence and protests against land grab to indigenous movements against the destruction of the rainforest.

In this volume we limited ourselves to selected movements and have left the selection to the authors of the volume. This selection is therefore to be understood as exemplary and by no means complete. Let this inspire you to continue your research on the topics that concern you and to think of them as interlinking with a social work that demands it.

Solo dancers in neoliberal dress

Paradoxically, the recognition of social work and the increasingly differentiated support system that goes with it have contributed to the fact that the treatment of social problems is outsourced to specific settings and is thought of in a more columnar than interwoven way. Both the profession and the discipline are repeatedly confronted with the statement that they have de-politicised themselves and show too little commitment against neoliberal political concepts or are even involved in the construction and implementation of neoliberal politics (e.g., Wagner 2009: 17). But as a solo dancer in neoliberal dress, social work loses its allies and cannot win any new ones. What is needed is a change of direction.

Against the backdrop of social work solo dances, it is not surprising that it was mainly the "new" new social movements that reacted to advancing globalisation and globally worsening inequalities from the 2000s onwards. The financial and banking crisis, neoliberalism, antifeminism, homophobia and transphobia, the climate crisis, wars and violence, and the widening gap between rich and poor bring together actors from different parts of the world. The protest is translocal and transnational, fluid and digitally supported. With flash mobs or art performances, parades and music, the "new" social movements show imaginative, innovative choreographies with political content that demand further analysis.

The social work environment increasingly demands that these "new" new social movements and international social work dance together. In view of the major problems in the world, social work should not be content with supporting individuals in coping with their lives – which is undeniably one of its important tasks – but must regain more political power and intervene in, and help change, social conditions (e.g., Thole/Wagner 2019; Kleibl et al. 2020; Lutz 2022). This is also regularly demanded by the international professional associations of social work, whose important positions, campaigns and resources are not always given sufficient consideration in teaching and training for social work profession. This is also a concern of the present volume: we would like to encourage you as students to look beyond the "national horizon", to perceive international positions and developments and to network and show solidarity across borders.

Let's dance: dare more movements (again)

Against this background, our textbook sees itself as an invitation to all of us – to cosmopolitan social movements and international social work – to dare more joint dances and movements again. If we need advices on how to initiate shared choreographies, we can find valuable experiences in history. At the same time we also need courage to dare new alliances, to get involved with each other and to try out common dances. Dancing means trusting the other person and forgiving each other if the partners step on each other's toes. Dancing generates energy and momentum, which we urgently need in times of global crisis. And in dancing, the roles of leading and following can change constantly, depending on which dance partners come together and how they inspire each other.

We can learn from the "new" new social movements – so we sum up – that working on changing inequality structures is not only meaningful but can also be fun, and that this does not necessarily mean that the important agendas have to take a back seat, but that digital, creative and cheerful forms of protest have the potential to open up new public spheres (e.g., Stauber 2013; Hill/Schmitt 2021: 18–20). What becomes clear here is: we are capable of action – individually as well as, above all, in the collective of social movements, which are always working on concrete utopias, even if these often cannot be implemented in the lifetime of the acting actors. This realisation is all the more important in a time of multiple crises and little encouraging prospects for the future, in which many people feel powerless in the face of the magnitude of the challenges. In this sense, the social movements represented here in the book are democratic antidotes, because they show what potential people can develop when they actively help to shape democracy. New public spheres and a sense of responsibility, civil society ambitions as well as a radius of action that extends beyond individual places, cities, regions and nation states are highly relevant for international social work in order to establish itself more and more as a profession and discipline without borders, to exert influence worldwide, to find recognition and to be able to take up the interlinked problem situations in the world.

The idea of alliance and a reflection on the diverse forms of social work can be found in the concept of popular social work, which we believe is important for the future direction of our discipline and profession (Lavalette/Ioakimidis 2017; Schmelz 2021). Popular social work takes the links between social movements and social work as a starting point, reads the international history of social work as the history of social movements and vice versa and appreciates the diversity of forms of support – from state-embedded social work to interventions in social movement contexts, to activist initiatives against racism, transphobia, nationalism and for peace, solidarity and the rights of marginalised groups such as refugee children, young people and adults, LGBTQI* or BIPoC.

International Social Work '… shall find itself in dancing …'[1]

We end this volume with a vision for an international social work that is closely interwoven with social movements. Such an international social work sees itself as a moving and agitating dancer between consolidated professional and disciplinary structures on the one hand and fluid alliance possibilities on the other, which it repeatedly subjects to critical, decolonial and inclusive questioning. These possibilities of alliance allow her to remain attentive to inequalities that are often particularly quickly denounced, scandalised and dealt with by social movements.

Between its institutionalisation – and thus its social legitimisation and the possibility of not leaving support to chance but transferring it into organisational structures – and its mobility and openness to opportunities for politicisation, intervention and protest, we see international social work as an actor that must also gather forces, but which, because of its mandate to work on inequalities and to stand up for participation together with the people we are working with, must not stand still.

Vision of a cosmopolitan dance hall

With this volume we would like to initiate old and new debates in international social work and open up a dance hall open to the world. Guests are not only important authorities, such as the "experts by experience", the service users, providers and community-based organisations, but also and in particular social movements, in order to tackle the major issues of our time together.

Feel invited to reflect in your studies and professional practice as well on what alliances you would like to form beyond your immediate environment and what social movements might be important for your field of action and work.

---

1 „… soll im Tanze sich drehen …" is a quote of a German folk song.

Bibliography

Hill, M./Schmitt, C. (2021 Solidarität in Bewegung. Neue Felder für die Soziale Arbeit. In: ibid. (eds.): Solidarität in Bewegung. Neue Felder für die Soziale Arbeit. Vol. 44. foundations of social work. Schneider Verlag Hohengehren: Baltmannsweiler, 11–32.

Kleibl, T./Lutz, R./Noyoo, N./Bunk, B./Dittmann, A./Seepamore, B. (eds.) (2020): The Routledge Handbook of Postcolonial Social Work. Routledge: London/New York.

Lavalette, M./Ioakimidis, V. (2017): Popular social work in extremis: two case studies on collective welfare responses to social crisis situations. In: Social theory, empirics, policy and practice 13(2),117–132.

Lutz, R. (2022): Anthropozän und Klimaverwandlung. Skizzen einer „transformativen Sozialen Arbeit". In: Pfaff, T./Schramkowski, B./Lutz, R. (eds.): Klimakrise, sozialökologischer Kollaps und Klimagerechtigkeit. Beltz Juventa: Weinheim/Basel, 370–394.

Schmelz, A.F. (2021). Rebellin gegen Klassenverhältnisse: Mentona Moser (1874-1971). Eine Pionierin der internationalen Sozialen Arbeit. In: Soziale Arbeit 70/9, 337–344.

Stauber, B. (2013). Jugendkulturell geprägter Protest: Eine Reflexion zum Zusammenhang von Solidarität und anderen Strategien gegen die Entfremdung. Oder: Solidarität ist auch da drin, wo sie nicht draufsteht. In: Billmann, L./Held, J. (eds.): Solidarität in der Krise. VS: Wiesbaden, 271–280.

Thole, W., Wagner, L. (2019): Von der radikalen Kritik zum politischen Dornröschenschlaf. In: Sozial Extra, 43, 35–39.

Wagner, L. (2009): Soziale Arbeit und Soziale Bewegungen – Einleitung. In: Wagner, L. (eds.): Soziale Arbeit und Soziale Bewegungen. VS: Wiesbaden, 9–19.

Index

The information refers to the page numbers of the book.

A

Activism 15, 33, 49, 67, 75, 98, 101, 117, 121, 122, 131, 138, 143, 144, 153, 163, 169, 175, 176, 178, 188
Advocacy 35, 173
Age of Enlightenment 45, 63, 193
Agency 111, 199
Artivism 15, 111, 119, 121–123
Asymmetric wars 188

B

BIPoC (Black, Indigenous and people of colour) 7, 61–63, 65–69, 71, 116, 133, 208
Buen Vivir 140, 145, 151, 157, 159, 163–165

C

Care chains 33
City 15, 50, 67, 100, 111, 114, 115, 117–119, 122, 125
City card 117–119
Civil society 9
Claim to hegemony 23
Climate justice 134
Climate Justice Programme 16, 131, 134, 135, 138, 143
Club of Rome 188
Community action 138
Convention on the Rights of Persons with Disabilities 169, 180, 181
Conviviality 199
Critical Whiteness 14, 61, 66, 68–70, 72
CRPD 169–171, 178, 182, 183

D

De-institutionalisation 172, 178, 183
Deep Ecology 134, 137, 140, 141, 151
Dichotomies 192
Disability Studies 173, 174, 184
Discrimination 48, 158

E

Eco-Spirituality 140, 151
Ecosocial Work 16, 131, 137
Environmental justice 134
Environmental racism 133
Environmental Social Work 16, 131, 137, 138
Eurocentrism 141, 155

F

Flight migration 93

G

Global Citizenship Education 17, 195, 199, 200, 202
Global Divide 201
Global Governance 20
Global North 23, 34, 35, 46, 53, 68, 69, 97, 112, 127, 131, 133, 134, 141, 143, 152–155, 163, 170, 171, 194, 199
Global South 16, 20, 21, 32, 33, 46, 47, 81, 97, 98, 133–135, 137, 141, 151, 153, 163, 170, 194, 199, 206
glocal 199
Green Belt Movement (GBM) 16, 131, 141
Green Social Work 16, 131, 134, 137–140, 145, 146

H

Hubris 196

I

Inclusion 125, 179
Information overflow 27
Internationalism 29, 30
Intersectionality 31

L

Lobbying 103, 117

Index

M
Mad Studies 173–175, 184
Migration 14, 15, 91, 94, 96

N
Negative peace 17, 187, 189
Neighbourhood work (community work) 24, 91, 125, 132, 142, 172, 206

O
Ownership 30

P
Para-social work 33
Paternalism 82
Peace as a process 17, 187
People-First-Movement 169, 172, 173, 176, 177, 180–184
Performance Art 12, 122
Personal assistance 180, 182
Popular Social Work 111, 125–127
Positive peace 189, 201
Post-growth 133, 143, 145
Proxy war 188

R
Racism 14, 61–63, 103
Ratification 170
Real economy 200
Realpolitik (political realism) 200

S
Sans-Papiers 117–119
Self-determined life movement 16
Self-empowerment 143
Service User Involvement 22
Settlement movement 91
Shrinking Spaces 9, 35
Social Development Goals (SDG) 22
Solidarity 8, 15, 100, 111, 115, 116, 122, 126
Solidarity city 111, 115, 117, 127
Sustainable Development Goals 43, 44, 126, 132, 145, 199

U
Ubuntu 145, 153, 164
UN Millennium Development Goals 22, 43, 44, 126, 132, 145, 199
United Nations Universal Declaration of Human Rights 76, 158, 170
Urban citizenship 113

V
Violence 41, 48, 49
Vulnerability 93, 97, 101, 139, 192

W
white supremacy 26, 61, 70